$844 ⁰⁰

D1243037

WITHDRAWN

William Dunbar

Guill.º Dunbar

WILLIAM DUNBAR

SCIENTIFIC PIONEER OF THE OLD SOUTHWEST

ARTHUR H. DeROSIER JR.

THE UNIVERSITY PRESS OF KENTUCKY

Publication of this volume was made possible in part by a grant
from the National Endowment for the Humanities.

Scholarly publisher for the Commonwealth,
serving Bellarmine University, Berea College, Centre College of Kentucky,
Eastern Kentucky University, The Filson Historical Society, Georgetown College,
Kentucky Historical Society, Kentucky State University, Morehead State University,
Murray State University, Northern Kentucky University, Transylvania University,
University of Kentucky, University of Louisville, and Western Kentucky University.
All rights reserved.

Editorial and Sales Offices: The University Press of Kentucky
663 South Limestone Street, Lexington, Kentucky 40508-4008
www.kentuckypress.com

Frontispiece: William Dunbar's signature. (Courtesy of the Mississippi Department
of Archives and History, Jackson)

11 10 09 08 07   5 4 3 2

Library of Congress Cataloging-in-Publication Data

DeRosier, Arthur H.
  William Dunbar : scientific pioneer of the old southwest / Arthur H.
DeRosier, Jr.
      p. cm.
  Includes bibliographical references and index.
  ISBN 978-0-8131-2455-1 (hardcover : alk. paper)
  1. Dunbar, William, 1749-1810. 2. Scientists—United States—Biography.
I. Title.
  Q143.D88D47 2007
  509.2—dc22
  [B]   2007019559

This book is printed on acid-free recycled paper meeting the requirements of the
American National Standard for Permanence in Paper for Printed Library Materials.

Manufactured in the United States of America.

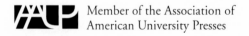
Member of the Association of
American University Presses

For my family—
Deborah DeRosier Lasseter, Marsha Carol DeRosier,
Brett Preston Scott, Melissa Estelle DeRosier,
and life's companion Linda Scott DeRosier

Dedicated to the memory of John Edmund Gonzales—
mentor, colleague, friend

Contents

Illustrations follow page 122

Acknowledgments

Though this volume would not have been possible without the assistance of many individuals, one of the problems faced in acknowledging those who contributed to this work—which took forty-six years to complete—is that memory fades, names slip away. Then again, how does one acknowledge all who contributed an idea, a pat on the back, an inspiration that helped one to take the next step—the right step? It is impossible to do so, but I can tip my hat to all who pointed me in the right direction, who scolded me when the easy route was sought or procrastination became a friendly associate. The helpful cast is filled with relatives, teachers, thesis and dissertation advisors, and those with faith enough to entrust a graduate program to my keeping, an academic enterprise to my care, and three colleges/universities to my guidance during twenty-five mostly turbulent years. I thank them all.

I recall fondly the encouragement received from a University of Southern Mississippi history colleague, John Gonzales, Mississippi State University historians John Bettersworth and Glover Moore, and University of Mississippi English scholar John Pilkington, as well as Dunbar descendants Marian Patty and Doug McQueen.

Equally important are numerous librarians and archivists in Edinburgh, Elgin, and Aberdeen, Scotland, and Liverpool, Manchester, and London, England. Librarians and archivists in the United States were as generous with their time, suggestions, and inquiries as those in the United Kingdom. I offer special thanks to librarians and staff in the Mississippi Department of Archives and History, the Library of Congress, and city and state libraries in Mississippi, Louisiana, Arkansas, Tennessee, North Carolina, Massachusetts, Virginia, Florida, Pennsylvania, and New York—libraries housing valuable Dunbar, Dunbar-related, and old Southwest collections used in this study. Librarians and archivists provided access to primary resources in the days before Xerox enabled us to copy a document and before fax machines and the Internet could put it in our hands almost before we asked for it.

When I turn to thanking others for making this book possible, I have to begin with past Rocky Mountain College board chairman Dorothy Metz for encouraging me to undertake the task. I appreciate the contribution of Victoria Cech, managing editor of Pryor Mountain Press, who played a significant role in helping make a pedestrian effort a better one, and I must salute also Rocky Mountain College provost Susan McDaniel, who edited the text, along with Professor Linaya Leaf and Idaho historian Judith Austin, for enhancing what is offered for reader contemplation. I am truly grateful to noted historians Charles Boewe and Edward J. Cashin for providing me with additional information and guidance and for calling attention to inaccuracies in my initial draft, and to copyeditor Anna Laura Bennett, without whose careful attention this book would never have seen the light of day. Special thanks go to Andrew Arkin for support and constant encouragement.

Introduction

Rediscovery

Ours is a young country peopled by citizens of differing colors, cultures, and beliefs who added much to a rich native civilization already populating the Americas from sea to sea. Some immigrants were attracted to one or another of the thirteen colonies founded along the continent's east coast after 1607. There evolved a once-in-a-lifetime opportunity for Europeans who valued land over all else and who equated opportunity with the availability of land, even though that land had to be stolen from native people who already owned every inch of it. The Indian removal story remains one of the saddest chapters in the history of our nation, but what migrating hordes from Europe did with the land taken and occupied became a story—thousands of stories—that allowed the emergence of a new nation and funded dreams impossible to realize in France, Scotland, Germany, or elsewhere on the European continent. The saga is a majestic one of individuals willing to chance the treachery of a vast ocean, the hostility of land that would not yield without a struggle, and the daily need to survive among tribesmen naturally resentful of the plunder of their homelands long occupied and treasured.

Some were successful in those thirteen colonies or on land westward, beyond colonial borders toward the Mississippi River; many others were not. Winners and losers alike were soon forgotten and ended life buried in simple graves that tell little of their struggles. Though most of those colonial pioneers have been forgotten, some—George Washington, Benjamin Franklin, John Adams, Patrick Henry, Thomas Jefferson, Alexander Hamilton—have become historical figures bigger than life. Others made significant contributions to the emerging nation, were applauded during their lifetimes, then nearly disappeared from the pages of history—remembered only fleetingly, if at all. Such a contributor was William Dunbar of Elgin,

Scotland, who sailed to Philadelphia in 1771 and, over the following four decades, emerged as a scholar, scientist, agriculturalist, and explorer without peer in the old Southwest.

This volume endeavors to rediscover William Dunbar and, more important, to evaluate his legacy to America's early national years. Some suggest that Dunbar has always been ranked among Mississippi's giants. John K. Bettersworth wrote that "Sir William Dunbar was unquestionably the intellectual giant of the Mississippi Territory," and Dunbar Rowland called him "the pioneer scientist of the state."[1] Mississippi historian J. F. H. Claiborne went so far as to laud Dunbar as "the most distinguished scholar in our annals."[2] Some would contend that he has not really been lost when such accolades have been heaped upon him and when no historian of the territorial era has suggested that others are his superior or even his equal. Be that as it may, Dunbar has been relegated to one or two sentences affording only passing recognition. Why have not the full dimensions of William Dunbar's contributions been explored in an effort to give meaning to Claiborne's words and Bettersworth's contention? This volume attempts to lay before readers the dimensions of Dunbar's interests and contributions, his standing among national peers from 1798 until his death in 1810, and a brief analysis of a life that grasped the opportunities available in America and would make possible achievements well beyond the goals he might have imagined as he sailed from London in 1771. This work attempts to pass on to students of the early national period—especially those studying Mississippi Territory—awareness of the accomplishments of a person who was educationally prepared and who took advantage of the opportunities America made available to him.

In 1959, as a young assistant professor of history at the University of Southern Mississippi, I was called upon to teach Mississippi history. While preparing myself for the task, I discovered William Dunbar and began to wonder why he had been highly praised by some but given little scholarly attention for 150 years. At first, I dismissed what Bettersworth had to say as exaggeration. After all, there were not many people in Mississippi Territory, and few of them were scientists or explorers, so perhaps it had been easy to excel in a place devoid of competitors. Yet to be considered the leader in many fields of interest, from surveying to exploring, from astronomy to planting cotton, was unusual to say the least. Dunbar was considered the premier scientist in West Florida by the British and then the Spanish, and he was touted by Andrew Ellicott, the American commissioner surveying the thirty-first parallel with Dunbar (who represented the Spanish government), as one of the finest scientific minds in all of North America.[3] Tributes to

Dunbar increased until Thomas Jefferson, arguably America's most intellectual president, became Dunbar's sponsor in the highest circles of American scientific thought and activity. It appeared to me that William Dunbar was surely a major figure in the nation's history as the eighteenth century gave way to the nineteenth. Moreover, it seemed an injustice that his life and accomplishments had been relegated to a few words offered here and there by respected historians. His historical significance deserved further study and analysis.

Before committing myself wholeheartedly to studying the life of William Dunbar, however, I visited with two colleagues and friends—John K. Bettersworth and Glover Moore, historians at Mississippi State University. These scholars knew much more about the old Southwest and Mississippi's territorial years than I, and both encouraged me to press forward with a full study of Dunbar's life. Both John and Glover advised me to begin my research journey by spending as much as a year in Scotland and England studying Dunbar's early years and his later cotton transactions with Liverpool and Manchester merchants and agents before giving serious attention to his American years and contributions.

Glover insisted that I start at the beginning because Dunbar was born early in the Scottish Renaissance of the eighteenth and nineteenth centuries, and it was important to know what that era of unprecedented scholarship had to do with Dunbar's ever-expanding scientific interests. After some initial research on the breadth of Dunbar's interests, then, I left for Scotland in 1964, supported by American Philosophical Society and University of Southern Mississippi research grants, to begin a journey that has resulted in this work. Both Bettersworth and Moore warned me that the journey would be long because of Dunbar's wide interests. They were right.

To uncover new information, a historian has to be tenacious and lucky. Early in my research, I found my way to Second Creek, Mississippi, and the remains of the fabled home of the Dunbars—the Forest. The dwelling itself burned to the ground in 1852, but along with some foundation work the porch columns had survived. Left standing also was the carriage house, an unattended graveyard, and the remains of orchards and gardens. At that time Dunbar descendent Marian Patty was living in the carriage house. Patty took me in, wondering aloud why it had taken so long for a historian to rediscover one of Mississippi's most famous citizens, and shared with me stories of her family, along with the hope that I would do more with Dunbar's life than previous historians who had only nipped at the edges of a life never fully defined. She gave me an introduction to Douglas McQueen, a descendent living in Birmingham, Alabama, who was also delighted to see a rekindling of interest in his fabled ancestor. As our friendship developed, McQueen shared with me a research tool beyond price: the manuscripts of his mother, Virginia Dunbar McQueen, who in 1883 began writing a journal dedicated to memories of her grandfather, William Dunbar. Douglas McQueen and his sister, Mrs. Pearce McDonald of Montgomery, Alabama, had safeguarded this valuable journal begun by their mother. Virginia Dunbar and Stewart McQueen had met and courted as fellow students at the University of the South in Sewanee, Tennessee, and married on November 1, 1883. The journal proved to be a rich source of information as well as a valuable research tool. I found it included both information that verified other manuscripts and family information not found in other correspondence or personal Dunbar journals. McQueen wrote about all of the appointive and elective offices Dunbar held in Mississippi Territory—particularly court appointments—his efforts to save hundreds of lives by personally financing the inoculation of all in the territory during a smallpox epidemic at a time when needles were suspect, his inventions and scientific improvements, and his publications in the *Transactions of the American Philosophical Society*. She noted that her grandfather's name became familiar and respected by academicians the country over.[4] The McQueen journal led me to other sources and, more significant, to other phases of Dunbar's life that I might otherwise have missed. The journal greatly expanded the research phase of the project, as it broadened both the scope and dimensions of a journey encouraged by fellow historians who urged me in 1960 to join a small band of dedicated colleagues who considered old Southwest history a fascinating chapter in the American story.

By choice, this volume is not simply about the public figure William Dunbar and the times in which he lived. It is about Dunbar himself and his legacy, for I have endeavored to rediscover a historical figure of significance, with some emphasis on his formative years and his rise to a position of importance in West Florida and Mississippi Territory. It is true that his American years (1771–1810) were interesting and tumultuous years in the history of the nation and Mississippi Territory. I chose, however, to include important national activities, such as the American and French revolutions, the Articles of Confederation years, and the evolution of the Constitution, only as they affected Dunbar's life. As she entrusted me with her journal, Virginia Dunbar McQueen expressed her commitment to the belief that William Dunbar should not be forgotten or neglected as historians and others seek understanding of an important region in America and the interests and accomplishments of one of its major territorial players. Dunbar did not live in a region where early national events improved or disrupted his life.

What affected his life were the international scene and America's role in it. His fortune depended more on the Mississippi River and New Orleans than it did on New York or the evolution of the Supreme Court. A naval war would disrupt the flow of goods to and from the East Coast and Europe, which, in turn, would affect his life. The expansion of Napoleon's appetite from Russia all the way to Louisiana lands also affected Dunbar's life and held his interest. Treaties that influenced trade, boundary lines, and land holdings were of keen interest to him, but failed Articles of Confederation and squabbles between Federalists and Democratic-Republicans were not. References to the old Southwest, major figures in the region, and Natchez itself are offered here as ways of introducing the activities of a man whose diversity has been nearly forgotten and whose contributions have been relegated to generalized paragraphs or footnotes.

This volume concentrates, in part, on the versatility of Dunbar. It challenges other Mississippi Territory scholars and graduate students to identify aspects of his life that deserve further study and reflection beyond this work and the 2006 study of the Dunbar-Hunter exploration of the Ouachita River–hot springs expedition.[5] It is important, I believe, to give form and structure to this figure in early American history and to discuss briefly his contributions in myriad fields of interest and importance. The questions addressed are three: Who was William Dunbar? What were the dimensions of his interests? What lasting contributions did he leave to a nation and its citizens whom he came to love? What one finds is an inventor whose contributions were more notable in the area of refining and improving than in discovering, an explorer whose scientific knowledge expanded the dimensions of information required of all future explorers, a citizen who advocated the value of education, and an agriculturalist who acclaimed cotton as the staple of Mississippi as the eighteenth century gave way to the nineteenth. His work with cotton—long grain, planting techniques, baling, multiple uses of cottonseeds, and selling and shipping—helped, unfortunately, to maintain slavery, an institution that would impact the South from that day to this one. William Dunbar was a citizen who influenced the road the South would take that led to Vicksburg, Atlanta, and a new nation after 1865.

1

The Dunbar Family
of Elgin, Scotland

As 1779 closed, William Dunbar stood silently looking at the rubble around him. In February 1778, the Continental Congress had sent an expedition, led by Captain James Willing, down the Ohio and Mississippi rivers. Willing was charged with capturing and securing Natchez and routing Loyalists all the way south to New Orleans. Willing was instructed only to secure control of Natchez, Manchac, and environs, and not to damage property. Against those instructions, Willing wreaked vengeance against known Loyalists, including William Dunbar. Burning and trampling with abandon, Willing and his troops destroyed much of Dunbar's new and growing plantation.[1] The next year, Spain joined the conflict on the side of the patriots to get even with the British over past defeats at their hands, and, from New Orleans, a second invading force reached Manchac and finished destroying Dunbar's holdings. Remaining buildings were looted, crops destroyed, and slaves freed. The invaders left Dunbar penniless, deeply in debt, and stripped of all he had worked for since arriving in 1773.[2]

It is true that Dunbar was a Loyalist; he had no reason not to be. He did not arrive in Philadelphia until 1771, a few years after Parliament had passed restrictive legislation to cow the rambunctious American colonies. But insurrection was in the air; the vocabulary on both sides of the Atlantic was filled with threats back and forth; and the patriots, though a minority throughout the 1760s and even during the Revolution, were gaining the upper hand. William Dunbar, twenty-one years of age at the time, wanted nothing to do with a brewing war over past indignities between parent and recalcitrant children, so he moved from Philadelphia to Pittsburgh and then on to Louisville. Yet the fever of war followed him to northern Kentucky and he did not feel secure there, so he negotiated for land in British West Florida,[3] believing the move would free him from the tumult in the East, and there he could get about building a plantation that would allow him to recapture that which was lost through primogeniture in Scotland. That was all he wanted—an opportunity to become economically successful so he could return his attention to the science he had loved since early youth.

Dunbar was born into a privileged "first family" in Duffus Parish near Elgin in northeastern Scotland, less than ten miles from the Firth of Moray and the North Sea. The town and environs are located in four parishes—Elgin, Duffus, Alves, and Spynie. The two parishes of William Dunbar's youth were Elgin and Duffus: Elgin was flat with some rich, loamy soil and clay, but also a great deal of sand blown in from the Firth of Moray; Duffus had been tilled so much through the centuries that by Dunbar's youth the land was exhausted. At that time, farming techniques all across northeastern Scotland were primitive; the land was pockmarked with small farms inhabited by tenants without leases, subject to removal at any time. A stranger traveling through Duffus Parish around the time of Dunbar's birth in the mid-eighteenth century was heard to say, "Is this the fine province of which I have heard so much? The meanness of the cottages, the leanness of their cattle, and the open unimproved appearance of the fields . . . present . . . a very unfavorable view of a country naturally rich."[4]

Elgin Parish was a bit better off. The parish was dominated by the town of Elgin, which in turn was overshadowed by its famous cathedral. In the mid- to late eighteenth century, Elgin boasted a glove industry, tailors, weavers, shipwrights, shoemakers, blacksmiths, and bakers. It had once had an extensive malt trade with Norway, but a high malt tax levied by the English Parliament had forced that trade to be abandoned. The one thriving industry—fishing in the Firth of Moray—was of no interest to the Dunbar family, despite that they owned the best fishing site with the deepest harbor in the area. Sixty thousand lobsters were shipped to London yearly, and whitefish and salmon from the Firth were much in demand.[5] Apparently the Dunbars preferred agricultural pursuits to the wealth others were reaping from the seas.

Elgin Cathedral was created by an apostolic bull dated April 10, 1224, took two generations to build, and became the seat of one of the great bishoprics of the medieval Scottish church.[6] It dominated the town for centuries, and as late as 1750 an observer referred to Elgin as "a monkish-looking town, most reverend to view."[7]

The leading families in Duffus Parish were the Gordons and the Dunbars. The Dunbars date their presence in the area to 1072, when King Malcolm III bestowed on a loyal subject, Gasparic, the name of "Dunbar with the adjacent land of Lothian."[8] The head of the family was titled the Earl of March, and the family was known as Dunbar from that time forward.

The history of the Dunbar family before William Dunbar's birth is filled with striking characters, wars, plots, and the general unruliness that infected the British Isles for centuries. For example, Black Agnes of Dunbar resisted nineteen British attacks on Dunbar castle in January 1337, while she taunted the enemy by walking, elegantly clad, in full view atop a rampart.[9] Two of the most interesting Dunbars were Archibald Dunbar, provost (mayor) of Elgin and justice of the peace of the County of Moray from 1714 to 1716, and his daughter, Rebecca. Archibald loved red wine and used his offices to smuggle it into Scotland through Dunbar harbor on the Firth of Moray so he would not have to pay British import duties.[10] The customs collector knew of the scam, waited to catch Archibald red-handed, and eventually found seven full casks of smuggled wine in the cellar of a Dunbar crony, William Crombie.[11] The collector turned the keys and evidence over to Archibald for prosecution, but Archibald procrastinated and then delayed some more. Finally, in frustration, the collector reclaimed the keys, opened the cellar, and found that the wine had been replaced by casks of water.[12] Archibald was removed from office in 1716, not because of his smuggling mischief but because he was an Anglican supporter and the Presbytery of Elgin demanded his resignation.[13] He is important because he cemented ownership of the three estates that were eventually owned by Dunbar's father.[14]

Rebecca Dunbar gained fame by becoming a Jacobite rebel in 1746. She supported the cause of Prince Charles, who was proclaimed the new sovereign of Britain. Scots from the Highlands and elsewhere gathered in Elgin, where Prince Charles himself took command of his supporters in March 1746. The battle for primacy was fought in April. Charles and his army suffered major defeats, and Rebecca hid Prince Charles in her house until she could arrange to smuggle him out of the country.[15] She never relented in her loyalty to the prince, and when she died twenty-five years later, she was, according to her instructions, wrapped in the sheets from Prince Charles's bed that she had carefully preserved since 1746.[16]

Of all the Dunbars from 1072 to William's birth, however, none was more complex and fascinating than Dunbar's father—Sir Archibald Dunbar, the son of Robert and Margaret Mackenzie Dunbar. Through the generations, many estates were brought to marriages by bride and groom and parceled out to children during later years. Thus even though holdings came and went, the Dunbars were always a respected first family of northeast Scotland and, indeed, the whole country. Robert inherited Newton from his father, and when his elder brother, Archibald, died on April 16, 1733, Robert succeeded as the male heir to the estate of Duffus and the patronage of the Parish of Duffus. Robert died in September 1742 at the age of seventy-two, and three months later was followed to the grave by his widow, Margaret Mackenzie. Robert and Margaret left two heirs, Archibald, who inherited Newton and Duffus, and a younger son, William, a captain in His Majesty's Forty-third Regiment who died in New York City in March 1763, a decorated veteran of the French and Indian War.[17] Growing up, the two brothers were inseparable,[18] and it was in honor of his father's brother that William Dunbar was named.

Archibald Dunbar was born in 1693, and in 1735 he married his cousin Helen Dunbar, one of the daughters of the wine-smuggling lord provost of Elgin, Archibald Dunbar. Helen brought additional titles and land holdings to her husband when she inherited the estate of Thunderton from her father.[19] Little is known of Helen, for she died thirteen years later. We do know that the marriage was a happy one and that she gave birth to three possible heirs to the Dunbar estates.

Fortunately, there survives considerable source material about Archibald, who is reflected in his letters as a most lovable and interesting person. He was a typical gentryman—masculine, a sportsman, and lover of the outdoors. He often mentioned his love of the sports of hawking, fishing, and "blooding dogs."[20] As early as 1702, he proudly reported that he had sold for a handsome profit two dogs he had bred and raised.[21] Though he enjoyed the lifestyle, Archibald could not abide the paperwork that accompanied being a large landowner. Often his record books were hopelessly incomplete, as he ignored them in favor of the company of friends, hawking, fishing, or simply riding over his domain. His friendship with fisherman buddies got him in trouble with British authorities in March 1757 when he refused to impress a number of them for the British navy.[22]

As a member of the landed gentry, Archibald believed that laws were meant for others and disregarded them whenever it suited his purpose to do so. He too often smuggled wine to avoid high import taxes; he brought in large quantities, kept what he wanted, and sold the rest to William Sutherland, a wine merchant in Elgin. Both men profited handsomely as Sutherland ordered the wine and Archibald picked it up. Their arrangement is noted in a letter from Sutherland to Archibald in 1710: "I have mentioned to order Skipper Watt how soon it pleases God he comes to the firth to call at Caussie and cruise betwixt that and Burgh-head until you order boats to waite him."[23]

Also as was a custom of the gentry for centuries, Archibald feuded with his neighbors, especially Sir Robert Gordon, who owned an adjoining estate. Neighbors reported that Gordon "terrorized his dependents and harassed his equals."[24] It is true that Gordon did all possible to annoy Archibald. His favorite trick was to wait until the wind blew from the east and then force his tenants to plow sand near Archibald's gardens so that sand blew all over his fruits and vegetables. Since the wind more often than not blew from the west, however, Archibald got the better of the "game" by plowing and returning more sand than he received. There is recorded one episode when the wind constantly shifted as the tenants of both men plowed at the same time while sand whirled and blew in every direction.[25]

To most, however, Archibald Dunbar was a generous man and a thoughtful friend. He loved people, and in one letter after another he is found going out of his way to help a friend or bestow a kindness. In 1758, the Earl of Moray requested Archibald's assistance in electing his brother to Parliament. Archibald answered by promising to write personally to every gentleman who was or might become the earl's ally, including all Dunbars. He wrote, with typical humility and sincerity, "Your Lordship I believe knows that I have not the ability of a politician: God Almighty has denied me the talents necessary for those ends . . . ; but if your Lordship is pleased to honour me with your foundation, plan of operation, and hopes of success, I surely will not hurt your interest."[26] During the following year he worked unstintingly for the earl, writing to hundreds of friends, visiting voters, and soliciting help from all quarters.[27] On another occasion, when his brother was stationed in Gibraltar, Archibald wrote to high-ranking friends in the area to "help better your position there."[28] William did not ask for this favor; the thoughtful gesture was typical of Archibald, who often offered assistance without solicitation.

Not only was Archibald generous; he was also humorous. He seemed never able to refuse a request, even when his help was not deserved. One of his useless tenants was moving elsewhere and asked for a letter of recommendation. Archibald wanted to refuse but could not, and he wrote this recommendation:

> To all of his Majesty's loving subjects who can feel for a fellow sinner in distress, I beg to certify that the bearer, W.J., is the son of my old bellman, a man well known in this neighbourhood for his honest poverty and excessive sloth, and the son has inherited a full share of the father's poverty and a double portion of his indolence. I cannot say that the bearer has many active virtues to boast of; but he is not altogether unmindful of scriptural injunctions having

striven and with no little success to "replenish the earth" though he has done but little to subdue the same. It was his misfortune to lose his cow lately from too little care. . . . [T]he poor man has no means of repairing his loss but the skins of the defunct and the generosity of a benevolent public whom he expects to be stimulated to greater liberality by this testimonial.[29]

Archibald and Helen owned three estates and lived in both Duffus House and Thunderton House. Duffus House, their main country home, was located six miles northwest of Elgin between an abandoned castle and the village of Duffus. The house was set back from the road and is, even today, very handsome and commodious. The building is three stories high with dormer windows. At the entrance is a massive porch with large windows above it. The public rooms, located on the north side of the home, are large, well lighted, and airy. In Dunbar's day, the south side of the house overlooked a park tastefully enhanced with flower gardens. Flowers, trees, and a well-manicured lawn surrounded the house, and an extensive and well-stocked orchard was located north of it.[30] It was a most livable house: comfortable, informal, large, and peaceful. It was the birthplace of William Dunbar, and one can see in Duffus House many qualities Dunbar later incorporated into his Natchez home, the Forest.

Located at the corner of Thunderton Place and High Street, the townhouse in which Archibald and Helen lived and reared their family was originally the Earl of Moray's town mansion, then called King's House.[31] The house was passed on to Lord Duffus in 1653, but he fell into bad financial circumstances and was forced to sell it.[32] In 1735, Thunderton House, as it came to be called, became the property of Archibald Dunbar; it remained in the family until 1800, when his Scottish heir sold it to auctioneer John Batchan. Batchan wanted the grounds more than the house; consequently, he tore down most of the old building. Since that time it has been a Holdanite church, furniture warehouse, preaching station, printing office, Masonic lodge, factory, and hotel. During the months spent researching the Dunbar family in Elgin and throughout northeast Scotland, I stayed in Thunderton Hotel, viewing the remains of the original structure while trying to envision its grandeur as the Dunbar home centuries earlier. I came to recognize its central location in Elgin and the power and influence exerted by a family that dominated more than a town in the eighteenth century—the century of Dunbar's birth. As one Elgin historian stated, "The destruction of this fine old mansion . . . was a great error."[33]

Thunderton House was ideal for Archibald and Helen's growing family.

It was three stories high, had large rooms with high ceilings, and was surrounded by picturesque grounds and gardens.[34] It was located in the center
of Elgin, on its main street, and was much more pretentious than Duffus
House. The latter was made for comfortable living; the former was a show-
place ideally situated for visitors and the constant entertainment of guests.
Thunderton House was highly ornamented from many architectural periods, and the two large sculptured lions that flanked the back entrance were
said to be the most treasured sculptural art in Elgin.[35] One need only read an
inventory of the house and its possessions to realize how regal Thunderton
House was in the eighteenth century. The architectural jewel of northeastern Scotland, it contained many large and elegant family rooms, quarters for
servants, a sizeable stable and coach house, a fine bowling green, gardens,
and a very substantial, fully stocked wine cellar. The house was lavishly furnished; even the ceilings were highly ornamented.[36]

Not only did Archibald Dunbar own and fully utilize these two beautiful homes, but he also possessed the extensive surrounding lands of Duffus,
Newton, and Thunderton, and he controlled all of the tenants and property
on those lands. Certainly William Dunbar was born into the most fortunate
of economic and social circumstances of that day. Wealth allowed him to
worry about other things, such as gaining as extensive an education as possible, and it allowed him to nurture his innate curiosity, which led him to seek
better ways of doing most things. This was what he lost when primogeniture
drove him from Thunderton and Duffus houses at age twenty-one, and this
was what he sought to recoup across the ocean in turbulent America.

On April 10, 1748, after only thirteen years of marriage, Helen died.[37]
Among the children she left behind were at least one girl (name unknown)
and three boys: Archibald became a captain-lieutenant in the Highland
Battalion and died unmarried in Madras on March 4, 1762; Robert died
unmarried at Duffus House one month earlier; and the youngest son, Alexander, lived to inherit the family estates. William Dunbar was the firstborn
child of Archibald and his second wife, Anne Bayne Dunbar. Alexander's
death in 1791 led some historians to claim that William, as the eldest remaining Dunbar male, inherited the family estates and titles in Scotland.
However, elder half-brother Alexander and his wife Margaret had three children, two of whom were sons. The elder son, Archibald, born on June 30,
1772—a year after Dunbar left Scotland for Philadelphia—replaced Dunbar
as the heir apparent. At his father's death, Archibald inherited all family estates
and titles. William Dunbar was not entitled to—nor did he ever claim—
either family possessions or the title of sir. As he often stated, he was William
Dunbar of the Forest. Over the years, however, historians and genealogists

have persisted in calling him Sir William Dunbar—a title invented, I suspect, by a later descendent seeking British status.

In studying William Dunbar's family history, I attempted to concentrate on determining what impact life in Scotland and family position had on a young man soon to leave for the English colonies in North America. To be sure, family standing, wealth, and name gave him great advantages, including a first-rate education. Though his older brothers had the same opportunities, they did not show William's thirst for knowledge and intellectual curiosity. They hawked and drank; William studied rocks and tested seawater. What created the difference between William and his elder brothers was very likely his mother, Anne Bayne Dunbar. Her emphasis on and respect for learning were more important than Dunbar titles, holdings, and money. He inherited from his mother an insatiable curiosity, a love for learning, and a desire to make a difference. What he got from his Dunbar ancestors was the economic and social security to make that difference. Those influences converged during Scotland's greatest century to produce a man of substance and achievement, not in Scotland but in the old Southwest of America.

2

The Youthful Years

L ife was hard in mid-eighteenth-century Elgin. Not only was agriculture unproductive and industry scarce, but, worse still, the educational facilities one needed to escape poverty and stretch the mind were practically nonexistent. As late as 1793, there were only two small schools in Elgin, each employing one schoolmaster.[1] That number would hardly be adequate for a sparsely populated rural environment; in a town of 6,306 in 1775, the lack of schools and teachers made opportunities for learning few. The absence of basic educational opportunities was perhaps one reason that the town was stagnant for decades. While much of the rest of Scotland was experiencing an educational and intellectual revolution—the famed eighteenth-century Scottish Renaissance—illiteracy and superstitions lingered in northeastern Scotland.[2]

In 1749, Anne Bayne became the second wife of Archibald Dunbar. Anne was the daughter of a minor English nobleman, Thomas Bayne, who had provided a good education for his children even though he was financially unable to rear them in an aristocratic fashion. Anne had supported herself by working as a governess, and in 1748 Archibald Dunbar hired her as a tutor for his children. Wealthy Scotsmen, unfortunately, cared little about the inadequate educational opportunities offered the masses because they could afford to hire governesses for their children. They simply did not see education as something of value for common folks.

Within a year of Anne Bayne's employment as the children's governess, Archibald married her—to the consternation of his children, who believed he married too quickly and beneath his station. They never forgave their father and, despite her brilliant mind and kindly disposition, never accepted her as a member of the family.[3] The marriage lasted until Archibald's death in 1769, during which time Anne presented her proud husband with three children. William Dunbar was the eldest child of this marriage. Anne also gave birth to a daughter, Margaret (Peggy), who died at sea on her way to America to live with Dunbar and his family in Natchez, and a second son, Thomas, who became a distinguished military officer and rose to the rank of major general in His Majesty's service. In 1775, Thomas began his military career as a young lieutenant stationed in Boston, Massachusetts. He participated in the Battle of Bunker Hill and spent the Revolutionary War fighting in Massachusetts, New York, New Jersey, and Pennsylvania. Thomas distinguished himself in battle, especially the Battle of Monmouth, and he rose to the rank of colonel by the end of the conflict. Thomas died on December 20, 1815, having not seen his brother since the latter's departure from Scotland in 1771.[4]

A careful search through four sets of parish birth certificates, which were hopelessly incomplete, did not yield William Dunbar's birth date. Nor is his date of birth listed on his tombstone. Some historians claim that he was born in 1749, probably because his gravestone at the Forest states that he died in the sixty-second year of his life. Though I cannot dispel this contention, I have reason to believe that it is not accurate. First, Archibald and Anne did not marry until 1749. Therefore, one would have to claim illegitimacy or premarriage pregnancy to support the 1749 birth date, and I found no such claim or evidence anywhere in the Dunbar papers. Second, if Dunbar were born in 1749, he would have been fourteen or fifteen in 1763 when he entered King's College, Aberdeen, yet the normal age for entering college at that time was twelve or thirteen. And, finally, if he had been born in 1749, he could have emigrated sometime in 1770, because he was bound legally to the family only until his twenty-first birthday. Dunbar, however, did not immigrate to America until 1771. If the above reasoning is correct, Dunbar was born in late 1750 or early 1751.

I found no manuscripts that specifically describe Dunbar's early years, but from his infrequent comments about his youthful years, from his correspondence with his mother until her death in 1780, and from his father's papers, a somewhat hazy picture of those years emerges. The relationship between Dunbar and his mother was very close, but he did not appear to share many interests with his father or half-brothers.[5] Whereas the older male Dunbars hunted, hawked, drank, and generally lived the lives of prosperous Scottish gentlemen, Dunbar was a quiet, serious lad who was curious about everything around him. His father ridiculed his silly and constant questions about stars, animals, trees, and grass. Archibald accepted nature as a challenge to be physically fought and beaten; Dunbar looked upon nature and natural phenomena as a challenge demanding respect and understanding.[6] So while many if not most of the gentry males in Duffus and Elgin parishes frolicked about, Dunbar studied rocks, analyzed seawater, and caught butterflies.[7]

Although Archibald found his son Dunbar different from other boys his age, there is no evidence in the Dunbar correspondence to suggest that father and son drifted away from each other. Archibald supported his son's fascination with science and nature while also attempting to steer him toward the path of his elder brothers. Dunbar's mother, however, appears to have better understood her son. Dunbar's interests mirrored her own, and she constantly encouraged him and her other two children to welcome curiosity and to allow it to guide their educational interests and pursuits. Anne Dunbar, without a doubt, was the critical influence in Dunbar's life; she gave him love, understanding, and encouragement, whereas Archibald, who may have loved Dunbar just as much, simply did not understand the boy.

Fortunately, William Dunbar was born during the Scottish Renaissance. Never before or since has Scotland produced so many significant leaders in so many different fields. William Cullen and John Hunter pioneered in the field of pathology, Joseph Black and John Leslie were world leaders in chemistry, James Hutton had few if any peers in the field of geology, and the brilliant James Watt was a leading engineer. When the Newtonian system was still unwelcome in Oxford and Cambridge universities, it was being taught by David Gregory at the University of Edinburgh. The eighteenth is the century in which Scotland gave Adam Smith to the field of political economy, David Hume dominated the field of philosophy, and historians William Robertson, Robert Keith, and Richard Rawlinson towered over others elsewhere.[8] An Italian traveling in Scotland wrote that a large part of Britain's reputation for scholarship in the eighteenth century was due to great Scottish thinkers. He claimed, "Two entire ages have elapsed from the time of the general revival of letters, before anyone could have imagined that this kingdom should have become so distinguished by science and erudition."[9] The eighteenth century in Scotland was, as D. B. Horn maintained, "unequalled in any other period of Scottish history."[10] William Dunbar was a product of that renaissance.

It is ironic that during Scotland's century of intellectual leadership the two schools in Elgin were declining. The English and Scots have always attempted to provide educational opportunities, and a 1496 act of Parliament required "all barons and freeholders of substance, to put their eldest sons to the schools."[11] The town council of Elgin established a grammar school, which grew to the point that a second school had to be created in 1550. Records show that both schools had strong academic beginnings, but oversight neglect led to hiring less-qualified teachers and lack of attention to deteriorating facilities.[12] By the end of the eighteenth century, however, newly involved citizens created Elgin Academy, an excellent school in the nineteenth century that employed as one of its teachers none other than Alexander Graham Bell.[13]

The Dunbars, both Archibald and Anne, possessed a keen interest in education, and, though not a scholar himself, Archibald made certain that his sons had every available educational opportunity. He took great care in selecting governesses and tutors and never relied upon the decaying facilities and minimal scholarship offered by the Elgin grammar school. Whenever Archibald found it necessary to hire a new tutor, he advertised for applicants and corresponded widely with friends who offered suggestions and recommendations. On April 23, 1754, William Falconer, bishop of Moray, highly recommended Alexander Diack, who had served as a tutor in the house of the Master of Elphenston. Archibald did not hire Diack, but the letter Bishop Falconer sent to Archibald reveals the qualities Archibald was seeking in a tutor, as well as what the bishop was recommending. Diack was described as an old-fashioned classical scholar who was at his best teaching languages and mathematics; he was reputed to be a young man of virtuous character, as well as a superior disciplinarian. It is worth repeating that the bishop stressed Diack's ability in mathematics, for it was that subject that most interested an excited young William Dunbar—an intellectual love affair that lasted a lifetime.[14]

The first of Dunbar's tutors was John Brulet, who had been hired before the recommendation from the bishop of Moray. Brulet lived with the family, receiving room, board, and a guinea a quarter for his pay, for one and one-half years, and during that time he had a profound influence on young Dunbar. Brulet was a Frenchman who excelled both in languages and mathematics. At Duffus House, he taught all five boys to speak French fluently. Brulet's influence on William, however, was more pronounced than on the others, for he found the boy more inquisitive than most. He and Dunbar would talk long past study hours, and together they explored the countryside.[15]

Though some Dunbar scholars have maintained that Dunbar attended Glasgow University,[16] such was not the case. In the fall of 1763, Dunbar entered King's College, Aberdeen.[17] At that early date, his potential was considered extraordinary,[18] and Reverend Lachlan Shaw tried to convince Archibald that St. Andrews was the only university for so promising a lad. Shaw wrote Archibald that King's College was weak in Latin and Greek and was too close to the main part of Aberdeen, which contained all too many diversions for a young scholar. St. Andrews, he argued, was more whole-some, more private, freer from diversions, and clearly superior in Latin and Greek. Since Shaw knew that King's College was historically the institution in which all Dunbars were educated, however, he reconciled himself to the fact that young Dunbar would probably not think of going elsewhere.[19] He wished the lad well and told Archibald, "I sincerely wish your son may meet with all encouragement in his studies and makes progress in learning and virtue."[20]

King's College was a superior institution of higher learning that boasted about the quality of its internationally respected faculty and offered a highly disciplined routine and a spartan existence for its students. It was small and had a carefully selected student population. Students' commitment to their studies was considerable; all were expected to subordinate outside and extra-curricular activities to an intensive four years of learning. Each year the col-lege advertised in an Aberdeen newspaper what was expected of its students and what each should bring to school with him. It was always emphasized that each student must be proficient in Greek grammar before arriving on campus.[21]

It is impossible to determine from the few records available how many students entered the school each year. During the 1760s, however, the aver-age graduating class was twenty-nine, and there were twenty-four in Dun-bar's 1767 class.[22] Dunbar's three half-brothers had attended King's College in the 1750s, and even though records are incomplete and confusing, it appears that at least two of them flunked out somewhere along the way. Dunbar's younger brother, Thomas, did not attend King's College.[23]

All King's College students were required to live on campus, even those from Aberdeen. Each professor saw his students approximately ten times a day at public prayers, in classrooms, at meals, and in their rooms. Dormi-tory rooms contained only the bare essentials, including a bedstead, table, chimney grate, and fender. Students were allowed to have personal posses-sions, but all must be provided by individual students and their families. They were expected to provide their own fires and candles and to do their own washing. In the classrooms, students were seated according to their current proficiency in that subject, and competition was keen for front row seats.[24] Though life at King's College was austere, it would be misleading to suggest that it was unpleasant; the college years of 1763–67 were memo-rable ones for Dunbar.

King's College had a competent and demanding faculty that taxed Dunbar's intellectual resources. He studied history, English, Latin, Hebrew, religion, science, economics, geography, philosophy, and mathematics. One of the most eminent professors was Thomas Reid, author of a number of highly regarded volumes, including *An Inquiry into the Human Mind.* In 1752, he was elected professor of moral philosophy at King's.[25] The most popular member of the faculty was the professor of mathematics, Alexander Rait. Other than Dunbar's mother, no person in his youth—and possibly his whole life—had a more profound influence on the young scholar than did Rait. His belief that higher mathematics was the key to civilized progress became Dunbar's belief for the rest of his life. Dunbar tried to apply mathematical principles to all manner of subjects and problems. In the yearbook dedicated to each graduating class, there was always listed, without comment, the members of the faculty and administration, plus their academic credentials. In the yearbook of the class of 1767, Rait was singled out for special mention: "Mr. Alexander Rait has for some years . . . taught mathematiks privately in this college with great approbation."[26] Another professor, however, failed to practice what he preached. Dunbar's religion professor, who taught at King's for thirty years, was suspended for three weeks in 1794 for repeatedly being drunk in class; he was fired on November 7, 1795, for "still frequently getting drunk."[27]

On March 30, 1767, Dunbar and twenty-three classmates were graduated with master of arts degrees.[28] It is impossible to determine from the graduation rolls how well Dunbar placed in his studies. Students in the class were simply listed alphabetically by the first letter of their first name in Latin form: in Dunbar's case, Giullemus. From all indications, he ranked very high in his class. A 1764 letter from his faculty advisor to Archibald Dunbar stated, "It gives me great pleasure to inform you that I continue highly satisfied with your son. He behaves very well, makes an excellent scholar and is very desirous to distinguish himself, so that he stands high in the class. One of his genius . . . will not fail to succeed in any study he shall engage in."[29]

One area in which it is most difficult to trace Dunbar family history is religion. There is no doubt the Dunbars were loyal supporters of the medieval Church of Scotland, for the graveyard at Elgin Cathedral is full of Dunbar tombs and gravestones. Ascertaining with certainty the religious preferences of the Dunbars who lived during and after the Reformation, however, is a nearly impossible task. Some joined the Church of Scotland; others affiliated with the Church of England. Some evidence indicates that Dunbar's father was a much-involved Presbyterian; other evidence suggests he was an Anglican. We do know that Dunbar's mother came from England and was not Presbyterian.

The evidence indicating Archibald was Presbyterian is impressive. Letters show that he was quite influential in acquiring the ministry of the Presbyterian Church of Duffus for Reverend John Bower in 1737.[30] To achieve that goal for his friend, Archibald used all of his personal influence with the synod and general assembly to swing votes for Bower over the objection of his old nemesis, Sir Robert Gordon. After three months of intensive politicking and letter writing, Archibald got Bower elected in May 1737.[31]

Another bit of evidence is excerpts from Presbyterian minutes of the Church of Alves that mention, under the subtitle "Heritors Present," Archibald Dunbar of Thunderton.[32] In addition, in a pamphlet titled *Parish Ministers of the Presbytery of Elgin, 1560–1912*, Archibald Dunbar is listed as having presented James Dunbar, a new minister, to his parish. He presented Bower in November 1736 and Alexander Murray in August 1748. His son, Sir Archibald Dunbar of Northfield, Dunbar's elder half-brother, presented John Reid in August 1778.[33]

The manuscripts indicating that Archibald Dunbar was Anglican by birth are, however, more plentiful than the Presbyterian evidence, beginning with the Anglican record of births and baptisms listing the baptism of Archibald Dunbar, William Dunbar's half-brother, in 1740. When the Dunbars purchased Duffus House in 1705, it was specifically noted that they were supporters of the Anglican church. In *History of the Episcopal Church in the Diocese of Moray*, the author stated, "The chief proprietor in the parish of Duffus is Sir Archibald Dunbar of Northfield, who resides at Duffus House. The Dunbars of Thunderton and Duffus have been steady friends of the church in her deepest depression, and have never belonged to the Presbyterian communion."[34] Shortly before his death, Dunbar's father turned over the Scottish family holdings to his son Alexander and retired to London. Archibald died on July 13, 1769, at the age of seventy-six, and was buried in the parish graveyard of St. Anne's, Soho, Westminster, on July 23.[35] St. Anne's is an Anglican church, and Archibald is buried in the churchyard proper, not in an area petitioned off for dissenters.

I have been unable to find whether William Dunbar made any statement in regard to religion. Knowing as we do that he grew up in a part of Scotland that was split between Presbyterian and Anglican believers who voiced opinions openly and loudly, it is perhaps understandable that he chose not to do battle on a subject that may have split his own family. It is possible too that he did not care one way or the other, for Dunbar lived in an age when Scottish deism, or modernism, was very influential, particularly in intellectual circles. His lifelong silence on the topic of religion suggests strongly that Dunbar was influenced by that movement. His faith in science and mathematics suggests a belief in natural laws imposed on earth by a deity who gave humans a mind to seek them out.

During the eighteenth century, there was a transition in Scottish literature and religion from orthodox thought to speculative thought. In 1607, Thomas Aikenhead, with the approval of Edinburgh ministers, had been executed for questioning the credence of the Christian Trinitarian belief. By the 1720s, though, clubs were being founded and debates offered that questioned various basic Christian beliefs. In 1739, there appeared David Hume's shocking and provocative *Treatise of Human Nature*, followed by Thomas Reid's *Inquiry into the Human Mind* and Adam Smith's *Wealth of Nations*, among several others. By 1750, deism reigned supreme in intellectual circles, and Allan Ramsay wrote that the prevailing thought was a pagan naturalism "for which Christianity was a temporary aberration of the human mind." John Gregory, professor of the practice of natural philosophy at the University of Edinburgh, wrote, "Absolute atheism is the present tone." By the 1750s, "new modernism" was in full bloom in Scotland. Adherents felt that modern churches should give free thinkers considerable latitude.[36] Accommodation in both church teachings and the standard of Christian life might well have been the beliefs they took to their classrooms and pulpits. It surely was the position they brought to their writings.

The freeing of man's thinking, including subjecting Christian dogma to the test of reason, was the prevailing goal among intellectuals in King's College as well as in Edinburgh, Glasgow, and London. One might assume that the rational approach already accepted in the colonies by scientific-minded men such as Thomas Jefferson and Benjamin Franklin was also accepted by the young Scot from Elgin who soon would join them in America. Part of Dunbar's presumed deism may well have been a reaction against the religious bigotry in and around Elgin.

During his last four years in Scotland, Dunbar was a busy young man. After graduation, he returned to Elgin to chart a course for the future. He spent much of his time with his mother, sister, and brother, all of whose company he enjoyed. Also, Dunbar engaged in natural science study and research, investigating earth formations and examining and classifying minerals, an undertaking he relished.[37] He corresponded widely with some of the leading scientists of that period, including the renowned William Herschel.[38] He also did a great deal of work for the Museum of Natural History in Aberdeen in conjunction with John Jeans, a friend associated with the museum. They collaborated on such subjects as crystallizations, granite, iron ore, dust, Scottish gems, taxidermy, and the products of the sea. Dunbar became an inveterate collector of everything, a habit he retained the rest of his life. Many of the natural curiosities he collected over the years were shipped to Jeans in Aberdeen.[39]

The breadth of Dunbar's curiosity is remarkable. No natural phenomenon was too petty or too uninteresting to deserve at least a fleeting perusal and written commentary. If he wanted something from the sea he could not secure himself, Dunbar bribed fishermen with a pint of whiskey to enlist their assistance.[40] He even became interested in elixirs and acquired from Jeans a recipe for D. Houghton's, the ingredients of which were "4 ounces orange Rhinds . . . 2 ounces Calamus aromaticus . . . 2 ounces Gentian root . . . 2 Drops English saffron . . . 2 Drops Cocheneal . . . 8 Drops Virginia Snakeroot . . . and 8 Drops Laurel Berries." The ingredients were mixed with a pint of white port or cherry wine and put into a cave for eight days, then mixed with a bottle of pure liquor and allowed to stand for ten more days. A wine glass full of this concoction was said to be excellent "for windy disorders of the stomach and belly."[41]

During much of the period between graduation and emigration, Dunbar worried about his mother, who was ill and never seemed to fully recover. He was fond of her as both a loving parent and as an intellectual whose discussions and opinion meant much to him, so he spent as much time as possible with her at Duffus House.[42] By 1769, as a result of their thoughtful discussions and her urgings, Dunbar had begun thinking seriously about leaving Scotland and his family for a life in the New World. He was devastated, however, by the reality of abandoning the person he loved most in the world when she needed him more than ever before.

Why leave Scotland for a British colony an ocean away? Reasons that a poor person from the highland country might want to emigrate were numerous: fighting in 1714–15 and again in 1745–46 in support of Stuart pretenders seriously disrupted normal agricultural life and caused much suffering; sheep were dying off and sheep farmers were poverty stricken; circumstances forced people to marry late, bear and raise unhealthy children, and die early; manufacturing in towns gave rise to unhealthy factory conditions, especially in towns that became overpopulated because farmers were driven from the land; primitive and wasteful farming techniques shackled agriculture; lack of fuel made life intolerable; and staying in a country devoid of opportunities for the young and ambitious was futile.[43] Commenting on the terrible agricultural conditions in late-eighteenth-century Scotland, an English traveler remarked, "The renters let the land out in small parcels from year to year to the lower class of people, and to support their dignity, squeeze everything out of them they can possibly get leaving them only a bare subsistence. Until this evil is obviated Scotland can never improve."[44]

These reasons, though they summarize conditions in northeast Scotland around 1770, do not answer the question of why Dunbar would leave.

True, the lack of fuel affected gentry as well as peasants, and economic depression affected all in the region—some, of course, more than others. Yet Dunbar cannot qualify for emigration under any of the reasons listed; these are a poor man's reasons. One historian has written that Dunbar migrated to America for his health.[45] Not so. It is difficult to envision anyone leaving the north of Scotland for the mosquito-ridden, semitropical, hot, cholera- and smallpox-infested region of the old Southwest for health reasons. A more accurate contention is that Dunbar left for a reason that applied to rich and poor alike: the desire to improve oneself economically. Reverend John Grant bemoaned that Scots were "incited by the prospect of making a fortune, . . . and so the flower of our young men, of every class and description, go abroad."[46]

In 1769, when his father died, Dunbar was approaching his twenty-first birthday. His half-brother, Alexander, inherited the Dunbar titles and property holdings, leaving William Dunbar with only the five hundred pounds sterling willed to him by his father.[47] Dunbar came to America for the same reason that motivated most other Scottish migrants—a better life for self and posterity. Dunbar wanted from America economic and social opportunities lost to his brother Alexander in Scotland, and he had the essential mental and physical equipment needed to achieve that goal in a new land that welcomed hard work and resourcefulness. By any measure Dunbar was bright, inventive, curious, motivated, and unafraid of any and all odds against success.

From our knowledge of Dunbar's character and the close ties that bound him to family, it is apparent that he would never have left Elgin unless his mother, brother, and sister had urged him to do so. During 1769–71, Dunbar prepared to depart. He spent all of his money on equipment, Indian trading goods, and a ticket to Philadelphia.[48] When the ship sailed from London in March 1771, a brilliant, young Scottish scientist was on board in the person of William Dunbar.

3

From Pennsylvania to Louisiana

As England disappeared and the wide open ocean surrounded the ship
Dunbar took on that long journey to Philadelphia, there is no doubt he
realized he was on his own. He was now twenty-one years of age and must
seek his place in an exciting and rapidly changing world. Clearly, he knew
also that moving half a world away was quite different from moving two
towns from home. One allowed the continuation of family ties, including
immediate help and advice; the other did not. Dunbar selected opportunity
over predictability, danger over sameness. He knew, as did thousands of
Scots before and since, that the American colonies were rich in just about
everything Scotland lacked and they offered opportunity beyond other possible destinations beckoning bright potential contributors in the late eighteenth century. No doubt Dunbar anticipated real possibilities of success in
Philadelphia or elsewhere in the colonies, but with the limited communication options of that day, those expectations were vague. What really did he
know? I believe he knew that there was danger everywhere: danger from na-
tives angered by losing land to encroaching settlers with guns and whiskey;
danger from animals still aplenty also protecting home turf; and, most of
all, danger from Americans picking sides in 1771 for or against the mother
country. Whatever path he chose held its own perils. Dunbar could be loyal
to Britain, or he could join the patriots in their dispute with King George
III and Parliament—a dispute he knew little about. Either way there were
risks he could not avoid. Dunbar was taking the chance of a lifetime, ready
to meet adventures not yet known but welcomed.

Throughout March and April 1771, Dunbar sailed the Atlantic Ocean
headed to America's largest and most exciting city, Philadelphia. We cannot help but wonder what he was expecting of himself. French interpreter
of America J. Hector St. John de Crèvecoeur wrote, "I wish I could be ac-

quainted with the feelings and thoughts which must agitate the heart and present themselves to the mind of an enlightened Englishman, when he first lands on this continent."[1] Crèvecoeur wrote that Scotsmen were more likely to succeed than Irishmen because they were more focused. He noted also that both might have stayed at home and continued predictable lives with "more civil advantages," but the Scots were frugal and laborious, and they usually knew what they were going to do when they reached their new homeland.[2] Dunbar had a plan, along with a letter of introduction to John Ross, a family acquaintance and successful Scottish merchant in Philadelphia. Dunbar would seek advice from Ross regarding what to do with his Indian trading goods; he would befriend this fellow Scot, borrow money from him, and follow his advice on how to proceed. Dunbar knew not where he wanted to settle, but the temporary life of an Indian trader would take him far and wide so he could look for himself as he sought an opportunity to secure land, build an estate, and become a successful farmer or planter in this land of opportunity. Dunbar did not prefer Pennsylvania over the Carolinas, New York, or anywhere else. He sailed to Philadelphia because John Ross was there, and he hoped that Ross would help guide his first steps.[3]

Philadelphia surprised Dunbar. By 1771 it was the largest city in North America, as well as the chief financial center of the colonies. New York stood second in population and was gaining on Boston as a business center. Philadelphia was well located in the center of the East Coast colonies, and it was peopled with hardworking folks who migrated there from Boston (including Benjamin Franklin), other colonies, and many nations. It was populated by "new men" who came from surrounding counties wanting only an opportunity to succeed, even if through illicit trade.[4]

Land in Pennsylvania was in demand and growing more expensive because people had begun, at the conclusion of the French and Indian War, to flock to the interior of Pennsylvania, attracted by the availability—and fertility—of land. Between 1769 and 1774, southwestern Pennsylvania became the first English-speaking trans-Appalachian frontier in America. George Croghan wrote on October 2, 1770, "What number of families has settled since the Congress of Fort Stanwix, to the westward of the high ridge, I cannot pretend to say positively; but last year, I am sure, there were between four and five thousand, and all this spring and summer the roads have been lined with wagons moving to the Ohio." George Washington speculated on land in the area, noting that Virginians had an interest in fertile soil all the way from Virginia to the Ohio River. By midsummer 1771, it was estimated that there were ten thousand families in the upper Ohio River country, and a good number were Germans, Scotch-Irish, and Scots.[5]

When he met Dunbar in late April 1771, John Ross liked the young Scot from Elgin, and he befriended him for life. He told Dunbar that if he wanted to participate in Indian trade, he should move to Pittsburgh, in southwestern Pennsylvania, and seek out his son, Alexander Ross, a successful land speculator and entrepreneur. What Dunbar found there amazed him even more than did the size and excitement of Philadelphia. When he presented himself to Alexander and shared his plan, however, one historian has suggested, he was not particularly impressed; he simply jerked a thumb toward the woods and told Dunbar to take his pack of Indian supplies and "get rid of it out there" as fast as he could. That could have ended the partnership before it began, but Dunbar did have a letter of introduction from John Ross noting that Dunbar was a fellow Scot, and he was a member of a Scottish family well known and respected in Ross's home country. As Dunbar took his leave of Alexander Ross's office headed for the woods and Indian trading, Alexander might well have thought that would be the last time he would see the young man. Months passed; then Dunbar appeared carrying a load of fine pelts for sale. Thereafter, Dunbar was welcomed with more enthusiasm, and the partnership between the Rosses and Dunbar was cemented for life.[6]

Dunbar participated in fur trapping and trading activities from 1771 to 1773, during which time he borrowed money from both John and Alexander Ross. An examination of Alexander's estate books in the 1770s suggests that he was a large and successful land speculator in the Pittsburgh area. When he died in 1806, he had 6,770 acres that reverted to the state. In accounts due his estate, the ledger included William Dunbar, who owed almost 224 pounds. Other references included gifts and loans from joint ventures with Dunbar in West Florida and Mississippi Territory—investments always recommended and monitored by Dunbar.[7] Alexander appointed Dunbar executor of his estate, a post Dunbar held until his own death in October 1810. (Dunbar's son-in-law, Samuel Postlewaite, completed the task of executing Alexander's estate.) Alexander and John Ross and Dunbar were plantation partners first in West Florida and then in the Natchez District from the beginning of Dunbar's Florida years in 1773 until the deaths of the two Rosses. It would be almost twenty years before Dunbar was able to repay the Rosses' investment in him, but he did. Their joint ventures over the years always left one owing something to the other, and payment of debts was never addressed in the thirty-five years they invested and worked together. There is no evidence that Dunbar's reputation for honesty and integrity was ever challenged by anyone.

For almost two centuries, a showdown between French, Spanish, and

British interests in North America seemed inevitable. All three nations practiced mercantilist economics and exploited their colonists and slaves to enrich business and political leaders back home. In Scotland, colonies were viewed as opportunities to invest money and time to make fortunes. The French and Indian War begun in 1754 was bitterly fought; until 1761 it was French and Indian allies versus the British, with heavy losses on both sides. By 1761, the French were exhausted and beaten and would have surrendered if Austrian allies had not refused to allow them to do so. In truth, British prime minister William Pitt did not want the war to end until the French were totally defeated and expelled from North America. In 1761, French and Spanish Bourbons secretly signed a family compact for common action against Britain. Pitt wanted to declare war on the family compact at once, but the new king, George III, desired peace and forced Pitt to resign. Nevertheless, to the chagrin of the Bourbons, the war machine Pitt had created quickly seized Florida, Cuba, and the Philippines. In the Treaty of Paris of 1763, the French ceded to Britain all of Canada, and Spain ceded to Britain all of Florida, which made Britain owners of all North America east of the Mississippi River. Britain did allow Spain to keep New Orleans and environs, partly as recompense for the loss of Florida and partly because New Orleans was unprofitable, an administrative nuisance too costly for Britain to govern in the future.

The Treaty of Paris created two new British colonies—East and West Florida. The British Privy Council issued instructions to the governor of West Florida to appoint a competent person to complete a survey of the colony and then recommend the best method of settlement. Knowing that a full survey would take a long time, however, the Privy Council authorized the governor to begin land distribution immediately. Because white settlement on what had historically been Indian land would endanger settlers, it was recommended that planters be settled in townships laid out in units of approximately twenty thousand acres each. Every township was to reserve space for the military and suitable land to provide naval stores. Every township was also to build a church with four hundred acres of adjacent land reserved for the maintenance of a minister and two hundred acres for a schoolmaster. In reality, the township idea was found to be impractical and was never implemented.

Every master or mistress in a family was entitled to one hundred acres for himself or herself and fifty acres for every other black or white man, woman, or child on the plantation. This was known in West Florida as "family right" land. Persons desiring more land than the family right entitled them to could receive one thousand more acres if the governor thought the petitioner was able to cultivate and improve it, provided he paid—to the receiver general of quit rent—on the day of the grant, five shillings for every fifty acres. Land acquired this way was called "purchase right" land. Two years after the grant was awarded, the grantee was subject to an annual quit rent. George Johnstone, the first governor of West Florida, established quit rent at the rate of two shillings per one hundred acres. Soon thereafter it was raised to a halfpenny per acre, or four shillings two pence per one hundred acres.[8]

Orders in the king's name issued by the Privy Council were called mandamuses. The terms in all mandamus grants in the Floridas were practically the same: the grantee was required to settle the land with white Protestants within ten years of the grant's date. The Privy Council wanted the land to be populated by whites as quickly as possible, so it was mandated that there be at least one person for every one hundred acres of land held by the grantee. As one historian noted, "The very circumstances of the creation of the province . . . made the distribution of land in West Florida a matter of fundamental importance."[9]

The acquisition of the Floridas through the Treaty of Paris made securing the lower Mississippi River an important matter for Britain. It sought to protect the new holdings by building four forts (Fort Charlotte near Mobile, Fort Bute on the north side of the Iberville River, a post at Baton Rouge, and Fort Panmure at Natchez) and offering liberal grants to rich lands from the Yazoo River to Baton Rouge. British officials also encouraged the introduction of large numbers of slaves—a practice prohibited by Spanish occupiers. From 1765 to 1773, growth was slow but steady. People came first from North Carolina and Georgia, then from South Carolina and even New Jersey. Some sailed down the Atlantic coast and entered West Florida from the Caribbean. More and more settlers began coming down the Mississippi River by way of the Tennessee and Ohio rivers. The more generous the British were with land grants, the more settlers came, urged on by the growing dissension between Britain and its colonies. By 1773, the number of settlers was significant, and most now came by the inland waterway route as Loyalists sought protection from a war soon to begin.[10]

William Dunbar was among the group coming not for protection from fellow colonists but for the plantation opportunities afforded by liberal land policies in West Florida. Before leaving Pittsburgh, he entered into an expanded partnership with John and Alexander Ross.[11] The Rosses loaned the money needed for the trip and instructed Dunbar to include them in all of his West Florida land activities. He was asked to select choice lands for them as well as himself. Dunbar descended the Ohio and Mississippi rivers with all his possessions secured on a crude flatboat.[12] He went to New Richmond, a settlement in Manchac near Baton Rouge, selected the land he hoped to secure, and sailed to Kingston, Jamaica, to purchase slaves before going to Pensacola to obtain a grant from Governor Peter Chester based, in large part, on the size of his slave purchases. Dunbar secured the land he wanted near Manchac and then traveled to his new home by way of Louisiana lakes and the Amite River.[13]

By 1773, the West Florida government was quite specific about the conditions for cultivation and improvement that must be met within three years. For every fifty acres deemed plantable, a potential grantee was required to clear and till at least three acres within three years. For every fifty acres considered barren, the petitioner was required to pasture at least three cattle. If no portion of the grant was fit to plant or graze, the petitioner must erect a house at least twenty feet long and sixteen feet wide. If the land was stony and unfit for cultivation or pasture, it was acceptable for the grantee to work at least one good hand in a quarry or mine within three years, and the same time frame and number of slaves, for every one hundred acres in the grant. Fulfillment of one or more of these conditions was considered sufficient to forestall forfeiture of the grant. After meeting the three-year conditions, the holder had to present proof of fulfillment to the county court and have that proof certified in the registrar's office. As a part of the granting process, "the governor was directed to see that each grant contained a proportional number of profitable and unprofitable acres; that the breadth of each grant be one-third of its length; and that the length of any tract did not extend along the banks of any river, . . . that thereby the said grantee may have each a convenient share of what accommodation the said river may afford for navigation or otherwise."[14]

The growth of West Florida was slow but steady until Governor Chester arrived in 1770.[15] The most desirous land was in the west, along the Mississippi River, particularly at Manchac, Baton Rouge, and Natchez. Manchac was considered a place of importance from the beginning; it was key to the only possible inland waterway communication between the eastern and western parts of the colony. It was strategically located to receive valuable furs from boats coming down the Mississippi River. From Manchac, trade could also be carried on with nearby Indians, with the British who were fast settling the eastern bank of the river, and with the French who resided in and around the prosperous village of Point Coupee, located on the west side of the Mississippi River and slightly north. Fort Bute, established at Manchac in 1765 for protection, was abandoned in 1768. A town was laid out at Manchac in 1770, and upon Governor Chester's arrival in Pensacola, it began to grow quickly. Chester was enthusiastic about settlement, especially in the west, and he advertised generous land awards far and wide hoping to entice an increasing number of settlers.[16] He was committed to starting settlements across the colony, and by 1773 the numbers of petitioners and awardees were growing steadily.

William Dunbar was one of the 1773 petitioners, and his award came just before Parliament curtailed westward expansion as colonial punishment. In a May 16, 1773, letter to Lord Dartmouth, Governor Chester mentioned that several speculators "from the north had come down to prospect" and had asked that land be reserved for them so they could bring several thousand people into West Florida. In a letter received late that summer, Dartmouth told the governor not to increase grants, so Chester refused to issue future warrants for purchase right lands until Dartmouth clarified his instructions. Dartmouth did so in a letter received in October in which he threatened to end all grants because of the unruliness of eastern colonists.[17]

In the meantime, Manchac and Baton Rouge both threatened to overshadow New Orleans in size and importance. As one descended the Mississippi River, however, it appeared that Natchez might be a better location for settlers than Manchac or Baton Rouge. It was on the Mississippi River, was located at the southern tip of rich Mississippi delta lands, and was the first port of entry into West Florida for those traveling south. It was called potentially "the most flourishing Country in his Majesty's dominions." The negative factors were that the government in Pensacola preferred giving large tracts along the river to speculators rather than to individuals, Natchez was a long way from Pensacola and was petitioning (unsuccessfully) to become a second West Florida capital, and most discouraging of all, the Spanish controlled New Orleans.[18] The discriminatory policies of Spanish New Orleans officials checked British trade to and from Natchez until 1783, the end of the American Revolution.

The great attractions of Manchac, Baton Rouge, and even Natchez—all along the river—were the fertility of the land and the potential to move goods to other colonies, the West Indies, and international markets. Some cotton was produced, but only in small quantities; it would not become the major crop in the lower Mississippi region until after the American Revolution. As early as 1722, indigo became one of the staples in the region, and by 1725 it was being exported. By 1754, there were forty-seven indigo plantations with an estimated total yearly output of 82,000 pounds. By the end of the century, however, the crop's importance was fast declining because of new staples (cotton and sugar), a serious depression, ravages by insects, and exhausted soil that was responding "less favorably than for-merly."[19]

Lumber was an important crop that complemented the production of naval stores much needed by Britain. The seafaring power urged all colonies rich with lumber to help meet constant and growing naval store needs. The French hoped to make tobacco a commercial staple in Louisiana. France imported large quantities of tobacco from Virginia and the Carolinas and aspired to end that dependency by encouraging its growth in Louisiana. By 1772, considerable tobacco was being produced, especially in the Nat-chez District, and the quality was better than that of Virginia's tobacco. The Spanish raised tobacco around New Orleans after 1763, and Governor Ber-nardo de Gálvez issued a seventeen-point proclamation on June 15, 1777, outlining the growing, pricing, quality, and export conditions for all using the port of New Orleans to ship tobacco overseas.[20]

Wheat thrived in upper, but not lower, Louisiana, and by 1760 planters in upper Louisiana were shipping 800,000 pounds a year. Corn was be-ing raised everywhere, especially for home consumption. In 1776, a planter observed that if any corn crop failed "the greater part of the Negroes would perish," because it was the staple food product in their lives.[21] Its use was as common among the rich as the poor. But because of the semitropical condi-tions of West Florida, corn deteriorated quickly and, therefore, was not a profitable export crop.

During the eighteenth century, rice never became an export staple; there was an urban market, and rice was a staple for soldiers in the various home forts, but that was about it. The quality of the lumber in the region for naval stores, plus the cultivation of indigo at Britain's urging, made them the lower Mississippi's two most important export crops in the late eighteenth centu-ry. As early as 1731, peas and beans were being exported to the French West Indies, and by 1744, they were the most important exports from Louisiana to those islands. The list of fruits and vegetables raised for home consump-tion was long, from cabbage and cauliflower to pumpkins and watermelons, from chicory and turnips to sweet potatoes and asparagus.[22]

In America, as in Britain, agriculture was the means of support for the wealthy as well as the poor in the eighteenth century.[23] Though Alexander Hamilton, who championed the growth of cities and wealth through busi-ness, would prevail as the nineteenth century progressed, agriculture was the primary source of revenue in Dunbar's time. When we think of George Washington, we think of Mount Vernon, and Thomas Jefferson brings to mind Monticello. The same will be true of William Dunbar. He will al-ways be associated with wealth through agriculture, especially cotton, and in his day, his home south of Natchez, the Forest, would define success in Mississippi Territory. Such was not the case, however, between 1771 and 1790—the testing and up-and-down years.

From the time he arrived in Manchac, Dunbar was not wedded to any specific staple. However, he could not experiment as much as he would have liked because he was dependent on money borrowed from partners in Pennsylvania. Dunbar had little personal wealth, and he was on a mission to amass a fortune that would allow him to recoup that which was lost in northeast Scotland. That could not be done by raising peas and beans for export. Governor Chester and other British officials tried to steer new planters toward indigo, the preferred crop. Dunbar did experiment with indigo, but the shrewd Scot discovered another possibility when he was in Jamaica buying slaves—barrel staves.[24]

Fortunately for those who study history, in early 1776 Dunbar began keeping a daily journal that continued for the next five years. The diary is logical and easy to follow; as a scientist, Dunbar wanted all entries to be precise and exact. Even in the days of his youth, especially his King's College days, Dunbar was a stickler for both accuracy and completeness. Though the daily citations in the diary are often brief, they cover numerous subjects, some trivial, and illustrate clearly what life was like in the late 1770s on a plantation in a remote area with only waterways offering communication and trade routes to other places. It was a land with fertile soil, slave labor, few whites, and danger from everything from copperheads to smallpox.[25]

More than anything else, it was a land of loneliness and exploitation. Dunbar was twenty-three years old and unmarried when he began his labors in Manchac, so had time to oversee everything. He did have an overseer, and from time to time Dunbar hired other whites, to supervise building a road and constructing slave houses, barns, smokehouses, and other facilities, but for the most part we find him an involved planter pushing slaves six days a week, punishing those who ran away, got drunk, or actually plotted insurrections. Life was hard and cruel in that environment. Now and again, Dunbar received a letter from his mother—a letter he must have read a hundred times before saving it. She wrote with facility and beauty as she reported news from home, relayed greetings from friends and family adventures (including brother Thomas's military activities in America), and inquired after his health, while sending gifts for his new home.[26]

Since the only friends Dunbar had were other planters—about eight—they held quarterly gatherings to discuss mutual problems and, perhaps more important, to socialize one with the other. On Sunday, September 1, 1776, Dunbar wrote, "This day Messrs. Poupet, Ross, Ward, Gordon,

Marshall, and Cumings the Younger . . . dined with me." On September 18, 1777, he mentioned, "Yesterday being the quarterly meeting, the . . . eight dined with me. We spent an agreeable day & got merry by the moderate use of Madeira & Chalet [sic]." On Sunday, March 9, 1777, Dunbar noted that he "went to Poupet to be present at a meeting of the Settlement to conclude on some necessary resolves for the benefit of our little Society." Dunbar's 1776 and 1777 journals reflect frequent social occasions and contain precious few references to his scientific interests. On November 22, 1776, he wrote, "Enjoyed the pleasure of making Poupet happy by putting a new glass in his Telescope or Spy Glass." And on January 22, 1777: "Spent the evening in microscopic observations."[27] Still, those moments of intellectual enjoyment were few. On July 24, 1776, he received a letter from King's College classmate and friend John Swift, who chided him for not keeping up their correspondence on scientific subjects. "It is so long since you favor'd me with a line . . . that I am fearfull for your safety," Swift wrote.[28] Dunbar's chronicles reflect that he did not have time to do the things he had loved best as a young man in Scotland. He appears to have been simply trying to survive—and hoping to someday prosper—in the wilderness.

The diary is filled with references to illness, especially among the slaves. The references are as simple as "3 New Negroes sick," or "Mary and Mama sick," or "a new Negro died." Some got sick from the heat and hard work, including from hoeing accidents; others, from diseases or encounters with snakes and rats. One citation noted, "Killed a vast many ratts"; another referred to "a Rattle Snake with 14 rattles." Dunbar noted his own infirmities as well. On one occasion he wrote, "I found myself still mending tho' very weak."[29]

The topic that dominates all others in the 1776–77 portion of the diary is barrel staves. From the beginning, there was no doubt that Dunbar's major production was going to be the manufacture of barrel staves and that a large number of his plantation slaves (those working outside the home) were going to be producing thousands of staves.[30] Hardly a day passed without Dunbar's noting how many slaves were working on staves or how many staves were being produced per day or week, and he even staged competitions between his best stave makers with a prize for the winner. On Monday, January 13, 1777, thirteen hands were making staves; Dunbar noted the names of the three most experienced and expert and suggested a weeklong competition. He "proposed a premium of a green jacket among the three . . . to be given to him who shall give the greatest no. of staves before next Sunday." In that week, the three hands made 680 staves, the winner having made 247 of them. It was noted that Pollux lost considerable time because he broke one of his tools and had to seek a replacement. Dunbar noted the problem and promised "a competent allowance shall be made at the end of the week."[31]

A typical citation about barrel staves is the following: "This day made an addition to the No. of stave makers, being 9 in all: 2 Boys riving, 2 bolting, one saping, & 4 women sawing. Made today 399 W.O. [white oak] staves and 108 pr. Heading." Another is "13 Hands at stave making / having added Castor to the bolters. The wood exceedingly tough today." (The thirteen hands made only 380 staves that day.) The number of hands working on staves might be as few as six during spring and summer cultivation months and as many as fifteen during fall and winter months. Staves were a first-rate staple because they allowed year-round work and because, especially in the West Indies, there was a continuous demand for staves. On November 7, 1777, the hands carried approximately 100,000 staves to the bank of the Mississippi River "all ready for delivery upon the first favorable occasion."[32]

Though staves were the staple, Dunbar planted many crops, some for export, most for consumption at home. There are references to cutting cane and harvesting rice, peas, lots of corn, and pumpkins. One citation, dated March 20, 1777, notes that he distributed eighteen new individual hoes for the cultivation season ahead. Dunbar did export some indigo and rice, but very little. Barrel staves were the bread and butter of his plantation, but other chores for the hands—female as well as male—were endless. In addition to cultivating crops and making staves, they constructed roads, built and mended fences, constructed and maintained buildings, including their own quarters, and did every other chore imaginable on a plantation.[33]

The notations make it clear that slaves did all the work on the plantation. Though one should use care in visiting the beliefs of the twenty-first century on the eighteenth, the truth is that the institution of slavery never was defensible. William Dunbar hailed from a country in which the few ruled the many and peasants were hardly a step above slaves. In America, Dunbar found a society that long ago had accepted the institution of slavery, and his thoughts and actions fit right in. Much of his journal relates directly to slaves, not as people but as property to be bought and sold. Yet from the day he purchased slaves in 1773 until his death in 1810, Dunbar truly believed that he was as fair to his "property" as any slave owner in the country.[34]

In Dunbar's journal are many notations of slaves bought and sold. The asking and buying price most often mentioned in 1776 was approximately $270 each. Notations were as simple as "sold two Negroes," "sold a negro to A. Ross for $260.00," "sold 1 new negro to Mr. Poupet for $270.00, will pay in Dec. next."[35] Often the implication in Dunbar's journal was that he could house, feed, and clothe only so many slaves. When that number was exceeded, he would sell good and able slaves to friends. If he ever wanted to sell a mischievous or disobedient slave, Dunbar noted that fact in his journal as well.

Dunbar was very strict with slaves he found drunk. When a slave named Adam got drunk, Dunbar confined him to the "Bastile," as his makeshift jail was called. The next day Dunbar sentenced Adam to five hundred lashes "to draw a confession from him how he came by the Rum—which had the desired effect." Adam confessed that he had stolen the key to a storeroom when he worked as a cook and had taken the rum from there. Dunbar ordered a large, heavy chain attached to Adam's leg on December 7 and did not remove it until December 12, and then only because the leg had swollen so much. Dunbar, who complained often of the lack of gratitude some slaves had for his kindness to them, ended his comments on the Adam episode by stating, "I intend carrying him up to Point Coupee, where I shall sell him if I find an opportunity."[36]

Throughout the journal, Dunbar discussed punishments meted out to slaves. One particular instance is telling. On March 16, 1780, Dunbar participated in the trial of a slave girl named Molly Glass. Molly had an argument with a white girl, the altercation turned violent, and the white girl died at Molly's hands. Since a black had killed a white, it was not surprising that Molly was tried, found guilty, and hanged. What made this case unique, however, was that Molly was sentenced to "have her hand cut off & afterwards hanged until she is dead."[37] Cutting off Molly's hand guaranteed that she endured severe pain before being hanged. This pain would not only make the punishment exceed the crime but would also serve to cow other slaves who might consider harming whites.

Dunbar handled other incidents of fighting and biting among slaves— one lost a part of his ear—but only once did he confront a serious potential insurrection. On Monday, July 18, 1776, upon returning from a weeklong trip, Dunbar was visited by three fellow planters who informed him of a conspiracy, just uncovered, that had been conceived at Dunbar's house. Three of Dunbar's slaves and two others from nearby plantations were the principal organizers. Dunbar was appalled because, again, he always felt his fairness should translate into complete obedience. He wrote, "Of what avail is kindness & good usage when rewarded by such ingratitude." When the three were identified, Dunbar was further shocked; two of the three "had never before misbehaved and never once received a stroke of the whip." He rounded up the three conspirators from his plantation and accused them, but they pleaded innocence, even when confronted by informers—slaves belonging to Alexander Ross. The planters decided to take the slaves to Poupet's plantation for trial. Dunbar transported one of his slaves by boat. The accused had his arms and feet tied, and he sat in the bottom of the boat, "ashamed perhaps to look a Master in the face," Dunbar wrote. In the middle of the river, the slave threw himself overboard and drowned. Notice was sent throughout the neighborhood that a trial was to be held for the remaining four, and all were invited to this "solemn occasion," no doubt to show other slaves what could happen to them if they dared to plot a conspiracy. The trial was held, and all four accused were found guilty and were hanged the next day. Others less guilty—those who knew and did not alert their owners or were thinking about joining in but had not—received lesser punishments, mostly whippings. Because slave rebellion was the most heinous of slave crimes in the province, the receiver general had to pay the planters the average price for replacing the executed felons.[38]

In the 1776–77 years, there were also numerous incidents of slaves running away and of new slaves getting lost. In every instance of a lost slave, Dunbar led the way in an effort to find him or her. There was no punishment for getting lost; running away was another matter. On July 29, 1776, Dunbar wrote, "This morning Ketty & Bessy ran away, because they had received a little correction the former evening for disobedience." Ketty came home on her own and received only a tongue lashing. Bessy was found on another plantation; she was put in irons and returned home to receive "25 lashes with a Cow Skin as a punishment & example to the rest." On May 12, 1777, Dunbar wrote in his diary, "Two Negroes ran away but were catched & brought back. . . . Condemned them to receive 500 lashes Each at 5 Dift. Times, & to carry a chain & log fixt to the ancle. Poor Ignorant Devils; for what do they run away? They are well dressed, work easy, and have all kinds of Plantation produce at no allowance. . . . After a slighter Chastisement than was intended they were set again at liberty & behave well."[39]

It was true that Dunbar's slaves were well fed and clothed; they did not work on Sundays and some holidays; and he gave each a parcel of land to cultivate on his own. There are many instances of older slaves' getting easier jobs, and one slave was freed during Dunbar's lifetime: on Saturday, April 19, 1777, he noted that "Mr. Ross set out for Orleans, sent Daphne with him, having given her freedom."[40] But Dunbar was generally strict and unfeeling with respect to slaves. Now and again in his journal, Dunbar used terms such as "hands," "stupid savages," and "slow." He was pleased when slaves overproduced or broke stave-making records, but he never showed compassion for the sick, never expressed sorrow over a death, and referred to them as property, not fellow human beings. In these aspects he was much the same as other plantation owners; the contention that Dunbar was a kinder and more compassionate slave owner than most others in the old Southwest is not supported by slave owner journals, correspondence, or his own reports of his actions. When he died in October 1810, Dunbar did not free even one slave.

4

The American Revolution
in Manchac

As 1777 gave way to 1778, William Dunbar seemed quite pleased with his progress to date. His journal entries from this period are quite short and matter-of-fact but positive. He had been in America for nearly seven years, and he had accomplished much. Since landing in Philadelphia in April 1771, Dunbar had befriended the Rosses, found land to his liking in West Florida, acquired that land and a slave workforce, and progressed as a planter far away from the colonial rebellion against the mother country that had gone from angry protest to armed conflict by the mid-1770s. If the American Revolution worried Dunbar because it might disrupt shipment of staves to the West Indies and elsewhere, or might actually spread westward to West Florida by way of the Ohio and Mississippi rivers, he did not pen those concerns in his journal.

Young Dunbar's fortunes were soon to change dramatically. American patriot leaders had become concerned about the increasing number of Loyalists leaving their homes in the East for West Florida, a colony still loyal to Britain. Governor Patrick Henry of Virginia petitioned Congress to organize a military force of three hundred men to journey down the Ohio and Mississippi rivers to capture Natchez and Manchac.[1] Goods were gathered at Pittsburgh, and Captain James Willing, a frequent visitor to various West Florida plantations, including William Dunbar's, was appointed to head the expedition, assisted by Lieutenant John Campbell. The raid began in February 1778. Willing's journey was uneventful until he and his men reached the Natchez District of West Florida. Willing's orders authorized him to capture and secure Natchez and then Manchac. Since he had visited West Florida often in the recent past, however, Willing had a personal checklist of known

Loyalists, including William Dunbar. He and his men took Loyalist prisoners of war in Natchez and then systematically plundered the countryside before heading south to Manchac. They killed stock, seized slaves, stole private
property, and burned buildings. A few settlers had time to move their slaves
and other property across the Mississippi River into Spanish territory; other
planters simply hid in the woods. On February 21, Willing offered settlers
in the Natchez District a neutrality pact if they promised never to take up
arms against the patriots or give assistance to their enemies.[2] With no other
choice except open resistance, most signed the pact.

While negotiations with settlers were under way, a detachment of Willing's soldiers left Natchez for Manchac, where they seized the ship *Rebecca*,
plundered local plantations (including Dunbar's), and imprisoned local citizens. They then proceeded south to New Orleans with their booty, needing
to resupply their force before returning to plunder some more. Captain
Willing and patriot soldiers appeared in Spanish New Orleans with stolen
slaves, household property, an armed ship, and irate British refugees demanding that the Spanish officials force Willing to return their property.
The American raiders not only disobeyed their orders not to rob, burn, or
otherwise destroy homes and settlements, but they left upriver—all the way
to Natchez—outraged settlers demanding protection and revenge.[3]

The raids took place on the British side of the Mississippi River, and
Dunbar was far too busy trying to save his plantation to offer day-by-day
comments. He suspended his journal notations in late February 1778 and
did not return to the journal until May 1. He noted that he was informed in
late February that a party of Americans had arrived in Manchac and seized
the community. Dunbar immediately moved his slaves to the Spanish side
of the Mississippi River and then went to Manchac to view for himself what
had happened. He found that the *Rebecca* had been taken by thirteen raiders, who moved the boat south of town for protection. Rumors abounded,
some suggesting that between five thousand and eight thousand soldiers
were on their way from Natchez. Dunbar returned home and then departed
for Point Coupee to get more accurate information about the size of the
invading force, "not suspecting that any mischief was intended to the peace-
able inhabitants."[4]

Near Fort Coupee, a fellow planter advised Dunbar to move his slaves at
least ten miles inland on the Spanish side of the river in case the Americans
were inclined not to respect Spanish territory and confiscated slaves from
both sides of the river. The friend also told Dunbar that American soldiers
were robbing and plundering every British subject possessing property, especially those on James Willing's blacklist. Dunbar moved his slaves inland

while damning Willing, a young man from Philadelphia who had often visited West Florida and had enjoyed Dunbar's hospitality on more than one occasion. Dunbar noted in his journal that Willing "frequently indulged his natural propensity of getting drunk—this was the gentleman, our friend and acquaintance, who had frequently lived for his own conveniency for a length of time at our house."[5]

When Dunbar returned home after moving his slaves inland, he found that Willing and his men had plundered his property: everything worth taking was missing, from silverware to sheets, from weapons to tools. Dunbar did find a letter from Willing pledging the safety of Dunbar and his slaves, and he found also that his home and barns had not been burned to the ground. Some animals had been shot, but he was lucky compared to other planters in the area. Always thinking, Dunbar left for New Orleans and obtained permission from Spanish authorities to buy plantation land on the western side of the Mississippi River. "I made a purchase in the Accadian Country & soon after brought down all my negroes & effects to form an establishment."[6] If he were to be denied economic success in America, it would not be because he succumbed easily to adversity.

In the meantime, Captain Willing was being frustrated by Spanish officials in New Orleans, especially Governor Bernardo de Gálvez. After several boats were sent up and down the river plundering and pillaging, Willing returned to New Orleans for protection. His plan was to eventually take plundered goods back up the Mississippi and Ohio rivers to Fort Pitt and to contribute all booty to the war effort, thereby emerging as a genuine hero of the American Revolution. He had a problem, however: the Spanish governor would not let him take goods and boats back up the river.[7] Gálvez feared a British attack on New Orleans if he allowed Willing to do so, and he could not fend off what surely would be a major assault. Then again, the British might be less likely to attack if he refused to allow plundered goods to get into the hands of rebelling colonists. The American agent in New Orleans, Oliver Pollock, pleaded, Willing threatened, and Virginia governor Patrick Henry requested, but to no avail. Gálvez wrote to Governor Henry, "I cannot agree to the proposal of commerce which your Lordship desires between the States and this province."[8] Willing's presence in New Orleans with plundered goods made life difficult for the wily Spanish governor, who saw frustrating the American colonists as the only safe course to follow.

Did the Willing raid accomplish its goals? History records that it did the American cause more harm than good.[9] The British came to believe that their previous judgment to abandon the colony was wrong and decided they should build strong forts on the lower Mississippi River to protect West

Florida and its citizens from invasion from the south and east. Therefore, Sir Henry Clinton, commander in chief of British forces in America, authorized sending one thousand soldiers under Brigadier General John Campbell to Pensacola. They were to build a "sturdy" fort at Manchac, and three hundred soldiers would be garrisoned there, along with two galleys for the protection of inland navigation "and the prevention of subsequent invasions."[10] The episode really ended on May 24, 1778, when Willing wrote Governor Gálvez, "It is with the utmost mortification I inform your excellency that the sudden and unexpected appearance of the Enemy in the Great Lakes has in a great measure frustrated my intentions."[11]

Even though the Willing raid was relatively unimportant when viewed within the fuller picture of the war for American independence, it cannot be summarily dismissed and forgotten. Maybe Willing's raid into West Florida was partially successful after all. His effort did force the British to dispatch troops and galleys to Pensacola to construct a fort at Manchac and monitor navigation of the Mississippi River, an annoying distraction to Clinton's overall plan for victory. Slightly less important, the Willing raid caused considerable hardship to William Dunbar and other Loyalists and their families who lived in the lower Mississippi region. Many planters did not recover. The ever-resourceful Dunbar did survive, but at a price. Though Dunbar had succeeded in hiding his slaves on Spanish soil west of the Mississippi River, many of them escaped during the confusion of February–June 1778. Dunbar had secreted away forty-one slaves, but the list of those remaining in October was considerably shorter.[12] In addition, all of Dunbar's personal property was confiscated or pillaged, his animals turned loose, and his fences torn down. He still had his land and his home—more than many others had—but he also heard rumor after rumor of American soldiers by the thousands descending the Mississippi River to secure the Manchac area for the patriots. The besieged Loyalists cheered the news that a fort was to be built by the British at Manchac to house soldiers and sailors patrolling and defending the area.

To hedge his economic bets, Dunbar secured a grant of land from the Spanish west of the Mississippi River and moved his slaves to the new holdings. He even moved a small house from his land in the east to the new estate on the Spanish side. It pleased him to learn that people were coming to the area—settlers, not soldiers.[13] They were Loyalist sympathizers from the Carolinas who were "desirous of settling in a friendly manner among the Natchez people."[14] With sympathizers moving into West Florida, with British soldiers due momentarily to build a fort and offer protection, and with the Willing raiders long gone in disgrace, 1778 ended in a more promising way than it began. On November 28, Dunbar went to Point Coupee to sell one of his plantations. Then, on December 13, he heard a rumor that made his heart sink: Britain and Spain had recently entered an alliance against the American colonies. The rumor proved to be untrue, as did dozens of other rumors circulating in this isolated section far away from the centers of combat in the East. On Christmas Day, "the Gentlemen of the Settlement dined with Mrs. Watts . . . and spent an agreeable day with great sobriety the gentlemen staying all night with me."[15]

For a time, it appeared that 1779 was going to be a better year than 1778. The plantation Dunbar had sold the previous November was replaced by a new one in the Acadian country. With the incoming soldiers (some arrived on January 29) and Loyalist settlers, Dunbar felt more secure than he had in some time, and in February he decided to return all of his possessions to his original plantation on the east side of the river. In August, Dunbar traveled to New Orleans with a raft full of staves for shipment. There he learned the devastating news that the previous year's rumor had the facts backward; Spain was joining the colonies against Britain. To make matters worse, Dunbar was detained in New Orleans as a prisoner until Governor Gálvez's expedition north against Baton Rouge and Manchac was finished. If the governor succeeded in taking the yet-unfinished Manchac fort commanded by Lieutenant Colonel Alexander Dickson of the Sixteenth Regiment and manned by 278 soldiers, Dunbar would be allowed to return home.[16] The fort capitulated on September 21, and the Spanish expedition returned, triumphant, to New Orleans.[17] Dunbar was free to leave, but when he arrived home he found that his plantation had once again been plundered. He was devastated. He had used what little money he had or could borrow to replace goods plundered in the spring of 1778 by Willing's men. Now all was gone, and he had no way to reprovision and rebuild. During the fall, he pondered his fate and possibilities for the future. On January 1, 1780, he wrote, "We are at present . . . Quiet upon our plantations tho' we are far from flattering ourselves with a Continuance of a state of Tranquillity. It is said Governor Galvez is now fitting out an expedition against Pensacola."[18]

There were many reasons that Spain joined France on the side of the colonies in the American Revolution. By 1779, both countries believed the colonists might actually win, and they saw a golden opportunity to retrieve land and privilege lost to Britain in the past. Spain wanted back the Floridas, and it yearned to see the Gulf of Mexico become once again a Spanish lake.[19] They cared little about the colonists. In fact, in many ways Spain hoped they lost the conflict, for colonists' gaining freedom from one country would set a bad example for colonists of other countries. Yet the potential for humiliating Britain and the lure of recovered land outweighed the fear of future colonial uprisings, so France and Spain, in a treaty signed by both governments on April 12, 1779, made common cause against Britain in America and around the world.[20]

The battle at the Manchac–Baton Rouge fort was an important moment in the American Revolution in the old Southwest and in the lives of Loyalist planters. Between February 5 and 25, 1779, 225 men had arrived to construct the fort. Rumor had it that 400 more soldiers were on the way, with possibly another 300 arriving by year's end. If the fort were completed and fully manned with 1,000 men, Gálvez would not be able to take the fort, so he asked for—and received—permission to take the offensive.[21] Gálvez attacked on September 3. The battle was fiercely fought, and the outmanned Sixteenth Regiment turned back attack after attack by Gálvez and his men. But the fort was unfinished and the garrison small, and the British soldiers simply could not win in the end. Gálvez signed articles of capitulation with Colonel Dickson on September 21.[22] Perhaps Gálvez exaggerated a bit when he wrote that "this victory should be placed in history among those of the first rank," but it did cost Britain control of the Mississippi River and New Orleans.[23]

So far as Dunbar and his fellow British sympathizers were concerned, after the capitulation of the Manchac fort, they were now on their own in hostile country that Britain had to abandon to continue fighting in the East. No wonder Dunbar sat and pondered, during the fall of 1779, seeking an easy answer to a monstrous dilemma. The answer as 1779 gave way to 1780 was not apparent to him.

5

From Darkness to Light

There is no doubt that 1780 was the darkest year in Dunbar's life; it was also the beginning of a much brighter chapter in his life. As his thirtieth birthday approached, this man of Scottish fortune who might once have expected that the world owed him an American version of Duffus House and titles lost in Scotland had lost almost everything in America, too. He had nothing but land, a personal commitment to succeed, and hope in an unforgiving, mostly undeveloped part of a continent where the certainty of British supremacy was crumbling and a new nation of disparate colonies was being born. To make matters worse, the Spanish, who had lost the Floridas in 1763, were getting them back, and the pesky French would eventually reemerge all around him. Captain Willing had begun the destruction of Dunbar's dreams of economic solvency, and the Spanish helped matters not at all by joining in the struggle against Britain and ransacking what was left of Dunbar's seven-year effort to succeed in West Florida. All those staves shaped of white and red oak—all for naught.

Dunbar's position could hardly have been worse than it was in 1780. All of his movable possessions were gone, most of his slaves had disappeared, his fences were no more, roads suffered from neglect, and his animals were scattered to the four winds. To make matters worse, the winter of 1779–80 was "the coldest ever known."[1] A lesser person might have given up and moved on to more promising pastures, and many planter friends did leave—broken or disgusted men. The Dunbar of, let us say, 1773 might have joined them, but not the Dunbar of 1780. He was not a whiner, and he was willing to deal with life as it was presented to him. He still had land, empty houses, and a few slaves. More than anything else, he had an impeccable reputation for honesty among his neighbors and the merchants of Manchac and New Orleans. He struck honest bargains, kept his word, and paid his debts.

His word was his bond. Yet perhaps chief among Dunbar's traits was an insatiable curiosity. He seemed always to wonder what was around the next corner. For example, as he pondered the future, his favorite slave, Cato, died "after suffering excruciating pains. Had he lived till next morning," Dunbar penned, "I intended to have had a Chirurgical operation performed upon him to set the imprisoned air at liberty, which had it been performed early enough would have had the desired effect." After Cato died, Dunbar performed an autopsy and studied the intestines in an effort to save others who might show the same signs.[2] As a result of this and other postmortems, he developed medical procedures he and others used in the future—procedures that were quite advanced for his day.

Every now and then, a historian has to rely on instinct and conjecture when specific facts are missing. Such is the case with Dunbar's life in the early to mid-1780s. Here was a man who had decided to try one more time to succeed in America. Dunbar was twenty-nine years of age, without a wife and family, thousands of miles from any people who really cared about him. Perhaps it was a plus that he did not have to concern himself with supporting a wife and children. In the past he had shown himself as a man of good judgment and intelligence, one who had an unwritten plan to guide him.[3]

What we find in the early 1780s is a man trying for a second time to build an empire. He cleared land with the few slaves he had left, bought more slaves, and planted crops for export. No longer was he the "staves man"; now he was a diversified planter who depended on tried and true staples while experimenting with other plants not theretofore grown in Louisiana. Roads were repaired, fences mended, equipment purchased on credit. His journal is filled with such comments as "clearing the woods," "making a post & rail fence," "finished fencing in the great yard," and "commenced planting corn, rice, peas & pumpkins on my Spanish plantation." Because of the terrible cold in the winter of 1779–80, a number of slaves fell sick and a few died. Neither terrible weather nor loss of workers, however, deterred Dunbar from rolling up his sleeves, joining in, and planting and selling. Moreover, he now treated his slaves better; he continued giving them Sunday off and occasionally Monday and Tuesday as well, so they could work their own plots of ground.[4] Dunbar also expanded his interest in agronomy and charted the progress of everything he planted. He began planting cabbage and experimenting with different varieties of rice. In addition, he started evaluating the quality of corn planted on low ground versus high ground, in dry versus wet areas.

Dunbar had always dealt with honest merchants in New Orleans, and he never let an opportunity pass to visit with them to learn their needs and to send gift goods to them. On September 21, 1780, he sent a merchant 230 pumpkins by way of a canoe taking a neighbor to the city. Out of that trip came an order for 1,500 to 2,000 pumpkins at $3 a hundred. Dunbar sent all he had.[5] He became convinced in 1780 that to prosper he had to plant what was needed and wanted, that he had to market and deliver on time, and, most important, that he had to have a semipermanent presence in New Orleans.

What made success possible for Dunbar after the American Revolution was the fairness of the mercantilist policies followed by the United States and especially Spain. The United States was still thirteen faraway states snaking down the East Coast, whereas Spain's reacquisition of the Floridas and continued presence in New Orleans made it a much more formidable nation with which Dunbar had to contend. Fortunately, the Spanish were conciliatory—even friendly—to Dunbar because of his growing reputation for evenhandedness in business matters, success as a planter, and willingness to meet Spanish officials and settlers as coworkers in a not-too-friendly environment.

From 1781 until the running of the thirty-first parallel by Andrew Ellicott and William Dunbar in 1798, there was constant friction between the United States and Spanish Florida over the exact location of the boundary between American and Spanish land. Disagreements often led to violence and death. On one occasion—the Natchez rebellion on May 2, 1781—the Spanish commandant at the Baton Rouge fort issued orders to all plantation owners to do several things, such as surrender powder, guns, and boats and stay at home, but the rebellion ended two days later.[6] The Spanish never enforced orders that would discourage hard work, planting, and vigorous exporting and importing. Spanish officials were happiest when the port of New Orleans was overloaded with activity. Whatever squabbles developed between Americans and Spaniards in the old Southwest between 1781 and 1798 usually had something to do with disputed land grants or the boundary line. The rest of the time, commerce was brisk and New Orleans grew.[7]

The Spanish were quite liberal in their regulations. For instance, ships could go directly to some French ports and return duty free within ten years; they were exempted from paying duties on barrel staves and casks going to Spain; and colonists could buy foreign vessels without paying duties for two years and import slaves duty free for ten years.[8] These and other encouraging exemptions for colonists, which went into effect on January 22, 1782, were supported by Dunbar and others trying to reestablish plantations in the colony. Dunbar noted that even though Spaniards were Catholics they dispensed justice to Protestant settlers in a most impartial way. "A remarkable tribute to the integrity of the Spanish officers," he wrote.[9] The truth of the matter is that it was good business for Spanish officials and merchants to encourage planters to produce, import, and export goods.

For planters and farmers in colonies, mercantilism could ruin those who blindly followed national whims and demands. For example, as we have seen, the British and then Spanish governing West Florida urged the planting of indigo and tobacco before the Revolutionary War. The facts that indigo was difficult to raise and was subject to blight and insects and that tobacco was hard on the soil were of little interest to merchants back home profiting from those staples. For his part, Dunbar continued to resist fad staples and national urgings and to exploit the lucrative market for barrel staves despite British urgings to raise indigo. Tobacco also held little interest for Dunbar, despite its high prewar price and a generous postwar Spanish government price guarantee. Tobacco was never one of the major crops grown on Dunbar's plantation before the war and was never the major crop in West Florida. During the American Revolution, the colonial tobacco trade suffered. When the war began, the colonies were exporting 101,337,361 pounds of tobacco yearly; in 1782 tobacco exporting was down to 1,082,067 pounds—a good reason to get out of the tobacco business in the United States. Even though the tobacco trade revived after the conflict, it was slow in doing so. It was reported in 1791 that the British tobacco trade during the previous six years had not reached the prewar average.[10]

The Spanish really wanted people in and near Natchez to use its rich land to plant tobacco for sale in Spain. To encourage tobacco planting, the government guaranteed ten silver dollars per hundred pounds—a most generous offer. That guarantee encouraged people in the early to mid-1780s to mortgage their homes and farms to take advantage of a guaranteed sale at a subsidized price. Farmers did all possible to grow more and more tobacco to the exclusion of other crops. Production in the Natchez District went from practically nothing in 1779 to 589,920 pounds in 1786 and 1 million pounds by 1789. However, the Spanish discovered tobacco as good but cheaper in Kentucky and in December 1789 ended the guaranteed subsidy, thereby destroying the economic base of those planters in the district who had allowed the Spanish price guarantee to convince them to plant tobacco as a major crop despite diminished demand. Historian Jack Holmes noted, "Having stimulated overproduction, deficit spending, and excessive credit buying, the Spanish government changed its agricultural policies and, in so doing, lost the loyalty of its subjects, at least in Natchez." Governor Manuel de Gayoso wrote in 1796 that his district no longer exported tobacco and produced hardly enough for its own needs.[11]

Rather than focusing on tobacco or any other single crop, William Dunbar made the wise decision to diversify. In 1780, he developed goals for the decade: diversifying what was produced on his Louisiana holdings and spending the money he earned to purchase equipment and additional slaves, making his mark in New Orleans with a mercantile house and a capacity to serve Spanish officials, and taking Natchez land in payment for services rendered. He would begin by growing subsistence crops on his thousand acres of partially ruined West Florida land, and he would ship those crops to New Orleans for sale and export. Dunbar also borrowed heavily from John Ross to open a small mercantile house in New Orleans.[12] He was constantly on the move from Manchac to New Orleans and back again. He spent a great deal of time ingratiating himself with Spanish officials, especially Governor Gayoso, bringing him goods from the plantation and, because of Dunbar's facility with several languages, serving as an official Spanish interpreter. He became a surveyor of some renown, doing jobs for Spanish officials and citizens, but he seldom took money from government officials for his services. Instead, what he wanted from them was land in the Natchez District. Dunbar wanted someday soon to sell his Louisiana holdings, close his New Orleans mercantile house, and move to Natchez, where the land was rich and the ability to ship crops excellent. Natchez was where Dunbar would realize the dream he had outlined as he crossed the Atlantic Ocean in early 1771.

For the historian interested in all facets of Dunbar's life, he could be maddening. Through the years, many Dunbar papers have been lost or borrowed and not returned, but the content of the remaining manuscript material suggests that the lost correspondence would probably shed little light on the private lives of the man and his family. Dunbar simply did not commit to paper personal feelings, except in greetings and salutations. He wrote freely and extensively about plantation news, experiments, neighbors, and his environment, but he offered hardly a word about his private life beyond confirming his love for his family.

We know that Dunbar married Diana Clark in 1784, but we know nothing of their meeting, their courtship, or the marriage itself. One historian claims that "Dinah" was the fifteen-year-old niece of John Ross; another says that she was a widow with two children and that her name was really Diana, not Dinah; yet another suggests that she was an Englishwoman of much charm and beauty.[13] Since she signed her letters Diana, I assume that her name was, indeed, Diana Clark Dunbar. However, since the name Dinah is used by most historians, has infiltrated the Mississippi Department of Archives and History, and is even so listed in Dunbar's will and on her tombstone, I shall use the name Dinah in this volume. Historians are also not in agreement as to the number of children Dinah bore, with numbers from seven to eleven being offered (possibly two from a previous marriage), according to one investigator.[14] The absence of background information on Dinah is discouraging, yet we do know significant things about the marriage. Diana Clark hailed from Whitehaven, England; she came to America at an early age and made her way to the Manchac region to visit Alexander Ross, a relative. We do not know with certainty whether her visit was to be of short duration or if she was planning to live permanently in West Florida. Alexander introduced young Dinah to Dunbar, and a short courtship followed. When they married in 1784, she was fifteen; Dunbar was thirty-four. They were married twenty-six years—until Dunbar's death in October 1810—and during that time she bore nine children, eight of whom were still living at Dunbar's passing. Evidence is clear that she was responsible for no small portion of Dunbar's success from 1784 onward. Dinah was bright, hardworking, focused, and apparently as aggressive and single minded as her husband. Yet she raised their children with love and attention, and all of them who lived to majority succeeded in life as citizens and as contributors in myriad fields of interest. Before marriage, Dunbar evidently shared with her his economic dreams and social goals, which she enthusiastically accepted and referenced often in her letters to him.[15] From the beginning of their marriage, Dinah was a much-valued partner who helped advance their goals far beyond what either of them might have hoped in 1784. She was from an English family of some wealth, but Dunbar insisted on signing away his property interest in her estate before the marriage.[16] The two of them were determined to make it on their own in America.

From the moment of their marriage, Dinah assumed considerable responsibilities. She took over the management of the plantation in Manchac while Dunbar ran the mercantile house in New Orleans, accumulated land in Natchez, and built a home there that they occupied in 1792. For seven years, he was away from Manchac far more than he was there, and he left Dinah responsible for the slaves, breaking ground and planting, harvesting, mending fences, and other plantation chores. She, of course, had an overseer, and Dunbar helped a great deal when at home. Dinah and Dunbar had three daughters before moving to Natchez, and with little help, she was responsible for their care and upbringing. Her days were long and arduous, but for the most part, she carried out responsibilities with little complaining.

Dunbar and Dinah stayed in touch through letters sent up and down the river between Manchac and New Orleans or Natchez by way of friends and ship captains. Dunbar always insisted that members of his family write long letters, and so Dinah began a letter on August 11, 1789, by saying, "I am going to take your advice about writing a long letter." She noted that she was living in a little world while he labored among thousands of people in a larger world. Dunbar often advised her to take it easy. She thanked him for thinking about her but then chided him, "You seem to expect my dear that we have a deal of time upon our hands to do everything necessary about the plantation." She went on to write about repairing roads and fences after a hard rain, planting tobacco, suckering the plants, planting corn, and tending animals of all kinds. To his suggestion that she stay out of the sun as much as possible, Dinah responded, "I would willingly follow your advice & not go in the sun if I could avoid it, but there is many things to do about a place, that you men don't think of & I have not many servants." Her letters are carefully drawn vignettes of life on a plantation that is growing and diversifying. She wrote about a tiger (probably a panther) killing lambs, about packing tobacco for shipment, and about a domestic disagreement between her and Dunbar the last time he was home. She apologized and hoped he was not still angry, and then added, "I think I have some cause to be out of humor too," and stated her case one more time.[17]

What is illuminating about this correspondence is that the Dunbars made comments on everything going on around them. Yet something is missing in the letters—discussions of their personal lives with friends and family and information about activities of neighbors and business acquaintances. In letters, as with journals, Dunbar and Dinah wrote at great length about public topics but not private ones.[18] Now and again a private comment about each other or their children is found in a letter. Having learned from couriers that Dunbar had been ill in New Orleans, Dinah wrote that if she had known, "neither children nor the length of the voyage should have kept me from you." In the same letter, she wrote, "My whole happiness depends upon your fulfilling the dear sweet promise that we shall always be together."[19]

Throughout Dunbar's many journals, and all through their correspondence, Dunbar's illnesses appear again and again without explanation. He had a fever, or he was dizzy, or had one of many other conditions, none of which were ever explained. At times, Dunbar appears to feign illness or to be too sensitive to a pain or a headache, but as I studied his life through available original sources, I came to believe that he was not strong physically and succumbed easily to illness. Even at his death, we are told only that the accumulation of past illnesses—none are identified—finally prevailed. No specific cause of death was listed, and throughout his life no specific illness was blamed for his inability to labor at some task for several days. The Dunbars' letters reflect that he was often sick and Dinah worried about his inability to stay healthy for more than a short period of time.

When Dinah complained in her letters, it was usually about Dunbar's absence from home. In one letter, imploring him to come home more often, she wrote, "A pretty husband indeed that does not stay with his wife above 2 months in the year." She wondered, "Can my dearest be constant & faithfull in such a vile place as Orleans, where there is so many temptations, don't be angry with me my love for expressing my doubts, tho in my heart I am persuaded I have little cause, for I think if there can be a husband true to his wife, it must be mine."[20]

Dinah had every right to express doubts with Dunbar gone most months of the year for the first seven years of their marriage. Life was hard for her, but she continued to oversee numerous tasks around the plantation. Dunbar sent her cloth to turn into clothes for him and the family, and she wrote back descriptions of the kind of thread to send along, as well as her need for shoes, penknives, and other goods. Dunbar also wrote of unfinished scientific experiments left behind for her to tend and complete, such as recording the temperature three times a day and the amount of rain left by each rainstorm—activities requiring ever more work and time on her part. Also, Dunbar did not hesitate to request special presents for Governor Gayoso; on April 4, 1790, he asked for some tobacco for "Govr. Gayoso, who stands always my firm friend. If you get some good fresh beef my love . . . that we may eat some of it together & perhaps it may be opportune to offer some of it to Govr. Gayoso for his passage."[21]

By 1785, Dunbar was resuming his scientific activities on a large scale for the first time since leaving Scotland. He felt guilty about bringing home equipment of every description while forgetting to bring a present for his young bride. When he needed to return to New Orleans to sell produce and run his business and, later, to travel to Natchez to build his new plantation home, Dunbar again left behind numerous half-completed experiments all over the house, barn, and yard. And, of course, he wrote instructions so that Dinah could continue the experiments "in her spare time." When he wrote these instructions in a letter, he usually added a postscript swearing eternal love and affection for her and the children.[22] The marvel of it all was that she not only did everything asked of her but did it well, working toward the day she would become perhaps the most envied lady in Mississippi Territory.

Both Dunbar's business in New Orleans and his Manchac plantation were moderately successful by 1786, affording him more time for reading, experimenting, and making more and more friends in New Orleans, with

Governor Gayoso his major benefactor. Dunbar became perhaps the most valued surveyor in West Florida. He studied horticulture and was bombarded with requests to design original formal garden patterns at high fees. He studied architecture and designed three plantation homes for friends. He served as a Spanish interpreter in German, English, and French. When funds were available, he ordered astral equipment, and he experimented with original ideas on better ways to fix exact latitude and longitude than had theretofore been possible. Dunbar also invented five kinds of plows, all designed for different depths and various land formations. By 1790, he was becoming quite interested in the possibility of planting cotton along the Mississippi River and suggested a prosperous future for the crop if the seed could be separated from the fiber. Dunbar also demonstrated an interest in botany and zoology by identifying and cataloguing, for the first time, the plants and animals of the old Southwest. As his economic endeavors succeeded and he prospered, Dunbar spent more and more time pursuing scientific activities. Mostly, though, he ordered journals and books, read constantly, and developed the finest personal library in the region.[23]

By 1788, Dunbar had acquired more than five thousand acres of land in the Natchez region from the Spanish government. He cleared portions of the land, purchased more slaves, and put them to work farming under an overseer. Now Dunbar divided his time among New Orleans, Manchac, and Natchez.[24] He was well pleased with the fertile land in the lower delta region, and in 1790 he began thinking about selling his business and Manchac holdings and building a plantation home for his family on the Natchez lands. Dunbar decided to design the house and landscape the grounds himself; he would fashion one of the most beautiful estates in the old Southwest. When he broached the subject with Dinah, she danced about and happily agreed. It was time for the growing family to settle down in one place, enjoy living together, and reap the fruits of their years of toil.[25]

By early 1791, Dunbar's architectural plans were prepared and the business disposed of, and he was ready to begin construction of his Natchez home, which he had already named the Forest. Until the discovery of the original carpenter's contract, little was known about construction of the Forest. That document sheds light on this remarkable home and grounds.[26] Pictures of the Forest are rare, the most accurate being a pencil sketch drawn by a family governess during the first decade of the nineteenth century. Unfortunately, the home was destroyed by fire in 1852, and only a handful of erect columns still reflect its previous grandeur.

Dunbar, Dinah, and the children moved from Manchac to the grounds of the Forest in 1792. They lived in the carriage house for three years, while

Dunbar and his slaves finished the structure. Dunbar used slave labor to make bricks for the columns. During the next fifteen years, he landscaped approximately 150 acres of formal gardens, a park, two orchards, a lake, and a garden for experimental planting.[27] Dinah supervised the construction of a spacious kitchen near the home, and Dunbar built a laboratory that would become the finest in Mississippi Territory by the end of his life. It was in that laboratory that he spent much of his leisure.[28]

What a difference a decade can make! In 1780, Dunbar stood destitute in the midst of ruined property and dreams; in 1790, he had a wife and children and was designing what would become one of the finest plantation homes in the old Southwest. His plan of action was working, thanks in part to a willing partner capable of joining him in executing that plan success-fully. He might ultimately have reached this goal as a bachelor; it appears doubtful, though, that he would have been living in the Forest as early as 1792 without Dinah laboring by his side.

6

A Dream Realized

One claim made by visitors to Natchez is that it is the most charming small city in America. It's not on the way to anywhere, so tourists must go out of their way to walk its streets, see its old southern homes, and cloak themselves in its distinctive history. Its unique features today are the same ones William Dunbar inherited in 1792—high hills on which stately homes were being built, with the largest river in North America flowing by; a lower level, Natchez under the Hill, to which ships of all kinds and sizes docked, depositing and loading goods to and from across the globe; a panoramic view to the west—and Natchez has always looked to the west—that was majestic, and even haunting; and soil rich enough to tempt folks from everywhere. Despite its westward vista, it was becoming, in 1792, southern in a way unmatched by any other southern community, even Charleston and Savannah, or any other town founded and growing along the Ohio and Mississippi rivers. Perhaps it was Natchez's inaccessibility, except by water or burdensome trails; maybe it was because of what William Dunbar and others did with cotton, and slaves, and equipment, and rich land. It might have been because tea, ham biscuits, and pretentiousness on the hill were matched by cornbread, sour mash, and boisterous people under the hill. It could be that Natchez's dimensions were open and obvious; whatever, in the old Southwest in the late eighteenth century, it was America aborning.

Though Natchez was still a Spanish district, there were not many Spaniards there. In 1785, the population included 1,121 whites, 438 slaves, and no free blacks. Baton Rouge and Manchac were much smaller, with only 68 whites, 100 slaves, and 2 free blacks.[1] And Natchez was growing; by 1790, the white population had grown to 2,000.[2] The absence of Spanish citizens in a Spanish district drew the ire of many Spanish officials. One wrote the governor in New Orleans that the greater number of those in Natchez "were vagabonds, dregs of Europe and America, . . . men abandoned of all vices, and capable of committing any crime. They . . . have devastated this district." He pleaded for a fort of thirty to forty men to keep down crime.³

Most, however, described the Natchez of the 1790s differently. Andrew Ellicott, a future professor of mathematics at West Point and Dunbar's fellow commissioner surveying the thirty-first parallel line in 1798, journeyed to Natchez in 1796 to prepare for the surveying assignment. Ellicott, originally from Pennsylvania, possessed a keen interest in agriculture and the growth potential of the country. He wrote in his journal that Natchez was the capital of the district and that eighty to ninety houses dotted the high hill overlooking the Mississippi River. He noted also that the streets were laid out logically and that there was "much ground" between houses. He visited Fort Panmure, on the highest point near the river, commanding both the town and the river. The fort was in disrepair and probably could not provide defense for even a short period of time. Ellicott praised the stewardship of Governor Don Manuel de Gayoso, noting that his enlightened policies were as responsible for the growth of Natchez as was the richness of the area's land.⁴

Ellicott wrote that the population of the Natchez District was about five thousand inhabitants in 1797; the houses, "not neat or clean," offered few comforts. "I have seen houses possessed by responsible people scarcely furnished beyond first stages of civilization," he wrote. He found Natchez's weather to be "delightful" most of the time, but he admitted that summers were "somewhat too warm." He commented on a number of things he found in Natchez: Roads were very good, especially since the mode of transportation was horseback. Cotton was taking over the district and several gins were in evidence; they could clean fifty pounds of cotton in a day, with the gin owner keeping one-eighth of the amount as his payment. Ellicott wrote also about the high quality of rice and tobacco but noted that both crops were dwindling in quantity.⁵

Ellicott, along with several others, noted that lodging and board were high priced but most primitive. A room with meals cost $1 a day—a sum many found outrageous, particularly since boarders had to pasture their own horses. All imported goods were very expensive, which did not surprise Ellicott, who suggested that they were "higher than need. Will be better after America fully takes over." He wrote that when the district became a part of America, it would "be the most flourishing in the south-west territory; and the town of Natchez far to excel every other on the banks of the Mississippi."⁶

Ellicott's comments regarding Natchez residents are perhaps his most interesting observations. He indicated that society in Natchez was low and without manners and that people lived a second-class existence. In Ellicott's view, what many called plantations were, in reality, log houses badly furnished, sitting on land worked by slaves, with a few cattle and primitive agricultural tools, but not much else. But he did think that the inhabitants were "generally a sprightly people. . . . Many of the planters are industrious . . . [and] possess the virtue of hospitality." Moreover, Ellicott said, "some sensible people and men of education" had migrated to the Natchez District; thus manners might soon change.[7] What he, among others, stated was that Natchez was a frontier outpost that was growing and had great prospects. It is not surprising that there were few inns in Natchez or other southwestern outposts, because the Natchez Ellicott discovered in 1796 was a fairly new growth settlement, theretofore on the way to nowhere, except the river.

What drew people to Natchez was not only the quality of the land but the prospect of securing grants to that land from the West Florida government. Captain Philip Pittman noted that Natchez was the "finest and most fertile part of West Florida." The land was high, with rolling fields and fine meadows.[8] Ellicott highly praised the location of Natchez on a mighty river upstream from the greatest seaport in the country—New Orleans. On January 10, 1799, after running the thirty-first parallel with Dunbar, Ellicott wrote in his journal that "no place upon this continent, and perhaps the world, can command the trade of an equal extent of fertile country as that of New Orleans."[9] One surmises from the comments of many observers that for the importing and exporting of goods, Natchez was a jewel within a jewel.

If one could remove 1778 and 1779 from Dunbar's adventure since leaving Scotland, one would conclude that he was more often than not in the right place at the right time. His association with the Ross family steered him in the right direction; he went to the colony of West Florida at the right time; and he became a favorite of the Spanish governor in the 1780s, leading to land cessions around Natchez. His migration there in 1792 was also fortunate timing. Natchez was emerging, and he profited by the advancements that he, as much as anyone else, would engineer. Arthur Herman, in his monograph *How the Scots Invented the Modern World*, writes about what migration from Scotland, the poorest and nigh-on-smallest European country, meant to the rest of the world in the eighteenth and nineteenth centuries. Primogeniture and poverty unleashed talented, inventive, and educated people who migrated to America, Australia, Canada, and most everywhere else. As Sir Walter Scott said, "I am a Scotsman; therefore I had to fight my way into the world."[10] That kind of spirit brought William Dunbar to America, first to West Florida and now to Natchez, and kept him from quitting in 1778–79. The precision of his plan and his partnership with Dinah turned the plundering of wartime into prosperity.

And Natchez played a role—an important one. Some commentators have painted a more idyllic portrait of old Natchez than did Ellicott. Anna Gillespie Haydn wrote of handsome homes, acres of fruit trees, landscaped gardens, happy children, and privileged guests.[11] There was some of that as Natchez aged, agriculture diversified, and cotton became a major crop in Mississippi Territory. There were orange groves, gardens, cattle, horses, sheep, and mules,[12] and there was nearby New Orleans, through which goods could easily be shipped both ways. There were a few lovely homes and producing fields in old Natchez, but for most, hardships associated with all early and isolated settlements plagued Natchez, and life was difficult though the future was promising.

Probably more than most places in America, the Natchez of 1792 was growing in importance on the backs and sweat of slaves as much as on the genius of men like William Dunbar. Of the 4,346 Natchez inhabitants in 1792, 44 percent were slaves; in the Second Creek area, where Dunbar lived, it was 53 percent, laboring in an almost exclusively agricultural environment.[13]

One might expect that Dunbar, Dinah, and the children finally settled down to a plantation life where Dunbar could, after two decades of absence, resume a life of scientific inquiry supported by the finest personal laboratory and library in the old Southwest, but such was not the case. He continued his constant journeys to Manchac and New Orleans, selling crops, settling loan accounts both owed by and due him, and working for Spanish officials. Nothing really changed from those years in Manchac when he traveled up and down the river all year long, except that now the trip was longer. He continued apologizing for being gone so much—at least half of every year— and Dinah continued complaining of his absences and her multiplying duties as a lady envied and admired in the district. Dunbar continued his instructions to Dinah on planting, harvesting, and other necessary chores to be carried out. He wrote Dinah, "I am of the opinion your indigo seed must be fit to cut," and noted that the "fence ought also to be made near your hill to enlarge the yard for beating indigo."[14]

Dunbar's trips were as essential to the family's economic progress as were his plantation instructions to Dinah as he became ever busier in a variety of pursuits. As we have seen, the family lived in the plantation carriage house until 1795, while Dunbar and his carpenters were putting the finishing touches to the Forest, including his laboratory and Dinah's kitchen. Dunbar purposely constructed a plantation home that would outshine Duffus House back home in Scotland, and it cost him a great deal of money to do so. His crops were also first rate, but they took managing and marketing. He shipped goods to New Orleans, sold what he had, spent that money, and borrowed more to purchase the goods he and Dinah wanted for the Forest. If his loans had been call loans, he might well have had to settle for less, but his integrity was unchallenged and his credit good.

Dunbar grew some tobacco, but not for export, only for friends and creditors in New Orleans, and he kept a sharp eye on the local market. For example, in 1792 the price of indigo was terrible, and he had to study the market to determine whether he should cut back production, end the planting of the crop on his plantation, maintain the current production level, or wait out a short-term consumer problem. He traveled by boat directly from Natchez to New Orleans, but on the more difficult return trips he went to Baton Rouge by boat and Adam, one of his slaves, brought horses there for the remainder of the trip.[15] Though his responsibilities had increased, he never complained of anything other than his extended absences from home.

Dunbar's letters were more personal now than they had been in the 1780s. Business still dominated, but now only 95 percent of the time rather than the previous 99 percent. Since he was truly interested in medicine, he spoke of experimenting with remedies for different illnesses and trying them out on New Orleans children. If they helped, he passed them along to Dinah for their children. "I am sorry to find the children have been so ill," he wrote in June 1792; "it would be good I think to make them drink some sassafras tea or other diluting liquor to purify their blood."[16] In a 1797 epidemic in Natchez—when even Andrew Ellicott moved seven miles inland—Dunbar refused to flee to higher ground because he intended to try out a bleeding cure for fever and headaches. In many of his letters, he implored Dinah to have the children write to him. "Kiss the little girls & Billie for Papa and ask them to write me soon," he wrote in February 1794.[17]

Travel on the Mississippi was dangerous and long, and overland travel was even more so, with marauders stalking the pathways.[18] Dunbar reached Baton Rouge from Natchez by flatboat. Even with the current, it took four days to make the trip, with 125 miles still to go to New Orleans. It took twice as long to navigate going upstream or by footpaths. Natchez to New Orleans and then back—there seemed to be no end to this time-consuming and dangerous travel. He was always happy to be home between planting and harvesting, and he wrote Dinah, "We shall then constantly be together until it is time to fetch down the crop."[19]

What detained Dunbar the longest in New Orleans was not selling crops or purchasing items but paying off and collecting debts. He wrote that he was sorry to be delayed but "there is yet 700 dollars of indigo seed money to be received & I still owe Mr. Neil 2000 dollars which must be settled here."[20] He spent much time buying the goods Dinah wanted—seemingly an endless list—and he had to see that the goods were shipped by water up the river to Natchez. Dunbar bought from England, France, and other countries, as well as America, and he worried about their safety with the Napoleonic wars in full bloom on the European continent. Yet he could write, "I have bought paper for your house & most of your commissions."[21] On May 5, 1794, he wrote, "I am upon the eve of finishing all of my business. . . . I hope to settle with every body else in a day or two."[22] Finally on May 19, 1794, he wrote Dinah the following happy news: "Your forbearance my dearest shall not be thrown away upon me, . . . I may now say that my business is finished, because I have received all the money that I believe I shall get at present." Of course, he had to add a few instructions for sending horses, ordering oxen, and punishing slaves. Dunbar wanted Dinah to be ready to hitch their oxen to wagons and to borrow three more oxen and wagons from neighbors to cart home all of the goods that would soon be arriving in Natchez for the Forest, including a small box of china for Dinah's tea table.[23] Slowly, long stays in New Orleans became shorter ones as business stabilized, but frequent trips to the Crescent City to buy and sell goods, and to ship purchased goods up the Mississippi River to Natchez, continued.

Life in Natchez was full, exciting, and ever diversifying. Dunbar came upon an early cotton gin, began tinkering with it, and, though he did not invent a new gin, made cotton gins more efficient. Horse racing got started on a grand scale in Natchez, and Dunbar participated with both horses and architectural expertise when he helped build the racetrack, Fleetfield. Andrew Jackson owned a quarter-horse track near Bayou Pierre, and, so it would seem, a number of the first citizens of the district were participating in the sport of kings. Dunbar was among them as his friendship with Governor Gayoso continued to hold him in good stead. Non-Spaniards were treated fairly by the Spanish justice system, and the governor continued his successful efforts to populate the district. Natchez did not have a jail, so under Gayoso's direction, Dunbar drew up the plans for a well-ventilated jailhouse. Also, the governor wanted to see political power in the hands of local settlements. Syndics were appointed to represent the people and to supervise local affairs. The governor created what today we would call a city council for Natchez District. It included eighteen elected members, with two coming from Second Creek; Dunbar was one of the first two elected.[24]

Two things Dunbar and Governor Gayoso had in common were a love of learning and splendid personal libraries. When the governor died, 411 volumes representing approximately 165 different topics were auctioned off to the highest bidders.[25] There was no count of Dunbar's growing library—surely the best in the old Southwest—but he had volumes by Thomas Ruddimanno, Jared Sparks, John Locke, M. L. Weems, and others, with an emphasis on astronomy, the natural history of the earth, minerals, great waterways, and terrestrial bodies. There were volumes from many different countries and in myriad languages, and they mirrored a mind never ceasing to grow.[26] Neither the Gayoso nor the Dunbar library was large by Philadelphia or Boston standards, but for an outpost on a dangerous river a thousand or more miles away, they were most impressive.

Dunbar was also a songwriter—one song, simply titled "Scotland," was a particular favorite of the family through the decades. Stories of his surveying and architectural skills abounded, even before he arrived in the Natchez District, and those stories became a part of the burgeoning Dunbar legend. The earliest story, and possibly the one that gave staying power to the Dunbar legend, revolved around the Forest—the architectural wonder of the district. Its grounds, gardens, and orchards were spectacular, and the home was stately yet inviting. At the heart of the legend of the Forest, however, was not the plantation home itself but the hospitality with which the Dunbars entertained individuals and groups. Shortly after they occupied the home, Dunbar wrote to Dinah that three ladies from London were in Natchez and might call on her. He urged her to invite them to spend the night and to dine with her. He told Dinah that they were going to be hospitable to everyone despite their station in life,[27] and that was the creed they followed throughout the remainder of their lives. Indeed, the Forest became the Southwest's yardstick for hospitality. A preacher friend from a neighboring community hinted broadly that he wanted to spend New Year's Eve at the Forest.[28] Remembering one of the parties, Dunbar's son, William Dunbar Jr., remarked, "I wish I had made somebody count the carriages & horses that arrived at a fine moonlight night." He estimated one hundred people attended, and he described the tables, the bar, and the desserts. They used "225 lbs. of ice buckets of lemonade which disappeared in a twinkling," and the noise of popping champagne corks reminded him of a bird hunting trip.[29] A newspaper called the Forest a "princely estate . . . a mansion . . . in the same bounteous fashion" as those of "Washington and Jefferson."[30] It was a welcoming beacon a short distance from Natchez.

It was easy for Dunbar, a Scot, to migrate to an English colony soon to be a Spanish colony and then live out his life as an American. There is no doubt that Dunbar was proud of his heritage, but he was always completely loyal to the country he served and in which he lived, and legend has it that his loyalties were reflected in a portrait that features him dressed in a black coat in the style of the day. According to the story, his coat was originally painted a British red but later was painted over because of the anti-British sentiment still strong in America.[31]

It would be difficult to overstate the affection Dunbar had for Governor Gayoso; they were the best of friends. Because the governor's policies were fair to all and because he made land ownership so easy, Dunbar could not do enough for his friend. In a June 1792 letter to Dinah, he asked about the quality of the yams and potatoes and added, "Suppose you were to send a bag to the Gov. if they happen to be very fine."[32] He considered the governor the ablest of all officials and "personally incorruptible."[33] In fact, the citizens of Coles Creek District even named a town Gayoso de Lemos, an honor that truly moved the governor. One of the petitioners in favor of the name was William Dunbar.[34]

The 1790s were good to Dunbar and his family, but a tragedy befell them—a misfortune that would sadden Dunbar for the rest of his life. Dunbar wrote to his beloved sister, Peggy, in Scotland, asking her to join him and his family in Natchez, and he sent along money to "fit her out genteelly." Peggy excitedly accepted the invitation and set sail for America. Dunbar awaited her arrival or word that she was on the East Coast and needed help making her way to Natchez. After several months had passed, he grew worried and sent word home to his mother asking about Peggy. Anne was shocked by the inquiry, for she thought Peggy had arrived in Natchez and was enjoying a new life in America. Lady Anne and Dunbar waited anxiously: no word from Peggy. Dunbar asked about the ship and learned that it had disappeared, apparently never to be heard from again; she surely died at sea. In a letter to Dunbar, his mother expressed trust in the Almighty and said, "Indulge me in letting me see you before I leave this world." That wish was to be denied. Dunbar never saw any member of his immediate family again.[35]

One of the hallmarks of William Dunbar was his ability to develop a plan and then to focus on it. He had many opportunities to cry "enough," or to retreat, or to change goals. After the American and Spanish invasions of 1778 and 1779, he could have retired to New Orleans and become a successful businessman. In part he did that, but only as a means of recouping what was lost in those two years and rekindling his dream of economic success in the old Southwest. If being a merchant in New Orleans would earn him money, get him land, and develop a network of supporters, Dunbar would do so for as long as it took to guarantee success. In short, he wanted to venture where others had not gone, and he wanted to advance mankind through science.

Yet Dunbar seemed not to care that the land producing the good life for him and his family had been taken from Indians who had occupied it for centuries or that those making economic and social success possible for the Dunbars were slaves. He must have sensed the irony in that reality, but he never addressed it in his journals or correspondence. Like most fellow planters across the South, he saw slaves as one sees a tractor or a harvester today—as providers of agricultural bounty.[36] He wrote to Dinah in April 1794, "If the Negroes are obedient . . . & show a desire to do their best, they may do as well as they can." He asked her to tell the overseer not to work much himself "but to give an eye to every thing & keep every body else at work."[37] Dunbar's rules of conduct for his slaves were a part of his focus, which left little room for concern about status or the possibility of freedom for others on some distant day.

7

Emergence on the National Scene

L and brings out the best and worst in humans, mostly the worst. Many
assertions have been made about religious and political freedom as mag-
nets attracting Europeans to our shores, but the truth of the matter is that
land—its lack of availability to Europeans, from Spain to Scotland—is what
whetted the appetite for migration. Land was dear, essentially because there
was not much of it for most folks in Europe; that which was available was
reserved for a precious few through the medieval practices of entail and primogeniture and the control of the Church. Land simply was not available
to the overwhelming majority, and since it was the yardstick by which worth
was measured in Europe, people gladly died in endless wars and border
skirmishes to secure access to some of it. Gentry deprived by primogeniture
and commoners alike learned that there was a continent to the west, across
a mighty ocean, where land was so plentiful that it stretched endlessly westward. What is more, unlike the piece of earth they came from, that new
land in America was not worn out by overuse. True, every inch was already
owned by native people, but that fact simply was a stumbling block to be
removed in due course.

So they came to America seeking land. Two of the most important
groups that emerged in colonial America were land speculators and surveyors. Just about everyone of prominence speculated in land, from George
Washington to William Dunbar's friends and mentors, John and Alexander
Ross. The first requirement for purchase was that the land be bought by
someone representing some country, state, or speculator-owner. Then it had
to be surveyed to determine where each individual property began and ended. The problem was that different nations, each with its own land policy,
owned portions of eastern North America, and measurements varied among
them. During the seventeenth and eighteenth centuries, nations fought

each other over American land, the victors then dictating who owned what piece of land until the next war changed possession. For example, as we have seen, Britain possessed West Florida in the early 1770s, when Dunbar sailed to Pensacola to receive a grant to land near Manchac. Would that grant be honored if another nation took ownership of that region? Maybe so; maybe not. There was little security in land ownership; it could be permanent or temporary depending upon conditions far beyond any individual's control. Who owned what, when was it secured, and whether an owner's saved and signed documents were legal were only the first questions in determining who had legal right to a piece of land. Even then, getting a new ruling country to recognize a legitimate grant made by another nation was always chancy.

As if that were not enough, there were endless disputes over where one nation's land ended and another's began—boundary disputes having to do with which nation had the right to sell or gift land near a nonsurveyed boundary and in which country a grantee's land was located. Problems and disputes were inevitable. That fact made surveyors valuable citizens in every colony. Knowing that, Dunbar became a knowledgeable and respected West Florida surveyor whose services were much in demand. He was known by citizens and Spanish officials alike to be honest, dependable, and timely in his work. I could find no case where his work was challenged either by a government or a grant holder. Dunbar emerged as one of West Florida's most trusted surveyors, and his friendship with Governor Gayoso cemented the influence he would exercise in West Florida, under English control until 1783 and Spanish domination for the rest of the century. Dunbar came to know the land of West Florida better than almost anyone else, and that knowledge led him to identify exactly what land he wanted for his own— land around Natchez. That is what he wanted, and that is what he got. Dunbar knew how that game was played, and he played it well.

Still, Dunbar and other non-Spaniards interested in Natchez holdings had a problem: they lived in a region where it was impossible to know with certainty who owned what and whose land titles would be seriously disputed. The region was home to Indian tribes, and it became French, English, and Spanish territory before becoming a part of the United States in 1795. To make matters worse, colonial charters were badly written, allowing, for instance, the state of Georgia to claim land from its eastern boundary on the Atlantic Ocean all the way westward to the Mississippi River—an area that would later be the states of Alabama and Mississippi. North Carolina claimed Tennessee, Virginia claimed most of the old Northwest, and Connecticut claimed the Western Reserve, around what is now Cleveland, Ohio.

The confused American land ownership picture was most confounding in the old Southwest, where several nations, in addition to Georgia, claimed and granted land. Which grants were legal? More important, which should be honored? In 1789, Georgia—a sovereign state within the new United States—sold vast tracts in what would become Mississippi Territory to three entities jointly called the Yazoo companies. Their efforts to sell land from the Yazoo River to near Vicksburg were premature, so in 1795 they reorganized into four companies and, through bribery unheard of even among land speculators, pushed land grants comprising 30 million acres through the Georgia legislature at a cent and a half an acre. When the people of Georgia learned of the blatant land grab, they swept clean the legislature and, in 1796, repealed the cessions. It was not until 1802, though, that Georgia reluctantly agreed to its current western boundary, leaving the United States a messy $4 million bill to be paid to holders of Yazoo scrip. How could an honest landowner like William Dunbar know whether the fraudulent Yazoo land sales included any of the land already covered by legal grants he held? Just as important, how would he and other planters so affected be dealt with by an American judge and land agents when contested ownership cases made their way to court?

Spanish officials were often paranoid, expecting a double-cross. At first, the United States entered the Napoleonic wars on the side of France's enemies, but in 1794 the United States negotiated the Jay Treaty with Britain. This reaction alarmed Spain, which suspected the possibility of a common American and British action against Spanish territory in the lower Mississippi region. There was much discontent in Spain over high taxes and military reverses, so Prince Manuel de Godoy tried to reduce concerns about war by signing a treaty with France and negotiating with the United States. In 1795 the Treaty of San Lorenzo, which opened the Mississippi River to American navigation, gave Americans—for a three-year period—the right to deposit goods in New Orleans for transshipment without paying duties and surrendered the disputed lands in West Florida, including Natchez and all land north of the thirty-first parallel.[1] These generous concessions placated Americans for a few years.

The dispute over the location of the thirty-first parallel should have been settled years earlier. The Treaty of Paris of 1783 granted to the new American nation all land north of the thirty-first parallel from the Mississippi River eastward to the Pearl River, with American and Spanish appointed surveyors Thomas Freeman and Stephen Minor leading the survey, but that boundary was not surveyed and determined for fifteen years. In the meantime, Spanish and American settlers clashed—sometimes bitterly—over the border between Mississippi and West Florida. The failure to establish that border caused trouble and cost lives. No one honored a territorial line not marked by surveyors and accepted by Spain and the United States. With the signing of the Treaty of San Lorenzo by Spanish and American officials in 1795, however, the time had arrived to settle the controversy. President John Adams appointed the American team: Andrew Ellicott as commissioner and Thomas Freeman (later surveyor general for the United States south of Tennessee) as surveyor. On May 24, 1796, their appointments were confirmed by the Senate, and they were dispatched immediately to Natchez to begin settling a controversy too long unattended. Ellicott was a highly regarded surveyor who was trained in medicine but preferred astronomy and mathematics. He was among the first men of science and mathematics in the young nation to devote his life to the public good. "His previous work at Niagara Falls, on the boundary line between Pennsylvania and Virginia, and on the surveys of the new cities of Washington, D.C., Buffalo, and Presque Isle" had caught the attention of many.[2] Ellicott was the right man to represent the United States in what would surely be a difficult surveying task. He and a detachment of soldiers arrived in the Natchez District on February 24, 1797. Governor Gayoso instructed Ellicott to leave his soldiers at the mouth of Bayou Pierre and proceed without them to Natchez. Ellicott was reluctant to do so but remembered his instructions to "preserve harmony." Even though he kept those instructions in mind, there began a war of words between Gayoso and Ellicott, the latter wanting to get on with the survey, the former taking his time about moving forward with the task. Ellicott accused Gayoso of needless delays. On October 7, 1797, after eight months of inaction, an irritated Ellicott wrote that "the business of marking the boundary was no nearer."[3] Ellicott told Governor Gayoso that local citizens were getting restless over his unwillingness to move expeditiously. Was Gayoso delaying because Spain was trying to back out of the treaty? Did the governor want to foment revolution in and around Natchez? Gayoso thought such accusations were nonsense.[4]

The truth is that Gayoso was not delaying needlessly. There were numerous details that had to be resolved before he could authorize Ellicott and Freeman to proceed. Gayoso had to satisfy his superiors that current settlers' debts had been admitted and would be paid, and he had to convince his immediate superior, Baron Francisco Luis Hector de Carondelet, that the United States and Spain should move forward. Gayoso next asked William Dunbar, who would eventually be appointed to represent Spain in running the line, to inform Ellicott that Fort Panmure would be evacuated and turned over immediately to the United States.

In retrospect, it was fortunate that "immediately" did not really mean right then. Gayoso did not evacuate Fort Panmure until March 30, 1798. In the intervening year, Ellicott and Dunbar met and soon cemented their friendship. Ellicott said that Dunbar was "a gentleman whose talents, extensive information, and scientific accomplishments, would give him a distinguished rank in any place or in any country."[5] They undertook experiments and shared information, particularly in astronomy and mathematics.[6] When Ellicott learned of Dunbar's appointment as the lead Spanish commissioner, he knew that they were likely to succeed in running the line with a minimum of squabbling. The rendezvous was to be at Bayou Tunica, six miles below Loftus Heights (Fort Adams). Ellicott left immediately and began the surveying process by May 6. He was joined by Minor on May 21 and by Dunbar on May 26. Minor brought with him a party of woodsmen to clear the underbrush. On June 21, Gayoso (also a scholar with scientific interests) and other Spanish officers joined the group.[7] The principal surveyors for the commission were Thomas Power (later emissary to the Ohio) for Spain and Thomas Freeman for the United States.

As when negotiating with Spanish officials in the past, Dunbar had not immediately accepted the appointment to represent Spain in the running of the thirty-first line, without requesting payment in land.[8] On April 4, 1797—eleven months before the actual appointment—Dunbar noted in a letter to Governor Gayoso that he was extremely busy diversifying and expanding his holdings and that it would be difficult to get away during the planting, harvesting, and marketing months. He reminded the governor that he had responded positively many times in the past to invitations to serve "without any gratification . . . otherwise than by the promise of a grant of land within this district." It might take all or most of 1798 to complete the task, and Dunbar could not give that much time to the project, so he asked that Stephen Minor (a good friend of Gayoso's) be appointed his surveying partner. Before the governor appointed Minor, however, Dunbar advised Gayoso to "grant him such gratification as he may judge proper," such as "in the vicinity of the City 20 or 30 arpents of vacant land, being a part of what was purchased for & paid for to Dr. Stephen Minor."[9] Such compensation to both of them would assure that Minor and Dunbar would be the Spanish team running the line. The governor honored Dunbar's requests, and both were paid in modest land grants.

On July 29, 1797, Governor Gayoso left Natchez for New Orleans, where he replaced Baron de Carondelet as the governor general of the province. In a tearful good-bye, Gayoso acknowledged the promotion but reflected on the joy of living among Natchez inhabitants for eight years. They would be missed, he said. Then he turned over the reins of government to Stephen Minor. The excellent commission teams were formed—Ellicott and Freeman for the United States, Minor and Dunbar for Spain.[10] All brought talent, integrity, experience, and commitment to the task at hand.

Before Dunbar's arrival at Ellicott's camp on May 26, 1798, the American commissioner erected a wooden building to hold and protect equipment. Ellicott had with him military observatory tents, but they were old and worn and probably would not withstand the unpleasant weather one must endure in south Mississippi during the summertime. He and his men started building the modest structure on May 2 and completed it on May 4. Because weather was "unfavourable," Ellicott did not begin observations until May 6; he completed them on May 16, proclaiming that he had found the demarcation point of the thirty-first parallel.[11] Dunbar was in charge of astronomical observations to determine latitude for the Spanish as was Ellicott for the Americans. When Dunbar arrived, he set his astronomical circle fifteen feet north of Ellicott's and undertook independent observations for several nights. He concluded that Ellicott's fix was north of the thirty-first parallel by only six feet.[12] In a later report to Spanish officials, Dunbar stated that he disregarded that small difference and approved the starting point Ellicott recommended. In many ways the immediate agreement on demarcation by commissioners representing governments that had been disputing ownership of the region for fifteen years was surprising. It was by no means unusual for adversarial surveyors to rant at each other for months, even years, seeking every possible advantage; not so with Dunbar and Ellicott. Those months of waiting to begin the important work had allowed the two to size each other up and to gain a great deal of respect for one another. That respect paid off in May 1798 and throughout the hot surveying days ahead. As proof of the goodwill existing between the Spanish and American commissioners, Governor Gayoso named the point of demarcation Union Hill at an elaborate ceremony he hosted to celebrate the beginning of a venture that would prove successful by year's end.[13]

Once the point was determined, the commissioners hoped to survey due west to the Mississippi River and then east to the Pearl River. They began cutting a trace sixty feet wide to the west across the high ground they occupied, from which they would start the survey. Before they could push on through the low grounds to the river, however, "the annual inundation" of rain made progress to the west impossible for the time being—the waters flooded the land to be surveyed. When the rains finally stopped, instead of waiting for the waters to recede, Dunbar recommended that they turn their attention to the east and begin surveying in that direction. He suggested that the fifty white laborers be put to work continuing to the east the sixty-foot-wide trace already started to the west. He offered to loan the commission twenty-two slaves and an overseer to clear the path so the surveyors could run the line westward when weather allowed them to do so. Ellicott thought the plan a good one and gave his approval.[14]

Had they decided to await improved water conditions to begin tracking the westward line to the Mississippi River, they would have lost June and July. Weather did not improve enough to allow them to move westward until August 1. They went from the highlands to the lowlands and then across to the river—a distance of more than two miles—by August 17.[15] Dunbar and Ellicott continued the practice of erecting square posts at a distance of from one to two miles apart, a practice followed to the east as well.[16] Eighty-eight French feet from the mighty Mississippi, they erected a ten-foot post and surrounded it with an earth mound eight feet high. On the south side of the mound, they placed a crown representing Spain with an R underneath. On the north side, they inscribed "United States," and on the west side of the mound, facing the Mississippi, they put "Agosto 18th, 1798, 31 Lat. N."[17]

Since Dunbar lived nearby, periodically he went home for a day during June–August to tend to business. He quickly returned to the survey, and as they had done since their marriage in 1784, he and Dinah kept each other informed by letters. Since he was borrowing so many of his own slaves to undertake the arduous and painful task of cutting underbrush and marking a trace, Dunbar always had a slave on hand to deliver letters to Dinah. His letters were remarkably similar to those written from New Orleans and Natchez. He asked about plantation problems, offered much more advice than Dinah needed—or wanted—and discussed his ailments (he was quite ill much of the time) while also describing the land, vegetation, animals, and whatever else he saw. He began one letter by telling Dinah that her limewater had helped him recover from "a return of my complaint," then described at length the uselessness of their white laborers and asked if she could spare him more slaves to take up the slack. On second thought, he noted that Dinah might not be able to "send some hands without injuring the crop and other works."[18] Periodically, he thanked her for sharing field hands with the commissioners and surveyors and apologized for leaving her shorthanded during the most demanding months of an agricultural season. He usually kept twenty-two slaves working on the line, and that number stayed with him most of the time. At first, Dunbar promised Dinah that he would need them only for a month when waters receded and they could survey westward; in truth, he "borrowed" them in June, July, and some of

August, but he rotated them so that all of their slaves worked both in the plantation fields and on the line.[19] Dunbar advised Dinah on how to salvage a good corn crop with fewer men and how one should chop cotton when shorthanded. On and on he went, page after page. Dunbar even wrote on June 6, "Do not forget to wind up your clock otherwise it will stop."[20]

Dunbar seemed always to be one step ahead of the rest. As he had since arriving in 1771, he was contemplating ways to become a favored citizen in his newly adopted country just as he had done earlier with Britain and Spain. Part of the motive for his friendship with Andrew Ellicott was the opportunity to curry favor with the United States. In particular, Dunbar hoped to be appointed surveyor of the region, and he enlisted Ellicott's help in getting that post.[21] Dunbar wrote to Dinah that if he were appointed surveyor, "I think it will be right for me to quit immediately the service of Spain."[22] He mentioned this fact in three different letters. Dunbar never claimed to be a politician, but his political instincts were keen, and he seldom lost a political goal to another.

While Dunbar and Ellicott took astronomical observations and Freeman and Minor and their assistants continued surveying the thirty-first parallel, seventy-five laborers—black and white—did the actual backbreaking work, the whites going east and the blacks west. In his letters during the summer of 1798, Dunbar often referenced Mississippi weather—hot and uncommonly wet. He commented also on the quality of the land: "The first twenty miles of country . . . is as fertile as any in the United States," he said, but he noted also its impenetrability. Workers attacked the foliage with cane knives and hatchets. Dunbar observed that the countryside was covered with canes from twenty to thirty feet high and matted together by different kinds of vines. To make matters worse, workers were constantly attacked by swarms of flies, gnats, and mosquitoes.[23] Ellicott wrote, "It is now 9 o'clock at night and my eyes almost put out by Musketoes." The white workers could not handle the bugs and undergrowth, prompting Dunbar to call them a "mutinous set not easily managed."[24] He fussed also, as he usually did, about one or more of his slaves. He wrote Dinah on June 23 that York was a disgrace to his plantation, and he did not understand why the overseer had sent him. Dunbar told her that he was returning York to the plantation and begged her to send down Joe to replace him. Still, Dunbar made an effort to be fair to most of his slaves. Because the commissioners drove the workers hard and made them work every day of the week, Dunbar told Dinah to direct their overseer to give all returning slaves a weekday off for every Sunday they had worked on the survey so that they could tend their own gardens. He constantly asked Dinah to check with Mr. Cooper (his main overseer) to determine how long field hands could be absent without injuring the crops. He, too, wanted to return home, Dunbar wrote, but noted that he was trying to build up favors with the Americans and dared not just walk away from the important task at hand. "I am by no means comfortable here, yet the hopes of making some considerable gains, would reconcile the sacrifice."[25]

One of the few times Dunbar went out of his way to praise his slaves was in an August 18, 1798, letter to Dinah. He told her how good everyone felt about completing the survey to the Mississippi River sooner than expected. "We have done more with 22 Negroes in the same space of time," he wrote, "than the whole gang of white labourers have accomplished." He explained, "The white people are not so tractable & obedient as the black people." He also told Dinah he was sending the slaves home and outlined seven chores he hoped she could complete soon, including plowing and sowing a rye patch, building scaffolds, and weeding.[26]

After completing the line westward to the Mississippi River, the commissioners turned their full attention to the east, determined to finish the job before cold weather settled in. Dunbar, on August 20, journeyed to their new camp at Bayou Sara, where he and Ellicott wrote journals and made plans. To date, they had written only memoranda to one another and to government and scientific officials. Journals had to be started and brought up to date as quickly as possible. Between August 20 and 31, the surveyors and workers moved the line from point no. 10 to no. 15, and the survey team was now approximately eighteen miles east of the Mississippi River, including all of the cultivated land. Dunbar told Dinah that he had informed Spanish officials he was leaving the survey team by the end of the month. He had kept both the time and distance commitments he had made to Governor Gayoso upon his appointment, and, accordingly, he said his good-byes to Ellicott, Minor, Freeman, and the others on August 31. He remarked that he had spent more than three months in "uninterrupted harmony . . . with the gentlemen of both parties," and if it were not for family duties calling, he would be with them until the end. Of Andrew Ellicott, he wrote that, because of his "communicative disposition, I am indebted for much pleasure, information and instruction."[27] Ellicott wrote in his journal, "I considered [Dunbar's leaving] a real loss to the public. To myself it was irreparable."[28]

The day after Dunbar's departure, Ellicott moved the camp to Thompson's Creek, where he and his companions continued until October 27, and then they broke camp and proceeded to the Pearl River. The terrain was difficult and progress was slow, but Ellicott meant to complete the survey in

1798.[29] By November 5, David Bradford, a surveyor on the American team, wrote his friend David Redick in Washington County, Pennsylvania, that progress was picking up and that "the Greatest Harmony subsists between the Parties from each Govt.,"[30] but he spoke too soon. On November 8 Ellicott reported the firing of his surveyor, Thomas Freeman, for verbally abusing Stephen Minor. Ellicott called Freeman an "idle, lying, troublesome, discontented, mischief-making man."[31] Tempers were growing short; the men had been working at a very difficult task for more than six months.

Finally, on Saturday, November 17, 1798, the party arrived at Cane Brake, on the west side of the Pearl River. The next day was "employed in opening a road to the river, making rafts, and ferrying our baggage over, and on the 19th encamping and set up the clock." Ellicott remarked that they were the first white people ever to explore this country. They finished their work, fought bad weather, floated to the mouth of the Pearl, and then dispatched a member of the party to New Orleans to secure a vessel to take them to New Orleans and Natchez.[32]

On February 23, 1799, with much ceremony, Commissioner Ellicott and Governor Gayoso signed four reports, two in English and two in Spanish.[33] Ellicott returned to Pennsylvania a hero and later became a professor of mathematics at the United States Military Academy at West Point.[34] Freeman, though he had been fired, was shortly thereafter given a prized surveying position. Stephen Minor returned to Natchez as a Spanish envoy to the United States. Minor became Gayoso's listening post among new Americans and chose to retain it even when Governor Winthrop Sargent of Mississippi Territory tried to bribe him into becoming an American official and taking command of a regiment. Minor also continued his friendship with new American William Dunbar.[35]

Governor Sargent reported to Secretary of State Timothy Pickering that Dunbar had left the survey team because he had a young family and was in ill health but that he left only after "having afforded all the astronomical work and was absolutely necessary in the view of the Spaniards."[36] During the next two years, Dunbar spent considerable time defending his land holdings from Britain and Spain against claims from some new Americans in the region, who charged him with everything from fraudulent claims to outright confiscation. Dunbar claimed correctly that his latest land acquisitions came from Spain for his work on the line. In May 1799, Dunbar sent a twenty-two-point report to the deputy of Don Carlos Trudeau, surveyor general of Louisiana, stating what he received and when and noting that it was payment for services rendered.[37] His records were accurate, and he was remembered in New Orleans as one who served Spain fairly and faithfully. Dunbar lost no land. To cement their friendship, Dunbar gifted to Governor Gayoso his own personal scientific equipment that he had used in running the thirty-first parallel line—an excellent sextant "which graduated by the vernier to 10 seconds" and an astronomical circle, constructed by Edward Troughton of London especially for Dunbar. It was in reality a portable observatory "and executed in a masterly manner."[38] These were the finest instruments of their kind in the old Southwest.

Ellicott praised Dunbar to friends back East, especially to the leadership of the American Philosophical Society, to which his journal and report were presented. The latter was completed and signed on April 9, 1800. He wrote Dunbar on April 18, 1800, "Ever since you left us, I have had reason to regret your absence." Now that Ellicott's work was done, he was on his way back to Philadelphia. He added, "You are doubtless before this time informed of your being elected a member of the American Philosophical Society. . . . [Y]ou will do credit to the society."[39] Ellicott wrote Robert Patterson, vice president of the American Philosophical Society, as he delivered his report, "To William Dunbar . . . I feel myself under the greatest obligations, for his assistance during the short time he was with us; his extensive scientific acquirements, added to a singular facility in making mathematical calculations, would have reduced my labor, to mere amusement, if he had continued."[40] Dunbar's leadership in running the thirty-first parallel line on behalf of the Spanish government lifted him from the ranks of interesting man of science to one whose talents were now recognized and whose potential for service was just beginning. Dunbar was on his way to recognition not thought possible five short years earlier. What a fiftieth birthday present!

8

Scientist

William Dunbar earned national recognition and status after 1798 based on the reputation he gained as a scientist running the thirty-first parallel line with Andrew Ellicott. As the lead U.S. commissioner laboring on a thorny boundary problem with another country, Ellicott gained respect back home in the East, and he emerged as the central figure in a successful endeavor. Dunbar emerged as a hero, too, particularly in Mississippi Territory, because the new, accurate boundary settled a dangerous local problem that had festered for years—and, more significant, because the border placed Natchez squarely in the United States, where its citizens had hoped it would be. Ellicott's good work surprised no one back East, because his talents as a surveyor and astronomer were well known and much appreciated, but Dunbar had theretofore been unknown in the United States, having labored in obscurity for twenty-five years in the backwaters of the lower Mississippi region. Both men offered excellent and accurate journals to the American Philosophical Society, but Dunbar's was broader, more descriptive. Ellicott's focused on running the line; Dunbar's described the world around him and offered ideas and projections to contemplate, secondarily zeroing in on the survey itself.

Soon-to-be president Thomas Jefferson was most impressed by Dunbar, and at Ellicott's urging, he introduced the nearly unknown Dunbar to scientific America through his sponsorship of Dunbar for membership in the American Philosophical Society. Dunbar was accepted readily, and his contributions from the date of his admission to the American Philosophical Society in 1800 until his death in 1810 were numerous and well regarded throughout the scientific community. During the early nineteenth century, the young nation boasted of a surprisingly large and growing group of self-taught as well as university-trained scientific scholars. These included

Charles Wilson Peale (who dug up America's first mastodon in 1801), David Hosack (who founded Elgin Botanic Garden in 1801), Robert Hare (who developed the prototype for the blowtorch in 1801, at age twenty), Nathaniel Bowditch (who authored *New American Practical Navigator* in 1802), Benjamin Smith Barton (who published *Elements of Botany* in 1803) and his son William Barton (who tutored Alexander Wilson and in 1805 was invited by Jefferson to lead the Red River expedition), Alexander Wilson (who published volume one of his nine-volume *American Ornithology* in 1808), Frederick V. Melshiemer (who published *Catalogue of Insects of Pennsylvania* in 1806), and Robert Fulton (who is mistakenly credited with inventing the steamboat but was the first to develop a steamboat—*Clermont*—to ply the Hudson successfully in 1807). These were but a few of the recognized scientists who contributed to knowledge during the first decade of the nineteenth century. They were led, of course, by America's most scientifically oriented president—Thomas Jefferson.

Unfortunately, few of Dunbar's East Coast admirers ever met him, not even Jefferson, for Dunbar seldom ventured far from home except for business; nor did he ever intend to do so now that he had arrived as a planter and was comfortably housed at the Forest. His traveling days were just about over, except for enticing exploration opportunities.

Dunbar was a Renaissance man, but he was best known as a scientist whose interests were ever expanding. Little escaped his view or his comment, and much that he saw gained his attention and study. His thirty-first parallel journal was so inclusive that as late as the 1840s scientists still pestered family members with requests to republish it.[1] Visitors to the Forest in 1844 were introduced to another of his passions—music—and invited to sing Dunbar's compositions. In 1810, a world-famous ornithologist, Alexander Wilson, journeyed to Natchez to visit with Dunbar. Wilson noted Dunbar's generosity in sharing both valuable time and specimens with him: "I am indebted for the opportunity afforded me of procuring this and one or two more new species."[2]

It is difficult, perhaps impossible, to determine whether Dunbar was interested in astronomy more than meteorology, botany more than Indian sign languages, for his interests seemed boundless. He appeared to be interested in science, period. He was perhaps best known, however, for his observations in the fields of botany and zoology that came from his thirty-first parallel line journal. While laborers were chopping cane and cursing vines, Dunbar undertook a study of the territory's flora, fauna, and natural features. Therein, he introduced the world to Mississippi in the summertime, with all of its natural treasures, including high-quality soil, birds, trees, weather, fish, and animals. Even today it is interesting to read Dunbar's perceptions of that land, Mississippi—its alligators and mosquitoes—written while those around him were laboring in sweltering heat and high humidity. The accuracy of his observations is surprising. In August 1798, he ended a lengthy discussion of Mississippi crops with a listing of products he found there as well as commentary on how well various plants did in Mississippi.[3]

Dunbar loved flowers. In his comments about Mississippi flowers, he identified the common varieties that grew both in the low country and on the high ground, but he focused his in-depth comments almost solely on the high-ground flower he loved the most—the flower of the handsome magnolia tree. He called the pungent blooms "the grandest" and "eminently beautiful." He described the tree's deep green, shining leaves, which enhanced "one of the most glorious flowers of nature . . . shedding a most delicious perfume." Ever the pragmatic scientist, he noted that he did not know "that any discovery has been made of its ability in medicine or otherwise."[4]

Dunbar spent a great deal of time describing trees, discussing carefully a species of horse chestnut introduced from the north of Asia during the previous century. He identified locust, black mulberry, wild cherry, sassafras, and black walnut bushes and trees as abundant and valued by the inhabitants for the quality of their timber. He remarked that the redbud, or Judas tree, was "remarkable for its elegant display of pale crimson blossoms," whereas dogwood trees were "entirely covered with dazzling blossoms." Dunbar not only wrote of the beauty and utility of specific species, but he also displayed a botanist's knowledge of them. He wrote, "The Bois de fleche, dogwood, being the cornus, or cornelian tree of the Botanists, so called probably from the fine cornelian colour of its ripe berry, is one of the most elegant ornaments of the Early Spring, it consists of two varieties, one furnishes a flower of a yellowish green, inclining to white, but the flower of the other is of the most resplendent white, and the tree seldom exceeding 50 feet in height." He offered scientific observations on all trees catalogued, including white poplar, yellow poplar, water poplar, sycamore, willow, bamboo, red oak, white oak, black oak, and cypress. He wrote that cypress was the "most useful . . . to the inhabitants of this country, being preferred . . . for house building, furnishing beams, planks, and shingles." The willow "hangs over the banks of the river and is eminently qualified to retain and secure the soil by its innumerable fibrous roots." He identified each tree's location (high ground or low), utility, beauty, and history. His descriptions offered the first inclusive picture of trees and bushes in Mississippi. He even described the tenacity of cane plants growing in close proximity to each other, offering a near-impenetrable barrier to travel.[5]

Of equal interest to Dunbar were fish and animals along the shores, in the rivers, and on the land. He began by offering a long essay on the difference between the alligators of the Mississippi and the crocodiles of the Nile. Mississippi alligators exceeded fifteen feet in length and were almost impossible to shoot with a musket ball. His essay included informed comments on their location, lifestyle, and function. He discussed also several species of turtles, most of which could be eaten. One species, he noted, was called the alligator turtle because of its scaly body and its size; it was known to grow to three feet in length and could weigh one hundred or more pounds. Dunbar had much to say about the abundance of food along the Gulf Coast and in the rivers of the territory, especially crabs, oysters, and varieties of fish, including sheephead, spotted trout, and flatfish. Introductory comments led to a lengthy list, with little discussion, of the fish available in Mississippi. The list included catfish, perch, sturgeon, eel, armed fish or gar, sunfish, black trout, bass, rock, choique or mudfish, spatula fish, a species of herring, a large fish called red fish, and a great variety of nameless others. Dunbar then discussed crayfish and shrimp, the latter "in such abundance . . . that they may be immediately caught . . . by sinking a net, bag, or basket . . . about a foot or two under water during ten months of the year."[6] In his journal Dunbar did not comment much about snakes, other than to identify copperheads, cottonmouths, and rattlesnakes. We do know, though, that he was fascinated by them, for over the years, friends brought him snakes they had killed or captured for identification or information.[7]

Other animals were a focus of Dunbar's attention as well. He wrote of seeing a large "tyger" (panther) during the running of the line. The animal was at least three feet high and seven to eight feet long. He had seen other panthers during his days in Louisiana and Mississippi, and he noted their deep chest, short legs, and astonishing strength. They were not very numerous, which was fortunate, he noted, because they killed sheep, calves, and hogs.[8] Dunbar also chronicled the presence of numerous black bears in the territory; he discussed "timid" foxes, "aggressive" wolves, short-tailed wildcats, wild turkeys, a great variety of cranes, woodcocks, and snipes.[9] Otherwise he said little about birds, except to note now and again that the fields were filled with quail and "an infinite store of birds, some remarkable for their song and others for the splendor of their plumage." During the years ahead, he would write often about Mississippi's bird population, and he even corresponded with famous ornithologists in the East, answering questions and inviting them to journey to the territory to study its bird population. One wrote in 1810 that he intended to visit in a year or so to compile "a complete collection of all the aquatic tribes of birds found in your rivers & bayous."[10]

Dunbar never lost his interest in botany and zoology. In 1807, a traveler brought him some grass seed that he thought might thrive in Mississippi's climate and soil. Dunbar eagerly analyzed the seed and determined that his new friend was correct. He prepared the soil as he thought appropriate, planted the seed, and cultivated the first patch of Bermuda grass—a grass still quite popular in the South today.[11]

Dunbar believed that a scientist could be no better than the instruments and equipment he used to undertake observations and experiments. His correspondence and journals are filled with orders and instructions to the finest instrument makers in Britain. The same is true of his orders for books through Philadelphia and London agents. Unfortunately, he never recorded in his journal, personal letters, or even acknowledgment correspondence whether the equipment or books were received at the Forest. Neither did he maintain a listing of his laboratory or library contents. He usually accompanied a shipment of cotton with orders for books and journals and for sensitive and expensive equipment that would enable him to improve his experiments and to undertake studies not possible without the equipment being ordered. Dunbar gave specific instructions to his agents and to the artisans building his equipment. On October 22, 1802, he wrote a friend, "I expect from London my State Telescope. . . . It is a Gregorian reflector of 5 1/2 or 6 feet length in the great tube with 9 inch aperture possessing 6 magnifying powers from 100 to 525." In 1803, he noted, "The small fortune which I have acquired by cultivating the earth alone enables me to procure many instruments of moderate expense which might facilitate my researches."[12]

Dunbar was proud of his ever-growing and ever-diversifying holdings and was generous in sharing his books and scientific instruments with scholars, students, and friends. In 1805, Thomas Rodney, a neighbor and friend, viewed Venus, the moon, and the North Star through Dunbar's new Gregorian telescope (which had not been delivered until 1804).[13] Dunbar ordered scientific equipment primarily through Edward Troughton in London, the best instrument maker in the country. Dunbar ordered reflecting circles, sextants, micrometers, and chronometers, among many other items. Most instruments, especially the reflecting instruments for astronomy, were large and bulky, and Dunbar was always experimenting with ways to downsize them so that a man on horseback could carry and use them. He even suggested that instruments be made in two parts so that each half could be carried in a separate box, one strapped to each side of a horse.[14] Generally Troughton was able to provide the new instruments and the size Dunbar requested, moving Dunbar to write, "You are the most eminent artist in Europe."[15]

Dunbar was mindful of the cost of his scientific interests, however, as on one occasion, he fired an English representative and his company because "they stole me blind, put on 12 or 15% duty besides all other charges." He expected to lose one thousand pounds at the hands of the company he fired. He hired a new representative and company and sent the agent one thousand pounds from which to draw on items currently on order or soon to be ordered.[16]

Most likely, Dunbar was the best-equipped scientist in the old Southwest. What he purchased enabled him to undertake research on more projects than others could, and it allowed him to publish fifteen articles in the *Transactions of the American Philosophical Society* and the *Philosophical Transactions of the Royal Society of London* between 1803 and 1810.[17] The articles published show clearly the breadth of his interests, including the following: Indian sign language; temperature, rainfall, and barometer; fossil bones; lunar rainbows; vocabularies; hydrostatics; eclipses of the sun; the comet of September 1807; and the rise and fall in the depth of the Mississippi River. In one article he noted the theory, since proven, that terrible storms (tornadoes) had centers of absolute calm—new information for fellow scientists to consider. Dunbar offered numerous meteorological studies of his region based on thrice-daily observations. At Jefferson's request, he invented the first procedure to find the longitude of a given place without knowing the present time. Dunbar wrote John Vaughn at the American Philosophical Society, "I just wrote Mr. Jefferson about new way of finding longitude by single observer without assistant or chronometer, if approved be useful to single people of scientific turn because with good portable sextant can do it. Depends solely on moon's meridian altitude at certain periods of her orbit, which at 1 each 10 days of each lunation."[18] His observations on the subject brought about interest and discussion among scientists of the day. Dunbar corresponded with many of the greatest English and American scientists, including Sir William Herschel, Benjamin Rush, John Bartram, George Hunter, David Rittenhouse, and Alexander Wilson.[19] He even found time in 1803 to help charter the Mississippi Society for the Acquirement and Dissemination of Useful Knowledge.[20]

Dunbar was not a physician by training, but he had a keen interest in health, in part because he was often ill and because he lived in a section of America continually subject to epidemics. Ships visiting the port of New Orleans often brought rats, goods, and crews carrying diseases such as smallpox, malaria, and yellow fever, formerly not common to the region. Epidemics spread quickly throughout the area, leaving death in their wake and destroying Indian communities. On his Manchac plantation, Dunbar performed postmortem examinations on slaves so that he might treat more effectively other people with the same symptoms. He also mentioned finding medicinal value in various roots, flowers, and grasses. In 1806, for instance, he wrote in his journal, "Among the plants growing on the margin of the river is the China root used in medicine."[21]

In the spring of 1802, a smallpox epidemic made its way up the Mississippi River from New Orleans. Dunbar met with Governor W. C. C. Claiborne and asked for permission to secure enough smallpox inoculum to immunize the entire Mississippi Territory population. On the frontier, however, people were often more suspicious of inoculation than of the disease itself. The legislature was permitted by territorial law to sanction inoculation, but only on the recommendation of a local physician. Dunbar secured no such recommendation. He argued against the need for legislative approval to save lives, but to no immediate end. Dunbar and Claiborne were close friends, and even though Claiborne wrote Dunbar that "inoculation will not be resorted to but by general consent," he did address the legislature requesting a general law to prevent the introduction of smallpox into the territory. The legislature overwhelmingly approved the request and passed a law stating that any person "willfully" introducing the disease into the territory would be subject to fine and imprisonment.[22] Legislators also considered a territorial quarantine, but they realized that an effective quarantine would be impossible to monitor or enforce in an agricultural environment. They came to realize that the only way to save lives was through inoculation, and, in May 1802, the legislature authorized inoculation on a voluntary basis. Dunbar secured smallpox inoculum, and he and Dr. David Lattimore inoculated approximately two-thirds of the people in the district. Of those inoculated, not a single person died. In an October 1802 report, Dr. Lattimore stated, "It is not easy to say what might have been the fate of this menaced country without the advantages of this invaluable preventative. . . . [I]t was William Dunbar who most earnestly suggested to the Governor the general application of the inocule preventative."[23] Historians of the period have noted Dunbar's personal medical studies and forward-looking recommendations.

Even though Dunbar never listed geology among his strong interests, his writings, particularly from his successful expedition to the Ouachita River country and the hot springs of Arkansas, are filled with geological observations. In describing the valley of the Red River, he noted that "beneath the marl stratum, of which the calcareous sandstone appears to form an inconsiderable part is seen the deep red or pale yellow clay, common to the adjacent hills, in which sand abounds."[24] He wrote a 114-page paper on the

Blue Ridge country he visited only as a young immigrant working around Pittsburgh for two years. In it he described the gold country of that area and exhibited a highly sensitive knowledge of its geography and geology. Dunbar seemed to believe, correctly, that to be a botanist or an astronomer, one had to build upon a knowledge of land formations, natural resources, waterways, and other geological features of the region being studied. In short, Dunbar took for granted that scientists had an interest in and a working knowledge of geology.

What Dunbar did not take for granted were meteorological observations—an interest cultivated early in Scotland that stayed with him every day of his life. He kept detailed daily records that were bound monthly and then yearly, from 1791 until his death. His observations were made at the Forest, four miles from the Mississippi River, at latitude 31° 28" north. When Dunbar was away from the Forest, as we have seen, he left specific instructions for others to continue his meteorological observations. Dunbar recorded temperature, barometer, wind, and a description of the weather three times a day: generally at 6 A.M., 3 P.M., and 9 P.M. What he left is a detailed record of the weather around Natchez District for that time; often the notes in the margins stray onto other topics as well. Dunbar described the condition of his crops and what grew best in a damp climate and observed that the dogwood was in bloom or "the wild cherry & weeping willows are covered with foliage." He offered the daily high and low temperatures in addition to the mean. He included daily observations on humidity and rain, which he measured in inches.[25] Dunbar was particularly interested in the depth of the Mississippi River, noting high and low months and carefully documenting monthly changes from one year to the next. He also kept comprehensive monthly records on rainfall. On August 22, 1801, Dunbar sent President Jefferson a monthly recapitulation of meteorological observations for 1800. Therein, he offered comments that enabled the president, a planter much interested in such matters, to gain a working knowledge of the climate in Mississippi Territory. In an earlier letter, Jefferson had asked questions about the Mississippi River. Dunbar meant to include a short account—kept since his 1773 arrival in Manchac—of his observations of the river; he noted, however, that his copyist was ill, so the river account would have to be sent along later.[26]

The letters between Jefferson and Dunbar were long, involved many subjects, and reflected the scientific interests of both men. They challenged each other's ideas, offered observations they hoped would lead to further challenges, and seemed to enjoy showing off for each other. Significantly, their observations demonstrated their love of science and a desire to learn much about America from each other. Meteorological observations dominated some letters, showing both their curiosity and their hunger to continue learning, but both men were keenly interested in other subjects as well, including fossils found along the Mississippi and other rivers west of it, Indian languages, flora and fauna, and lunar observations.[27] In one letter, Dunbar stated that Jefferson's "observation of the Lunar rainbow is entirely new to me" and then challenged Jefferson's position, offering comments on phenomena he had observed in Mississippi.[28]

Often Dunbar closed his daily meteorological observation notes with a comment or two on something that caught his fancy. A typical closing reads, "1803, June 30th, at 7 1/2 P.M. The sun being just set, a beautiful rainbow was painted in the heavens forming a complete semi-circle. . . . As a rainbow is a reflector by which we can find the place of the sun, we must conclude from this phenomenon, that the horizontal refraction of the atmosphere had produced two images of the sun."[29] Dunbar had noted his interest in rainbows before. On August 12, 1798, while running the thirty-first parallel line, he wrote, "I had the happiness of viewing a most beautiful phenomenon" following a rainstorm—a rainbow. He offered Sir Isaac Newton's observations on rainbows and then described what he saw in minute detail, proclaiming it "the most beautiful one I ever beheld."[30] His words were those of an accomplished scientist who knew that there was an explanation for the existence of rainbows, but he still was moved to remark on the aesthetic value of such an occurrence.

Whenever a natural phenomenon appeared or was predicted, neighbors and friends flocked to the Forest to view it through Dunbar's six-foot Gregorian telescope. Such an occasion always seemed to be accompanied by a party to celebrate the majesty and might of nature. In September 1807, a comet appeared in the sky, and Dunbar tracked it from September 22 till February 3, 1808. During that time it went into a 140-degree arc, which Dunbar traced every day. The comet traveled from the southwest to the northeast, and people journeyed a considerable distance to see it through the Dunbar state-of-the-art telescope. Dunbar's notes and observations on the comet's journey were published, and his astronomical offerings were considered important because even the most skilled astronomers "have very strange and absurd ideas about comets."[31]

To Dunbar, the most exciting natural event of his life took place on April 5, 1800. What Dunbar simply called "the phenomenon" passed Baton Rouge, streaking from the southwest, heading northeast. It moved so rapidly spectators had only fifteen seconds to observe it. It flew low in the sky, about two hundred yards above the ground, and it appeared to be about the size of a large house—seventy to eighty feet long. It was "wholly luminous" and resembled the sun. In passing it emitted a considerable amount of heat, and the light it gave off resembled sunbeams as it traveled to earth. After it disappeared to the northeast, "a violent rushing noise was heard as if the Phenomenon were beating down the forest before it, and in a few seconds a tremendous crash was heard similar to that of the largest piece of ordinance, causing a very sensible earthquake." A meteorite had hit the earth, and Dunbar was there to record its speed, power, and potential for danger.[32]

From his correspondence with Thomas Jefferson, it is clear that Dunbar submitted all of his American Philosophical Society articles through Jefferson, seeking his honest opinion on subject matter, evidence, and presentation. Jefferson then shared the offering with trusted friends in Philadelphia, seeking questions and comments. Then Jefferson would submit the article to the *Transactions* on Dunbar's behalf, sometimes after making a few changes to improve it. He always sought Dunbar's permission to make changes, and Dunbar was forever grateful for Jefferson's advice, whether or not he took it. The authors expressed no rancor over points of difference; instead they learned from each other. Dunbar's sphere of influence was not limited to Jefferson. In one article, Dunbar instructed fellow scientists as to the best location for measuring temperature—in the shade away from direct sunlight, "but not so as to exclude all influence by reflection."[33] That became the standard for taking air temperature after 1801.

Dunbar undertook a comparative meteorological study between Quebec and Natchez through newspaper and scientific article notations. After scanning the study, Jefferson wrote, "I have often wondered that any human being should live in a cold country who can find room in a warm one. I have no doubt that cold is the source of more suffering to all animal nature than hunger, thirst, sickness, and all of the other pains of life and death itself put together."[34] Dunbar's choice of a place to live might suggest agreement with Jefferson.

As an involved and observant scientist, Dunbar addressed no topic more frequently in his journals than Indians. He did not write about them as human beings who owned every inch of North America before Europeans came to their lands and began wars of conquest that lasted for four hundred years. He did not note what tribe owned the land he farmed around Manchac, nor did he record what happened to the Natchez tribe on whose ancient land he built the Forest. He did not even write that the Choctaws were quite upset in 1798 that American and Spanish commissioners were running a boundary line through part of their homeland. No, Dunbar treated Indians as things—interesting and strange things that walked about, farmed a bit, and (particularly those west of the Mississippi River) communicated with each other through an intricate sign language. It was that sign language that interested him the most and led to a decade-long study and an article in the *Transactions*.[35] He got Jefferson, Ellicott, and others back East interested in Indian sign language, and he included an observation or two in most letters he wrote to them.

Dunbar also undertook a study of tribes' locations, migration habits, sizes, and especially their communication with other tribes. He knew that all negotiations between whites and Indians were accompanied by much liquor for the Indians and that American negotiators treated them as children—requiring only their X on a treaty they could not even read.[36] Dunbar knew this, yet he said nothing about it in his correspondence, perhaps because he, among others, was benefiting from policies leading to the forced cession of more and more tribal land. Though I can find no record that he ever made such views explicit, Dunbar seems to have considered American Indians (as he did Africans and African Americans) inferior to whites. In this he was no better or worse than his contemporaries, unless one believes that education and an inquiring mind should lead one to take some responsibility toward other humans regardless of color or heritage—a responsibility boldly stated by Dunbar's friend Thomas Jefferson in the Declaration of Independence but not much practiced during his presidency.

Dunbar's writings on the Indians of America as far north as the confluence of the Ohio and Mississippi rivers, on both sides of the Mississippi River, are astonishing for their breadth and accuracy. This knowledge held Dunbar in good stead during his 1804–5 expedition to the hot springs of Arkansas. He knew the location, disposition, size, and history of all tribes around him. There is little doubt in my mind that William Dunbar was the leading scientist in Mississippi Territory and one who gained the respect of his peers across America. He was interested in all areas of science, but his interests were pragmatic: he applied his understanding in making practical decisions that furthered economic goals, always important in his life. In addition to expanding scientific understanding in many fields of interest, Dunbar would change farming and planting in Mississippi for decades to come as he helped usher in cotton as a major agricultural product.

9

Land Policies

To understand William Dunbar's rise to wealth and influence in Mississippi Territory, one must first explore the importance of land and policies that governed its granting. The land policies adopted by different nations did not include automatic recognition of prior grants by one or more other nations, in part because the changes in national authority over a region usually had something to do with winning and losing wars. Nowhere in America were land policy difficulties more complex and more unsolvable than in the old Southwest. At various times, the lower Mississippi region was owned by different Indian tribes, Spain, England, France, Georgia, and the United States. Each followed a different policy, and each wanted to cancel what previous authorities had granted to grant land to someone else. The subject is difficult to understand and explain, but the acquisition, holding, and cultivating of land are so important to the Dunbar story that it must be addressed in detail. Dunbar's goal was to secure and protect holdings no matter which nation was presently in charge of making land grants. He was the master of recognizing what he must do to secure land and how to manipulate policies to his advantage.

The Spanish arrived in Florida in 1539 and concentrated their interest in the peninsula and eastern Florida. They lost Florida to the British in the 1763 Treaty of Paris but were allowed to keep New Orleans and Louisiana land on the west bank of the Mississippi River. Although Dunbar registered his 1773 land titles with the new owners—the British—he maintained a close and friendly relationship with the Spanish because the port of New Orleans would be critical to his business operations. He was good at maintaining relationships at all levels with whatever nations had colonies or controlled land in the area; these long-term relationships were beneficial to him personally and to his business interests throughout his life.

The location of Manchac and Baton Rouge put Dunbar in close proximity to Spanish settlers, officials, and settlements, and he was wise enough to use his knowledge of Spanish language and history to become a good neighbor and a friend to many Spaniards, especially Spanish officials. From 1773 to 1798, he formed relationships with several Spanish governors. The first governor after 1763 never ventured to New Orleans to take office. He was followed by Alejandro O'Reilly, who arrived on July 24, 1769. After serving only three years, O'Reilly was replaced by Luis Unzaga y Amezaga, who served until May 1779 and was replaced by Bernardo de Gálvez. Seven years later, in July 1786, Esteban Rodríguez Miró took office, and he served as governor for five years; he was replaced by Francisco Luis Carondelet in March 1791. In October 1796, Manuel Luis Gayoso de Lemos was transferred from the Natchez District to the governorship in New Orleans. He was replaced three years later, in October 1799, by the last Spanish governor in West Florida, Juan Manuel de Salcedo.[1]

Unzaga was governor when Dunbar entered the region in 1773, but Dunbar had no contact with him. He did, however, come to know well Gálvez, Rodríguez Miró, and Carondelet, and Gayoso became a close friend. Gálvez was governor when Spain declared war on Britain in 1779 and his soldiers sacked Dunbar's plantation near Manchac, but he was also governor as Dunbar regrouped and rebuilt after 1780. These were the men charged with implementing and enforcing Spanish land policy during the years when Spanish rulers played a major role in Dunbar's rise to economic and social prominence.

The process of securing a Spanish grant in New Orleans was complicated, expensive, and slow. On February 18, 1770, O'Reilly issued a proclamation stating Spain's land policy.[2] All land was to be granted in the name of the king by the governor, who would appoint a surveyor charged with fixing boundaries in the presence of a judge. The surveyor would make three copies of the survey—one to be deposited with the governor's secretary for safekeeping as an official record, another for the governor, and the third for the grantee. Those holding French or English grants in territory now clearly Spanish were required to go through this process and pay the required fees. New petitioners followed the same process, which seemed simple on paper but not in implementation. From the beginning, Spanish land policy was administered in a "very loose and inefficient manner"[3] that attracted settlers but also frustrated them.

There was not even a general land office. A person wanting a grant drew up a petition that included a statement of eligibility for such a grant and a request for a certain number of acres. The petition was first read in provincial council, which recommended to the governor that the petition be accepted, rejected, or postponed. If approved—and the vast majority were—a warrant was issued by the governor authorizing the surveyor general to mark off the land and to return the survey, which must include a general description of the land's natural features along with a plat, within six months. A survey was made—seldom within the required six months—and given to the governor, who then issued a fiat to the secretary and the attorney general instructing them to draw up a grant. The final printed patent contained a description of the land and the terms of the grant. In 1774, for a grant of five hundred acres or less, seventeen different fees were due the governor, secretary, and messenger. The total cost was nineteen Spanish dollars and eight and one-half reals, of which approximately one-third went to the governor.[4]

Through the years, Spanish officials also made deals granting vast holdings of land to speculators who promised to recruit a certain number of settlers in a specific time period. For example, Baron de Bastrop negotiated a colonization contract with Carondelet in 1796 that granted to Bastrop 846,281 acres on the eastern side of the Ouachita Valley. He agreed to bring in five hundred families, mainly from Europe, during the next three years. Male heads of families were to be granted 336 acres (400 square arpents), and male children, upon reaching their twenty-first birthday, would also be granted 336 acres. If Bastrop did not bring in the required number of families, he would forfeit his grant rights,[5] but the inefficiency of Spanish officials in implementing land policies and the lengthy amount of time it took them to make grants made the enforcement of contract requirements impossible, particularly since Spanish authority soon ended in the old Southwest.

Among his other talents, William Dunbar was an excellent student of people. He noticed that Spanish authorities simply disregarded earlier British grants—which caused little trouble because, to the Spanish, "settlement was a title in itself." He noticed also that the Spanish played favorites. If a Spanish official liked the would-be grantee—for any one of several reasons—the seemingly endless process could be sidestepped or totally eliminated. For example, in 1789, Samuel Foreman came to Natchez to visit his uncle, Ezekiel Foreman; it was just a visit and he had no intention of staying. Because Ezekiel was a Spanish favorite, however, Governor Gayoso sent another favorite, Surveyor General William Dunbar, to visit with Samuel and to present him with a tract of land—and a bill for sixty dollars, Dunbar's surveying fee. Dunbar told Samuel that the governor had selected eight hundred acres of the best land available and was offering it as a present. Samuel was stunned. He accepted the gift, stayed around Natchez for about a year, and then left—thereby forfeiting title to the land.[6]

Dunbar had no problems with his land grants so long as Britain controlled West Florida—the first ten years (1773–83) of his time in Manchac. His grant was processed legally, and he worried not about its authenticity. In 1783, when the signing of the Treaty of Paris ended the American Revolution in favor of the colonists, Britain surrendered the region to Spain, the owner prior to 1763. Dunbar could see that his future prosperity depended on the new Spanish landlords' authenticating his holdings. Since Spain desperately wanted settlers and considered settlement as title, Dunbar had no problem getting Spanish endorsement of his British grant.[7] Still, as we have seen, Dunbar went much further in land dealings with the Spanish: he opened a mercantile establishment in New Orleans, left his new wife, Dinah, in charge of the Manchac plantation during long absences, became a Spanish surveyor, served Spanish authorities as an official interpreter of many languages, and studied architecture and designed homes and gardens for Spanish leaders—always taking land as payment for his services. Dunbar grew what was needed for plantation consumption and for sale in New Orleans and elsewhere, used some of the earnings from services and sales to help rebuild his Manchac plantation, and saved the rest to begin constructing the Forest on lands near Natchez granted by the Spanish. He and Dinah had a plan, and they stuck to it. No non-Spaniard was more trusted and admired by West Florida Spanish officials than William Dunbar. He showered officials with gifts—usually agricultural produce—and lost no opportunity to be of service, as the value of the land accumulated in the Natchez District increased yearly.[8]

After the Treaty of San Lorenzo was negotiated and signed in 1795, wise Spaniards and non-Spaniards in the Natchez District recognized that the area was now a part of the United States and that establishing the thirty-first parallel would certify that fact. Therefore, before the United States assumed control of Natchez and surrounding territory north of the thirty-first parallel, non-Spanish local families began bargaining with Spanish officials for land grants. No one bargained better than Dunbar, and in those negotiations he usually won. For example, as we have seen, Governor Gayoso wanted Dunbar to become Spain's commissioner running the line, but Dunbar played hard to get until a land grant became a part of the offer for his services.[9] One problem that later developed came out of a stipulation in the Treaty of San Lorenzo requiring that Spanish officials refrain from granting any more land five days after the treaty was ratified. Spanish officials did not heed that requirement, and the practice of antedating grants to make them appear legal proved to be a difficult problem for the U.S. government to solve after the border was confirmed in 1798.

Most Spanish officials liked their government's policy and process in granting land, but Gayoso took advantage of it by authorizing several grants in and around Natchez to favorites without the approval of any supervisor. Spanish intendants—district administrators representing the king—always maintained that they were the legal grant-making authority in Spanish colonies under an order signed by the king on October 15, 1754. The intendants maintained that they and they alone represented the king in this important matter. Still, since Governor O'Reilly decided in 1770 that governors were in charge of land grants, they had functioned in that capacity while intendants whined. What Gayoso was doing in 1797–98 was the last straw to Intendant Juan Ventura Morales, and he wrote West Florida governor Don Pedro Varela y Ulloa a long letter bitterly denouncing Gayoso's actions. Accusations went back and forth, and the acrimonious dispute was not settled until the king, on October 22, 1798, decided in favor of the intendant.[10] The decision came too late: by that date, Commissioner Ellicott was completing the running of the thirty-first parallel line, and Spain had been replaced as the owner of any and all land above that line, including Natchez. Morales's victory was a hollow one in West Florida.

Many American settlers in and around Natchez were jealous of Dunbar's success in securing land from Spanish officials, and indeed his success was extraordinary. In a letter to American general George Mathews, Dunbar wrote that he had heard that Mathews was concerned about charges of Spanish antedating and he, Dunbar, wanted to clear the air. After the Treaty of San Lorenzo had been negotiated, but before it went into effect, the Spanish government kept Dunbar—the surveyor general—working and on the payroll. "I thought myself bound to obey them when required by the parties," Dunbar wrote. "If the transaction be unlawful, the criminality is not in me." Dunbar asked the general to study all of his Spanish patents in New Orleans to ascertain if any were antedated, and he suggested to Mathews that he would not find a single one. Dunbar was too wily to antedate anything or to leave tracks that showed he was rewarded above and beyond services rendered.[11] He believed that he had worked long and in good faith and had earned all Spanish favors that came his way.

The Natchez Court Records: Abstracts of Early Records, 1767–1805 contain thousands of grant claims by Spanish officials to settlers in the Natchez region who, after the signing of the Treaty of San Lorenzo, applied for recognition by the U.S. government under An Act Regulating the Grants of Land, and Providing for the Disposal of the Lands of the U.S. South of the State of Tennessee. Those chosen to separate bogus from honest claims had a herculean task before them. For example, during 1789–97, there were eighteen Spanish grants of land to William Dunbar for himself and at least two of his children, Anne and William Jr.[12] The abstracts simply identified the land, sometimes its location, and always the date of the grant. A few examples follow: "William Dunbar, one thousand arpents granted to him on the Old Fork of Bayou Feliciana, 31st December 1791." Another stated that Dunbar was given one thousand arpents of land in November 1793 by Governor Carondelet in New Orleans "for services rendered." The interesting thing about that grant was that Dunbar did not file it until March 30, 1804. It was not like Dunbar to have allowed a land matter to go unattended for such a long time. Another abstract simply stated "400 arpents of land to Dunbar verified by Spanish Government." Most abstracts, though, included as much information as possible. One representative example stated, "William Dunbar, the lot N.A. of the square No. 6, in the city of Natchez, granted to him Petition Dec. 6, 1794, Warrant Dec. 8, 1794, Certificate Dec. 10, 1794, Patent Dec. 15, 1794. Signed by J. Girault."[13] Throughout the long, laborious process of checking thousands of abstracts relating to Natchez area land, I did not find even one of Dunbar's petitions rejected. He was the master of combining service and land grants, and he always seemed to know what land he wanted and why.

Between the ratification of the Treaty of San Lorenzo in 1795 and the confirmation of the thirty-first parallel in 1798, most Natchez residents were excited about becoming a part of the United States. If there was any uneasiness, it had to do with the possibility of losing title to their land.[14] Would federal agents try to deprive them of their lands? Were the titles they held secure enough to qualify? How would the United States handle the claims of Georgia and the improprieties of the Yazoo defrauders? There were two main kinds of grants. The first were the older titles granted by the British, which represented the majority of the occupied land around Natchez. That group had two kinds of holders: those who continued on British grants after Spain assumed control of the region in 1783, and those who bought deserted British grants from His Catholic Majesty after that date. Andrew Ellicott wrote in his journal that those holding grants to their families by the British had nothing to worry about because "there cannot possibly be any doubt as to the validity of their titles." Ellicott maintained that those who had bought deserted British titles need not worry either: "Upon the principles of justice and equity, [they] are perhaps equally safe." His prognostications proved to be correct, but the word "perhaps" did worry more than a few people. The second main kind of grant in and around Natchez were Spanish grants to land not included in prior British grants.[15] William Dunbar was a major beneficiary in both categories.

Because of the chaotic land conditions in Mississippi Territory, made more so by pesky Georgia land speculators, the federal government did not quite know how to proceed. Officials set aside a minimum of $4 million to buy their way out of the dilemma, beginning with the Georgia claims. The government was able settle the difficulty in 1802, but it cost the taxpayers $1.25 million to pay off holders of fraudulent Yazoo grants. After the payment to Georgia, the federal government inherited 5 million acres of Yazoo lands and decided to use the proceeds from the sale of those lands to settle land claims. "The Federal government agreed to extinguish . . . all Indian land claims in Georgia, and promised to cede to Georgia any claim or right to land located within the United States and lying south of Tennessee, North Carolina, and South Carolina, and lying east of the territory ceded by Georgia."[16] Finally, the territory ceded by Georgia would, in due course, become a state (actually two states—Mississippi in 1817 and Alabama in 1819).[17]

Having solved the Georgia land problem, on July 26, 1802, the government told Governor Claiborne that land commissioners were being appointed, and he was to give them all of the information he possessed on land in Mississippi Territory ceded by Indians. The commissioners were also to be given information about settlers' claims to land relinquished by Georgia, claims under the French prior to the Treaty of Paris of 1763, and claims under the British and Spanish governments before October 27, 1795—the date of the Treaty of San Lorenzo. They were, in other words, to be given everything the governor had and could find that related to land distribution since the French settled in the area in 1699.[18]

Claiborne did everything possible to comply with the directive, but because papers—even important land titles—sometimes were misplaced or lost, particularly since so many granting governments had been involved during a century, obeying the directive was nigh-on impossible. Within two weeks, Claiborne sent a handbill to everyone in the territory telling them to register their land claims with country clerks by November 1, 1802, less than two weeks away.[19] The response was predictably light: many did not even receive the handbill; others did not take the mandate seriously. On November 5, Claiborne reported to federal authorities that he knew of many people—a majority, in fact—who had not filed their claims. Many did not file claims because land speculators spread rumors that settler "rights would be greatly jeopardized by registration."[20]

Probably as thorny a land problem as the commissioners were going to face related not to past grants from Britain or Spain but to Choctaw Nation land cessions in the territory. In 1802, in the Treaty of Fort Adams, the Choctaws ceded to the United States 2,641,920 acres of land along the Mississippi River. In 1803, in the Treaty of Hoe Buckintoopa, Choctaws ceded 852,761 acres along the Mobile River. In 1805, they ceded 4,142,720 more acres in southern Mississippi and western Alabama. Between 1802 and 1830, the Choctaws ceded all of their Mississippi lands—nearly 40 million acres—which would cause a future land granting problem of monumental proportions.[21] The land ceded along the Mississippi River at Fort Adams was fertile and very valuable. How would illegal British and Spanish grants to Choctaw land made long before cession be handled? Claiborne urged the government to make provisions "for people who had settled on vacant land," and he expressed hope that "these citizens may be secured in their improvements."[22] In short, Claiborne adopted the Spanish philosophy, which maintained that "settlement was a title in itself." Land problems across America were, indeed, many and complex, but none more so than in Mississippi Territory.

Governor W. C. C. Claiborne never underestimated the task before him, and he became the first person in the territory to undertake a comprehensive study of all land claims. His long, involved reports to Congress made it possible for the federal government to formulate its first land act for the territory on March 3, 1803. The act stated that heads of families and those over the age of twenty-one who held British or Spanish grants prior to October 27, 1795, would have them confirmed. Another provision allowed squatters on land without title to that land to claim preemption rights to as much as a section (640 acres) of it, provided that land had been occupied and under cultivation before October 27, 1795. The act also provided for the creation of two land offices "to dispose of nationally-owned lands" in the territory. One office was to be opened in Adams County; the other somewhere east of the Pearl River. Two registrars (or land agents) and four commissioners were to be assigned to the two offices, and a surveyor general was to be appointed for the territory.[23]

The position of land agent in so large a territory with some of the richest land in the country was an appointment many people in the Democratic-Republican Party sought. Joseph Chambers was appointed to the eastern land office, while the western land office was given to Edward Turner, a former aide-de-camp to Governor Claiborne. Thomas Green, the territory's nonvoting delegate to the U.S. House of Representatives and a member of a powerful and influential Mississippi family, secured the seat for Turner, despite Claiborne's efforts to secure the post for his brother, Ferdinand.[24] There followed a donnybrook between supporters of Claiborne and Turner that, sadly, tarnished the image of the governor. No one in the territory worked more diligently at the difficult job of settling conflicting land claims than did Claiborne.[25]

The land act of March 3, 1803, was pretty clear cut;[26] sorry to say, resolutions of conflicting claims were not. For example, the Spanish regranted British grants that had been abandoned after 1783. Unfortunately, in too many cases, enthusiasm of Spanish officials for land granting caused mistakes; they made grants haphazardly and included a number of British grants that had not been abandoned. They also had the bad habit of granting the same land to more than one person. To stir the pot even more, the squatters who earned preemptive rights were, in some cases, squatting on land already owned by another person, and their claims had to be adjudicated.[27] Then there was the problem of Spanish antedating. As we have seen, though Spanish officials' granting of land was to end five days after the signing of the Treaty of San Lorenzo, Spanish officials were still granting land in 1796 and 1797, and Dunbar was one of the people getting some of that land. Nowhere in America was a land mess more complicated, more hopeless.

Since the claims were more numerous and more confused in the western land office, in Adams County, their work was more difficult by far. As R. S. Cotterill put it, "Into this slough of despond, the two commissioners waded valiantly and, after long delay and eminent exertions, emerged with a verdict."[28] They succeeded by giving petitioners, whenever possible, the benefit of the doubt—decisions that probably could not be defended or supported in a court of law. The land agents were each assisted by two commissioners. The March 3 act stated that the president would appoint the commissioners to the two land offices, giving him an opportunity to dispense a bit of patronage. To everyone's amazement, President Jefferson appointed Thomas Rodney, a friend of Dunbar, but one who had failed at just about everything he had attempted in life, especially business. Rodney had become a laughingstock in Natchez—a dreamer who tried to implement dreams—before leaving the region in disgrace. Historians called him "a toothless old failure living on romantic and mystic dreams," an "old derelict." The success he soon had as a western commissioner led historian William Hamilton to write, "This great republic blooms from the dust of some peculiar blossoms."[29]

Rodney had left Mississippi Territory and retired to the original family home in Delaware. Jefferson, likely at Dunbar's urging, considered Rodney a suitable choice and returned him to Adams County, where he displayed a new, serious-minded personality, indefatigable energy, ability, and a sense of fairness. After reviewing Rodney's decisions, Hamilton wrote, "In the delicate work of settling conflicting land claims under grants from five governments and in the important task of building the common law into an institution of Western society, he served his country well."[30]

From 1803 until his death seven years later, Dunbar was often called upon as a witness in land dispute cases and as an arbitrator.[31] In addition, he defended all of his own grants before the land agent and two commissioners. One claim in dispute was a tract of one thousand arpents in Wilkinson County dating back to 1793. It was a tract that Georgia had regranted during the time of the Yazoo frauds. On July 9, 1805, Thomas Rodney, Robert Williams, and Thomas Williams all signed a certificate stating, in part, "We do certify that the said William Dunbar is confirmed in his title thereto, by virtue of the Articles of Agreement and Cession, between the United States and the State of Georgia."[32]

From his earliest days in America, William Dunbar knew that the acquisition and cultivation of good land in a country aborning and growing would make possible the scientific life he craved. He never lost interest in buying and selling land or recommending acquisitions to others. Dunbar knew the importance of water, so he sought creeks, lakes, and, always, access to the Mississippi River. Friends elsewhere in the country may have wondered why he chose to live so far away from "civilization" as they defined it. Yet Dunbar knew that the Mississippi River gave him access to the world and gave the world access to Natchez. He knew that fertile land, abundant water, dependable labor, and a plan would make success possible. Far from being isolated in a region without civility and luxuries, Dunbar had much to sustain himself (and his family), both body and mind, as he wandered the grounds of the Forest, worked in his scientific laboratory, and read or wrote in his extensive library, all of which helped him recapture the good life that had been his in northeast Scotland. Land made all of this possible, and he knew it.

10

Cotton and Slavery

As Dunbar's agricultural pursuits in Natchez evolved, cotton became his most important staple.[1] When he arrived in Manchac in 1773, British authorities were urging settlers to cultivate and ship indigo, but Dunbar preferred barrel staves. Not only was indigo a difficult crop to cultivate because of its susceptibility to insects and bad weather, but producing staves was a year-round activity needing only oak trees and labor. Moreover, staves were in high demand. Then came the Spanish with their pet agricultural products, always indigo and often tobacco; both were tried in the Natchez region, and with some success. Dunbar was planting on his Natchez land long before the Forest was under construction; in 1789, of 262 farmers reporting the growing of tobacco, Dunbar raised the sixth-largest crop, 17,000 pounds.[2]

Dunbar grew many different crops, mainly for plantation consumption and the New Orleans trade, but he was always looking for just the right staple to be shipped worldwide. He knew that, for Natchez and environs, tobacco was not the right staple. It was hard on the soil, and the price fluctuated too much for his liking. He was looking for a crop much in demand worldwide that suited the weather of Natchez and its ability to ship large quantities of a staple easily and quickly from Natchez under the Hill to New Orleans and the world. Dunbar wanted to conduct business as efficiently as possible to free up his time to engage in other activities he loved, as reflected in a letter to Governor Winthrop Sargent: Dunbar noted that he "always looked forward to the day when I could spend time with natural history and philosophy."[3]

In the late 1790s, Dunbar knew that the Natchez District was poised to help New Orleans assume a major commercial role in the United States—one that would rival Philadelphia's. He had learned much about New Orleans's potential when he owned and operated a mercantile store there in the 1780s. Natchez had the Mississippi River at its doorstep, and it led to a port growing and prospering as the interior of America grew along rivers that led to the Ohio River and then the Mississippi River. A provision of the Treaty of San Lorenzo gave Americans the right to deposit goods in New Orleans free of charge while awaiting transshipment, leading one observer to suggest this "country is going to become one of the most prosperous in the world" and that New Orleans would rival any other American port quite soon. In 1799, 78 oceangoing ships entered the port of New Orleans, compared to 31 in 1794, the year before the treaty. In 1799, 110 river crafts came down the Mississippi to the Crescent City, compared to only 23 in 1794. And in 1799, 66 outward-bound vessels left the port of New Orleans, compared to 26 five years earlier.[4]

The British and Spanish staple of choice was indigo, exports of which from New Orleans in 1769 amounted to $400,000, but because of bad seasons and insects, indigo exports declined yearly until, in 1801, there was exported through that city only 80,572 pounds, worth less than a dollar a pound.[5] In the early 1800s, cotton was quickly replacing both tobacco and indigo as the top staple in the Natchez District. Prior to 1815, the upland cotton-producing region of the country was South Carolina and the eastern portion of central Georgia. It was estimated that out of a total of 40 million pounds of cotton produced in the United States in 1801, South Carolina produced 20 million and Georgia 10 million. Ten years later, the nation was producing 80 million pounds, of which South Carolina and Georgia produced 60 million pounds.[6]

In 1797, Francis Baily, an English observer who kept a journal as he roamed the lower Mississippi country, wrote that the land was excellent and the Mississippi River and New Orleans made a great combination to meet the import and export needs of the region. Land was cheap, about $1 an acre. Five acres in town cost $150, while one could purchase 150 acres near Natchez for $4 per acre. Baily noted that Natchez was an excellent place for a person to settle "if he can bring himself to give up the advantages of refined society." He remarked also that even though Spain did not believe in slavery, it allowed the practice in West Florida, and undoubtedly, Americans would continue the practice north of the thirty-first parallel and elsewhere "till they have adopted some measure for the utter annihilation of it from the country." Baily camped on the Homochitto River approximately thirty miles from Natchez and pronounced the land "the most fertile" he had ever seen. (The ground is level until one gets to within a few miles of Natchez; then it gets hilly.) The land was sandy and overgrown with large pines called "pitch pines" by the inhabitants, he observed, because some had used the pines to make pitch, tar, and turpentine—naval stores—for ships in New Orleans. Baily pointed out that New Orleans was only two hundred miles to the south, requiring six days to get there by river. Overall he appeared to be greatly impressed with the region.[7]

Cotton had at least two advantages over other potential staples for the region: it could be grown on just about all tillable land in the South, and it did not exhaust the soil. Moreover, planting and cultivating were quite simple. After the land was prepared for cultivation by breaking down the cotton stalks from the previous year, the field was laid off in beds by plowing a furrow between the old rows; seeds were sown, usually by female slaves; and furrows were closed by a harrow. When the plants were several inches high, the laborious task of thinning began, done with a hoe, followed by a plow to round up the ridges and weed the rows. Thinning required leaving first two plants, then eventually one, in hills approximately twelve inches apart. Cultivation was repeated approximately every twenty days (four to five times a season) until nearly picking time. In the southeastern states, planting began in late February or early March, whereas in the Natchez—southwest—region, the middle of May was planting time. First blooms usually appeared in June, and picking began in mid-August in the old Southwest and continued until the middle of December. Picking cotton was a laborious and tedious task undertaken by women and children as well as men. An average picking day for an average hand was about fifty pounds of cotton.[8]

In the old Southwest, William Dunbar became a leading pioneer planter of cotton. As early as 1735, the French farmers planted a small amount of cotton in the area, and Louisiana governor Jean Baptiste LeMoyne, Sieur de Bienville, noted that "the cultivation of cotton should be most advantageous."[9] Dunbar was impressed with the crop and its seemingly natural relationship to climate and soil. He did not cast his lot with cotton, however, until he saw England gearing up a textile industry to take advantage of the increase in cotton production after the invention of the Whitney gin in 1793. Fertile soil and favorable climate notwithstanding, a hungry market was necessary for success. From 1771 to 1775, Britain imported less than 5 million pounds a year worldwide, and from 1776 to 1780, an average of 7 million pounds yearly. In 1784—the year after the Treaty of Paris ended the American Revolution—the amount imported into Britain rose to 18 million pounds. By 1800, Britain was importing a minimum of 56 million pounds of cotton yearly.[10] America saw no such increase in textile manufacturing, perhaps because of President Jefferson's desire to keep America a society of yeoman farmers. Since Jefferson considered the city the personification of evil—a potential cesspool of political bosses, a proletariat, and mob rule—he thwarted the growth of cities any way he could.

Another bit of good fortune for Dunbar and fellow planters living north of the thirty-first parallel was a new Spanish policy that invited Americans to import goods through New Orleans literally free of charge. The policy was included in a letter from Juan Ventura Morales, intendant of Louisiana and West Florida, to Daniel Clark Jr., acting vice consul of the United States, which stated, in part, "No duties shall be collected on articles exported to the American settlements situated above the thirty-first parallel of North latitude."[11] The liberal statement of policy reflected the desire of Spanish officials to encourage commerce up and down the Mississippi River, thereby promoting settlement and agricultural pursuits to the benefit of New Orleans and its Spanish governing officials, setting the stage for agricultural expansion in Mississippi Territory. William Dunbar has been given credit for encouraging the cultivation of cotton over all other agricultural options and becoming "the planter pioneer in cotton."[12] Though exaggerated, the statement certainly can be defended, but the real father of cotton expansion in the South was Great Britain.

Since no gin had yet been perfected, cotton arrived irregularly during the year for general merchants in Glasgow, Whitehaven, Lancaster, Liverpool, Bristol, and especially London. Merchants in those cities bought cotton, stored it in their warehouses, and sold it to regular customers. By 1756, there were general brokers selling cotton at auction, but only a small amount of available cotton was sold that way, probably only damaged goods seeking a quick sale. In Liverpool, in 1766, there were twelve brokers—useful go-between people whose chief duties were buying, selling, forwarding, insuring, and collecting outstanding debts for merchants. By 1790, successful brokers started specializing. Four brokers were listed in a 1790 directory as cotton brokers.[13]

What gave Liverpool the opportunity to become the cotton import city of Britain, and indeed the world, was its proximity to Manchester, a city desiring to become the textile capital of the country. One could add to the plus side Liverpool's inland navigation, the convenience of Liverpool to West Indies and American trade, progressive policies, and excellent docks and warehouse facilities, yet all of those pluses could be duplicated by other cities, especially London. What other locales could not duplicate was the presence of nearby Manchester and its desire to become a major manufacturing metropolis. In 1788, twenty-six cotton merchants and twenty cotton dealers worked in Manchester; by 1804, there were more than sixty merchants and forty dealers in cotton alone.[14]

Until the late 1790s, the United States was a minor cultivator and exporter of cotton, much of which was raised in Turkey, India, the West Indies, Smyrna, Cyprus, Macedonia, Brazil, and other nations around the globe.[15] At that time and during the Jefferson presidency (1801–9), the Democratic-Republican Party advocated a nation made up of yeoman farmers and small towns. Federalists of Alexander Hamilton's persuasion preferred controllable cities to the "least government" advocated in rural environments. Democratic-Republicans did not anticipate that America would become a cotton empire encouraging the growth of cities.[16] Despite that fact, by 1800, thanks to Eli Whitney, the nation was exporting yearly 18 million pounds, about 45,000 bales weighing approximately forty pounds each, as compared with 57,000 bales from the West Indies and 28,000 bales from Brazil. Of the 45,000 bales exported by the United States, 40,000 went to Britain. America's entry into the cotton export business as a major player infuriated growers in the West Indies. In a circular dated November 2, 1801, a West Indies export company stated, "The quality produced in Georgia and Carolina, and on the banks of the Mississippi, in favourable seasons, will, in point of weight exceed all the West Indian Islands put together." The next year, for the first time, British importation of cotton from America exceeded that from the West Indies; by Dunbar's death in 1810, the United States provided 53.1 percent of all British imported cotton, while the West Indies supplied only 16.2 percent.[17]

In the early 1790s, Liverpool tried to combine the importation of cotton with the manufacture of textiles, but the effort failed because Manchester and the villages around it were much better suited to excel in manufacturing. Liverpool simply did not have enough skilled laborers to compete with Manchester. Liverpool imported its first cotton in 1758. Sir James Pecton recorded an isolated advertisement of November 3, 1758, offering to sell at auction twenty-five bags of Jamaican cotton,[18] and from that date forward phenomenal growth was recorded. The rate of increase from 1781 to 1791 was 320 percent, and it passed all competing English cities in 1795. In 1801, of 260,485 bales imported into England, 98,752 went through Liverpool, which maintained its supremacy throughout the rest of the nineteenth century and much of the twentieth century. In 1927, a newspaper listed Liverpool as the greatest cotton market in the world; the city's warehouses had space for 2 million bales.[19]

The rise of Manchester as a cotton-manufacturing center did not just happen. Merchants in that city worked hard and smart to make success possible; they sent agents to the source of supply. They had connections in all cotton-producing countries; some English merchants had large plantations in various countries, including the United States. From the early 1790s,

Manchester agents were in New Orleans working to increase the amount of cotton consigned to particular companies, and by the mid-1790s, cotton brokers appeared on the scene to act as buyers or agents on behalf of clients in Manchester. They were different from general brokers, who concentrated on selling, not buying. Liverpool and Manchester merchants agreed that those agents played a key role in the distribution system. They wanted a minimum number of hands through which cotton flowed on its way to the spinners: grower, middle man, importer, dealer.[20] It was important for Dunbar and other shippers to know all of the people with whom they were dealing, if they hoped to be treated fairly along the way.

Dunbar and others in Mississippi Territory abandoned other staples in favor of cotton in part because Mississippi was an ideal place to raise cotton, but also because the hunger for cotton in British ports and cities like Manchester made growing cotton wise, as did the attractive price raw cotton was demanding by the turn of the century. A profit could be turned at twelve cents a pound, but when Dunbar entered the cotton arena it was demanding thirty-five cents per pound. As with other commodities, the price increased and decreased quickly. In December 1803, cotton was being quoted in New Orleans at fifteen cents a pound and was at sixteen cents per pound the next year. The per pound price rose in 1804 and 1805 only to plummet again to around fourteen cents by 1809.[21]

Throughout his plantation years, Dunbar maintained that he knew very little about business. He said he was a planter, not a businessman, yet his reputation preceded him. Whether buying land or ordering scientific equipment from Philadelphia, New York, or London, Dunbar drove a hard bargain, and he kept track of all orders, receipts, and delivery promises. He was continually informed about happenings in the world—and was able to keep up with ships, cargoes, and prices—by reading newspapers from New Orleans, New York, and elsewhere. Dunbar did the same thing as a cotton producer, by choosing his American and European agents carefully (he worked only with proven agents and companies in Liverpool and London) and staying in touch with them. He insisted upon knowing the whereabouts of his goods at all times, and his reputation for honesty and prompt payment of debts was known far and wide. Agents and companies known to take advantage of clients wanted nothing to do with him or his business, but honest brokers knew that Dunbar was the largest and most successful planter in the Natchez region, that his cotton was first rate, and that he would pay all bills as soon as possible. In Dunbar's eyes, integrity on one side of the table must be matched by integrity on the other side.[22] This is not to suggest that he was never cheated; he was, but not often.

One factor that made Dunbar's dealings difficult to follow was that he did not simply sell, receive money from the sale, and then go home. He kept money with his agent in New Orleans, Chew and Relf, for insurance and goods he and Dinah might want from that city. Dunbar also had agents in New York City, Philadelphia, and even Charleston on the East Coast, and he kept funds with each of them—the last for the purchase of slaves and the former two for personal and scientific equipment and for shipping expenses. He drew on these accounts simultaneously. On January 12, 1802, Dunbar wrote to Philadelphia attorney Samuel Breek Jr. that he was forwarding money owed to the Ross family for years, and he wanted Breek to handle the matter for him. In the letter he stated, "I am shipping cotton at New Orleans for Lond. & am privileged to draw upon N. York."[23] It must have been difficult for someone residing in Natchez to keep up with the pockets of money deposited in many locations, both in the South and on the East Coast, and it took an individual with business talents to handle all those accounts. Dunbar knew exactly what he expected of each agent, and he knew, too, the dollar amount each kept to cover the expenses of other assigned duties.

Dunbar expected a lot of himself and others, and he was not above berating agents or companies who were inefficient in their practices. On July 5, 1802, he scolded Bird and Company for rating his cotton at twenty-five cents a pound when it was shipped at thirty-two cents and upward, and he haggled over the price they quoted for sundries. Bird and Company asked him what price he was willing to pay for, let us say, Irish linens or elegant sheets. He responded, "I am not a merchant. My occupation is agriculture."[24] Then Dunbar would haggle over the quoted price. On one occasion in 1802, he wrote his agent that a buyer had not yet paid him for the cotton shipped to him because the agent had not yet provided a bill to the purchaser. He ended the angry message by writing, "I hope the next accounts I shall receive will be more satisfactory."[25]

More often than not, though, Dunbar wrote to his agents in New Orleans, Philadelphia, and Liverpool or London to inform them what he was shipping, to pay a bill, to purchase goods, or to request being paid as expeditiously as possible. On November 11, 1802, Dunbar wrote Pearce and Crawford in Philadelphia, "Shipping some bales of cotton to your address for acct. of my debt to Chas. Ross Esqr. . . . Twenty-three bales will be shippt"—6,900 pounds of cotton.[26]

Dunbar very seldom commented on national or international politics in these strictly business missives. In a January 1803 letter about articles he wanted to purchase, he did add that French officials and soldiers had not yet arrived to take over Louisiana from the Spanish and commented that the troubles Napoleon was having back in Europe made it highly unlikely he could spare any troops to hold North American outposts an ocean and a sea away.[27] Dunbar was right. French officials came to Louisiana only long enough to sell not only New Orleans but all North American land claimed by the French to the United States in the much-celebrated Louisiana Purchase of 1803.

From 1802 until his death in 1810, Dunbar did business with at least eleven companies, and he alone seemed to manage every transaction.[28] He believed in insuring each shipment of cotton or other goods, and he worked closely with Chew and Relf in New Orleans to do so. If something was shipped uninsured or underinsured to or from the East Coast or Europe, Dunbar more often than not dropped the offending agent or company. He ordered blankets for his slaves, carriages for Dinah, numerous household goods, and, of course, scientific equipment and books, the orders that apparently pleased him the most. Dunbar used different agents for different goods, and he judged their worth by the quality and price of their purchases on his behalf. Significantly, he controlled the timing of his exports and imports to take advantage of the best price in both directions and neighbors tended to watch when he exported before they moved their own goods down the river to New Orleans.

Dunbar was particularly knowledgeable about when to hold his cotton and when to ship it. He listened to the advice of trusted agents and studied worldwide trends through newspapers, but he mainly depended on instincts and personal history as a planter. Sometimes, but not often, he failed to ship when he should have and had to unload his cotton later at the same or—more likely—a lower price. Still, he was right much more often than wrong, and friends learned to trust his judgment when it came to holding or shipping. He knew that he was primarily a planter whose livelihood depended on things that he could control as well as matters that were out of his hands. He could not control the weather, but he could plant in a way that minimized exposure. His meteorological records guided him in deciding when to plant, and he challenged nature as little as possible. Yet there was much he could control—what type of nonperishable crops to plant, what agents and companies with which to do business, which overseers to hire, and how to tend to the needs of his slaves. He could also increase the odds of his success by keeping up with national and international news, studying seasonal prices for goods, and learning how to improve his land and equipment. He may have been, as Dunbar Rowland maintains, "recognized throughout the United States as one of its leading men of science,"[29] but he was smart enough to know that he was a planter first and that shoddy agricultural practices and inattention to plantation business were the best ways to fail economically, thereby depriving himself of the opportunity to study the sciences he so loved.

One cannot contemplate cotton without considering slavery. The labor-intensive planting, cultivation, and harvesting of cotton required a constant source of labor. Even though the Spanish abhorred the institution of slavery and barred it from the Floridas before losing that territory in 1763, they did not abolish it after regaining the Floridas twenty years later. The British not only allowed slavery, they encouraged it, and William Dunbar began his plantation activities in 1773 with slaves purchased in Jamaica. By the time he married and was on his way to economic recovery in 1784, there were more than 16,000 slaves in West Florida, and by the time he was thinking about building the Forest and moving to Natchez, there were as many slaves in West Florida as white people.[30]

When Frederick Law Olmsted toured the South early in the nineteenth century, he pronounced slavery a mockery of good order and effective farm and plantation management. He declared slavery a wasteful economic system and exaggerated the responsibility of slaves for making the system ineffective. He saw slaves as shiftless and careless and a deterrent to success.[31] Other historians have maintained that American-born slaves, circa 1800, were "primitive" but with training could be as productive as free blacks.[32] Still others have suggested that the tendency toward "aimlessness" noted by observers resulted from slaves' desolate lives, which led not to freedom and individual enterprise but to the sameness of existence mandated by bondage from birth to death.[33] Some, with justification, have suggested that the availability of free land to white potential farmers and planters made slavery inevitable in the South and very profitable to plantation owners. The cost of slaves kept increasing, and by 1800 American-born slaves were selling at higher prices than African-born slaves. In 1800, a prime field hand was considered in the marketplace to be worth about 1,500 pounds of ginned cotton. By 1809, the figure had increased to about 3,000 pounds because of improvements in the gin and improvements in baling—both made by William Dunbar.[34]

The truth of the matter is that by the 1790s slavery was entrenched in the South; all it needed was a reason to stay. And cotton was so dependent on a constant and predictable labor force that profit would not allow the institution to die. White people were seeking their own welfare and comfort,[35] and a staple in demand the world over would provide that comfort. White planters already had in place a labor system controlled by the planter that would make production possible and profitable. By buying and controlling his labor force, Dunbar could work within predictable boundaries, absent, of course, predictability of weather and the marketplace. Instead of wages, he gave food, clothing, shelter, and medical care.[36] That was the constant cost of slave labor, and Dunbar could control it by controlling the number of slaves and the quality and amount of the food, clothing, medical care, and shelter provided. Since he did not skimp on those needs, and since he gave each slave family a bit of land for personal cultivation and Sundays off plus an occasional Monday, Dunbar felt that he was among the most generous of slave owners and that his slaves—young and old, female and male—should feel obligated, motivated, and thankful. He thought that in 1773; he thought that in the last year of his life.

Another reason slavery was profitable for Dunbar was that cotton needed year-round attention, and during slack times fences needed mending, corn needed to be grown, and a hundred odd jobs needed doing. Therefore, his slaves were busy twelve months a year, and constant expense was turned into probable profit. The cost of maintaining one slave was close to minimum subsistence. A planter who had forty slaves working diverse crops figured a yearly expense of $3.46 per slave in Louisiana and Mississippi Territory, whereas a planter who had one hundred slaves working primarily in cotton (a periodically labor-intensive crop) reported a yearly cost of $17.50 per slave in a budget that allowed $20.00 per slave. It was estimated that each slave would turn out seven bales each year. If one estimates sale cost at eight cents per pound—a conservative figure—the total income from those seven bales was $225.00—a nice return on a $17.50 expenditure.[37] Slavery may have been unprofitable for planters who preferred large numbers and had too many slaves for the jobs at hand. That was not so on the plantations of the business-conscious William Dunbar.

Cotton, as the amount produced increased, demanded more slaves, until by 1796 the crop in the Natchez region exceeded 3,000 bales. In 1801, Governor Claiborne estimated that the cotton sold that year brought in $700,000, the equivalent of 3 million bales. By 1802, cotton had become so important in Mississippi Territory that a proposed bill prohibiting the importation of more male slaves was rejected by the legislature. In that year, an improved plantation of six hundred acres near the Mississippi River represented an investment of approximately $21,000. The annual cotton crop was estimated at 30,000 pounds worth $6,000. Expenses, including overseer ($1,265 a year), left a net profit of $4,735, or 22.5 percent return on investment. Even before 1803, wealthier planters, led by Dunbar, were producing crops worth as much as $16,000 a year.[38]

Regardless of economic considerations, thoughtful, educated, moral-minded Americans during William Dunbar's maturity were, in growing numbers, suggesting that slavery should end in the United States. The French observer J. Hector St. John de Crèvecoeur described slavery in Charleston as a melancholy, evil scene. "You planters get rich," he wrote, but if he, Crèvecoeur, were "to be possessed of a plantation, and my slaves treated as in general they are here, never could I rest in peace."[39] In 1794, George Washington wrote, "Were it not then, that I am principled against selling negroes as you would do cattle in the market, I would not, in twelve months from this date, be possessed of one as a slave. . . . I wish from my soul that the legislature of this State, could see the policy of gradual abolition of slavery. It might prevent much future mischief."[40] Dunbar's scientific sponsor, Thomas Jefferson, wrote in 1795 that "interest is really going over to the side of morality. The value of the slave is every day lessening; his burden on his master daily increasing. Interest is, therefore, preparing the disposition to be just; and this will be goaded from time to time by the insurrectionary spirit of the slaves."[41] More and more southern leaders were suggesting that slavery was an economic burden on planters and farmers and that it would soon disappear, but they were wrong.[42] Cotton made slavery profitable, and even where slavery was not profitable, it was a social institution that slowly came to replace economics as the main reason to hold dearly to what eventually had to go. That logic was not Dunbar's, however; to him slavery was good economics.

The sad truth is that William Dunbar, one of the leading lights in Mississippi Territory, was not an antislavery leader. Though he did not openly advocate slavery in correspondence or scientific articles, he never questioned its need or morality. In all of his writings—back in Scotland and during his life in America since 1771—he left no clues as to what he thought of the institution of slavery. Slaves were property to be bought and sold, with no more rights than cotton gins, scientific equipment, or land. They were property, pure and simple, and should be treated as property to be used and cared for. Seldom in his writings did he register that any particular slave was doing a good job or deserved credit for something. As we have seen, however, he meted out punishment with severity. From 1791 to 1810 in Mississippi Territory, as had been the case in Manchac earlier, Dunbar made numerous notations in his journals and correspondence of slaves disobeying or running away. In March 1807, Dunbar wrote Winthrop Sargent about a slave Sargent was returning. "You may rest assured," he wrote, "that Aquilla will receive a very severe chastisement, which I presume will have upon him and as an example to others, a full & complete effect could be derived from the tardy civil process of our country." He accused Aquilla of "being a finished rascal[.] I will make him declare under the lash what he has done."[43] Harsh punishments were accompanied by statements denouncing the accused for not understanding that a Dunbar slave was a fortunate slave because Dunbar clothed, fed, and treated all slaves better than did anyone else. Slaves were not to be commended; instead it was their obligation to obey and produce. Dunbar did not invent the institution of slavery, but he indirectly helped it continue. After Whitney's gin and Dunbar's bale, cotton became such a profitable crop in the South that individual economic greed triumphed over doing the right thing.

After Dunbar and Ellicott settled the thirty-first parallel dispute between Spain and the United States, slaves were able to escape across that line to freedom in Spanish territory, while Spanish prisoners crossed into safety the other way. Thus resulted a diplomatic problem that Dunbar suggested be addressed by the legislature.[44] In 1806, Dunbar sold a number of slaves to a Colonel Morehouse, who defaulted on his payment for the slaves and was ordered to return the slaves, paying Dunbar $12 for each month he had used the slaves. Dunbar found out, however, that the colonel had sold one of the slaves. Quoting property law to Colonel Morehouse, he demanded not only the $12 per month payment for use of the slave but also retrieval of the slave, or the payment of $1,000 plus interest from January 17, 1806, to the date of delivery and "compensation for this trouble, time and commission."[45] For Dunbar, such situations were purely business and legal matters; there was no humanity in any of his references to slaves. He wrote to a friend that if Colonel Morehouse "returns the slaves to you I beg you to try to sell them, but if there is no opportunity, you may send back to me the younger one called Bill but I prefer that the other whose name is Sampson be hired out for the harvest, if an opportunity to dispose of him does not present itself."[46]

When slaves ran away, Dunbar, as did other planters, advertised that fact in local newspapers. Dunbar advertised on June 17, 1806, that a husband and wife recently purchased in Kentucky had run off and were probably headed back that way. He offered a $20 reward for the return of either of them. In describing the pair, he noted what were to him their relevant attributes—"straight limbed" and "low and well set."[47] As late as 1807, Dunbar was still ordering new slaves; he sent money to Chew and Relf to order slaves from Charleston, South Carolina. In describing what he wanted, Dunbar noted that he preferred twelve- to twenty-one-year-olds, "well formed & robust, & the proportion of females about 1/4 to 1/3 of that of males."[48]

William Dunbar was an enlightened scientist whose accomplishments still are recognized. The breadth of his interests was amazing, and the accomplishments he achieved in many arenas are more than impressive. In the personal arena, however, Dunbar was only economically successful. He came to America to achieve economic success, and in doing so, he represented the plantation class that refused to allow slavery to disappear until a bloody civil war forced its abandonment fifty-five years after his death.

11

Agricultural Experimenter

It was not easy to be a successful plantation owner. Those, such as William Dunbar, who became well known understood the ingredients necessary for success. Though it all began with the best land available, many planters who worked fertile land failed; success required business and financial skills as well as an understanding of fixed plantation costs. For example, sugar mills, cotton gins, rice irrigation ditches, and tobacco barns were costly items but essential to growing each of those staples. Such fixed costs forced owners to increase the size of land holdings and the number of slaves in an effort to increase the production needed to pay the costs. Successful planters paid close attention to the relationship among labor costs, production, and expansion. Important economic questions followed other questions: When did a planter have more slaves than he could afford? When were fixed costs too much for the quality and amount of land available? Once there were enough slaves to require daily supervision, a plantation owner needed to add the cost of drivers and overseers. They had to be dedicated and talented supervisors if the plantation owner was to guarantee that the output of an enlarged slave population was economical. The fertility and productivity of the soil and the mildness of weather made possible using and managing large slave gangs within a short distance of the plantation, so the planter was anxious to secure the best soil available in his region.[1]

Even if a planter happened to be a good judge of soil, hired high-quality managers, had a hardworking slave population, enjoyed pleasant weather, and followed sound economic practices, he still might fail. He had also to be a bit of a gambler, and he had to constantly experiment with ways to do everything better. That was particularly true with cotton—a fluffy, light product with tenacious seeds that had to be removed, a packaging process that confounded most planters, and a market controlled continents away that needed to be understood and managed as much as possible. Mississippi Territory produced a significant number of cotton "geniuses" who made that staple critical to the economy of Mississippi. Dr. Rush Nutt experimented with Mexican cottonseed and began the systematic selection and improvement of that seed. Colonel Henry W. Vick earned an enviable reputation for the work he did on seed improvement. Samuel Postlewaite, Dunbar's son-in-law, experimented with a roller fitted with knives to cut up cotton stalks.[2] The names of many others dot the pages of old Southwest history books. In 1854, B. L. C. Wailes, a Washington, Mississippi, planter and naturalist, published a geological survey of the state, authorized by the legislature, titled *A Report on the Agriculture and Geology of Mississippi*. Wailes began this monumental work by borrowing from the Dunbar family all of William Dunbar's correspondence, for he considered Dunbar to be the most successful planter during the territorial years.[3] Still, other historians have not included the name of William Dunbar in inventories of great agricultural reformers in the antebellum South. In listing fifty great southern reformers, Avery Craven did not include Dunbar's name, perhaps because most of those on his list hailed from the Southeast and labored after the 1820s.[4] Dunbar's activities were significant, however, particularly as early notions and improvements were realized later in the nineteenth century.

As cotton cultivation spread from South Carolina and Georgia, a demand arose for different and better varieties of cotton seeds to meet the conditions of different soils and climates. When farmers and planters started planting cotton in the old Southwest, they found that there were only two breeds available—Georgia Green and Creole Black. Neither was satisfactory because both were difficult to pick and clean and were less productive than desired. Worst of all, they were very susceptible to plant diseases. Both were inferior in length, Dunbar suggested, and he believed new breeds had to be developed to meet the needs of the lower Mississippi region. Many planters and farmers cultivated cotton in the antebellum South, but those who made cotton into an industry, shipping massive amounts of product down the Mississippi River to New Orleans, and then on to Liverpool or London, lived in the lower Mississippi area with easy access to the river. The strain that was developed to meet southwestern needs was the Mexican hybrid, and the extent to which it improved the quality and yield of American cotton suggests that its development was almost as important as the cotton gin in the spread of cotton planting throughout the South. It originated on plantations near Natchez and Rodney, and most of the name brands that came from the Mexican hybrid were developed as well on plantations in that region.[5] Mississippi became as internationally famous for the quality of its cotton as for the number of bales produced.

The development of Mexican hybrid cotton in Mississippi Territory happened by chance. Mississippi planter Walter Burling, while on a trip to Mexico City in 1807, bought some seeds that produced a fine, long-staple cotton that had been cultivated for centuries by Indians living in the central Mexican plateau. Burling smuggled the seeds out of the country and gave some of them to his friend and neighbor William Dunbar to study and evaluate for Mississippi Territory use. The following year, Dunbar began experimentally cultivating Burling's cotton, along with seeds of the tan-colored Nanking breed. He watched both daily, took notes, and at season's end sent samples of the lint from both varieties to Liverpool for examination by textile experts there and in Manchester. They returned to Dunbar a favorable, even enthusiastic, report on the Mexican cotton, which Dunbar described as a "fine rich color, very silky, fine & strong & rather a little longer—tho' not by much—than our own staple."[6] By his death in 1810, Dunbar had increased his annual crop of the Mexican variety to more than three thousand pounds of ginned cotton, and the variety was being grown in the lower Mississippi in increasing quantities every year.

The Mexican variety that was so successful in Mississippi Territory had one serious flaw, however: it could not be left unpicked for very long. Once the bolls began to ripen, planters had to put aside all other chores and turn everyone to picking. If the bolls were allowed to fall to the ground of their own accord, they would be severely damaged and even ruined.[7] That meant planters cultivating a large amount of the Mexican hybrid had to have available more slaves than might have been needed for the cultivation of other varieties. Even still, if early fall winds and rains hit at the wrong time, the whole crop could be ruined. Nevertheless, the variety was so good that planters continued to take a chance, hoping that bolls might not be damaged in their fields.

From the time cotton became Dunbar's staple, he constantly experimented with different seeds. His breakthrough regarding the Mexican variety was his greatest seed accomplishment, and it made him a cotton planter above all else. He also constantly experimented with plows and plowing techniques and found that by applying science to agriculture he could develop better farm implements based upon scientific principles. Dunbar developed plows to do different things at different depths, and he introduced horizontal plowing to Mississippi Territory. As ambassador to France, Jefferson had noted that the French plowed horizontally on hills, and he recommended that Dunbar experiment with horizontal plowing on the rolling hills around the Forest. Inspired by Jefferson's advice, Dunbar started running his rows along the contour lines of hills and found that doing so was useful in two ways: level rows reduced erosion, and horizontal plowing allowed plows to be used on fairly steep hillsides. Dunbar well understood that all power for gins, presses, and various kinds of mills was provided by mules and horses, and as early as 1805, he was tinkering with the possibility of attaching a small steam engine to a cotton gin.[8] He was not successful in doing so, but, as in so many other fields of interest, Dunbar simply was ahead of his time. His head said something might be possible, but technology did not support the dream—yet. It was not until the 1830s that steam engines began replacing draft animals in gin houses on large plantations.

Tools used in cultivating cotton were usually made by the local blacksmith. Dunbar, again using scientific principles, developed a scooter, or bull tongue—a four-inch strip of iron that was pointed and bent and used to open furrows into which seeds were placed—and a sweep, with two wide-cutting blades forming two sides of a triangle, used to clean weeds from the rows. He also developed a scrapper, which covered the furrow once seeds had been sown.[9] These tools did not totally replace the backbreaking iron plows or hoes, but they were important in expediting work and in allowing a hand to accomplish much more in the field than before. Most such progress in tools took place on large plantations, such as the Forest, because not many smaller plantation owners either traveled far or read widely, much less both. Northern writers blamed the lack of southern farming sophistication on the institution of slavery, but such was not really the case. The culprit was a lack of knowledge by most farmers and some planters, and even more the lack of a local marketplace where farmers might see and purchase improved implements.[10] Dunbar had an advantage in that he could afford to purchase implements manufactured elsewhere to his specifications; most farmers and planters could not.

It is almost impossible to overemphasize the breadth of agricultural, mathematical, and natural science activities Dunbar pursued throughout his life. If anything, his interests broadened as time passed, and he was as involved with all around him the day he died as he had been ten years earlier. Until his death, he experimented with products he might plant on one or more of his four plantations. By 1798, he had planted sugar cane, indigo, cotton, tobacco, corn, rice, okra, squash, sweet potatoes, Irish potatoes, millet, pumpkins, musk melons, watermelons, tomatoes, eggplant, quinces, almonds, plums, peaches, pears, and apricots.[11] The varieties did not all produce to his satisfaction, so he abandoned the less productive and went on to something else.

Dunbar experimented with crops that could be planted early—during winter months, in some cases—so that he could harvest some crops at about the time other crops were being planted. Thomas Rodney wrote to his brother, Caesar, in March 1804 that the month was quite cool and frosty in Natchez and some were wondering whether it was safe to begin garden planting; Dunbar would be harvesting peas in early April.[12] Dunbar wrote to Governor Winthrop Sargent on February 14, 1802, thanking him for the fine cranberries the Sargents had sent, and he added that he did not see why "the cranberry may not be introduced here by planting the seeds of the fruit; but it will be necessary to know its natural soil & position. . . . I have been told it grows in marshy ground." He also asked for grapevine cuttings when Sargent pruned his vines—and, while he was at it, the governor might send along flower seeds, for the Dunbar girls had started a flower garden.[13] Dunbar shared his own plants and cuttings with Sargent in return.

On one occasion, Dunbar and Governor Sargent wondered why the temperature varied a good deal between the governor's home and a grove four miles away. Dunbar explained the different temperatures by noting that they lived high above the river and were less exposed to colder temperatures because warm vapors rose from the river and spread out over nearby hills, diminishing the cold a bit. As a scientist, however, Dunbar needed to prove his contention to a skeptical governor, who believed it got colder as one went uphill. So, with a gardener as an assistant, Dunbar undertook an experiment. On a night when a frost was expected, Dunbar asked Governor Sargent to leave one thermometer in its usual location at his home, and he instructed the gardener to take a second thermometer—a half hour or so before sunup—to the lowest part of a swamp field below Sargent's residence. Dunbar wrote to Sargent, "Now if the warmth which is communicated to your hills be received from the river and swamp, the mercury will stand higher in the swamp field than on the hill but if the cause of your milder temperature be as I suppose, the reverse will be the consequence, and the thermometer on the hill will indicate a lesser degree of cold than that near the swamp."[14] He was right; the latter was the case.

In the agricultural arena, Dunbar played a significant role in advocating cotton as the staple crop of the lower Mississippi region. The invention of the cotton gin by Eli Whitney in 1793 had helped Dunbar make the commitment to cotton.[15] The problem with Whitney's cotton gin was that it was primitive, ripping seed from fiber and leaving somewhat damaged goods. A bankrupt planter, John Barcley, left Natchez for North Carolina in April 1793 but returned the following spring determined to improve Whitney's gin. It is likely that he had met with Whitney sometime that year and observed the process of teeth pulling seed from cotton. In 1795, Barcley invented a new gin and had it inspected by a group of Natchez planters (including Dunbar); they watched the machine remove seed from fiber, yielding 18 3/4 pounds of undamaged cotton in forty-five minutes. Governor Carondelet was impressed and gave Barcley an exclusive franchise for five years; anyone wishing to use the machine or another similar to it needed to pay Barcley a $10 fee. No one paid the least bit of attention to the governor's order, and many planters tried their hand at improving the gin further.[16]

Dunbar contemplated what Barcley and others were doing, and he, too, worked on the ginning improvement effort. In the meantime, he supported what others in the region were doing to improve the entire ginning process. He wrote to John Ross on March 23, 1799, that cotton was "by far the most profitable crop we have ever undertaken. . . . I have reason to think that the new gin has been greatly improved here."[17] His goal was to help develop a ginning process that injured cotton as little as possible; by 1802, he could boast of some success. He wrote Matthew Pearce and James Crawford that he held up shipping that year's crop because he had just successfully completed a process that improved the cleaning of cotton by moving it "over an inclined plane" which gently cleaned the cotton so that it was "perfectly separated from the seed." Dunbar believed that it greatly improved the ginning process and thereby significantly improved the final product. He ended by saying, "Our assembly is preparing an Inspection Law for Cotton, which we hope will put a stop to fraud & give to our Cotton that reputation abroad to which its intrinsic quality so justly entitles it."[18] Dunbar's contribution to the improvement of the gin, therefore, was allowing a cleaner separation of fiber from seed. His work on the gin was slow, methodical, and successful. On February 25, 1806, he wrote to Green and Wainwright in Liverpool, "I am now completing some improvements to the Cotton machine, by which it will be twice fanned and skreened & afterwards hand picked upon a moving web, which conducts the cotton from the machine."[19]

Problems in the baling of cotton concerned Dunbar even more than the difficulties with ginning it.[20] Whitney's gin invention and the improvements made by many in the lower Mississippi region and elsewhere had solved most of the ginning problems. But progress in solving baling dilemmas was slow, for the problems were many. An inhumane baling practice in use before 1800 required a large round hole to be cut in the floor on the second story of a barn. A large bag was attached to the lip of the hole, with most of the bag dropped through the hole to the first floor. Then a slave dropped down into the bag with a broad swatting paddle, and raw ginned cotton was dumped into the bag while the slave swatted it down as best he could, inhaling cotton fibers into his lungs while he labored.[21] In the end, the planter had a very sick slave and a great big, fluffy bag that took up a great deal of space and weighed little. On most plantations, this appalling baling practice ended by 1800, but on small upcountry farms and plantations in South Carolina and Georgia, the practice was still in use as late as 1842. It took one man fourteen days to pack as many as twelve bags by this unhealthy and unsatisfactory method.[22]

A Natchez mechanic, David Greenleaf, invented a press. He developed a rectangular-shaped box whose sides were lined with a hemp cloth. Cotton was poured into the box, and a large wooden screw press manned by two persons pressed the cotton into a rectangular shape in the box until it was full. Then two sides of the box were removed, and the exposed cotton was tied and sewn into place by the hemp cloth on which it lay. At that point, a number of hemp ropes were drawn through grooves cut into the face of the press box and tied around the bale, helping it keep its rectangular shape. The rest of the box was then withdrawn, allowing the cotton within the bale to expand, stretching the ropes tightly. The problem with this method was it was labor intensive; only a few bales could be processed each day. It was nonetheless a great improvement over the previous practice, and the Greenleaf press was to be greatly improved by Dunbar and others in the years ahead.[23]

Dunbar studied the Greenleaf press, even tried it, but was dissatisfied with the speed of the process. So Dunbar drew up specifications for a much more powerful press, sought advice from Ross on who should manufacture the machine, and signed a contract with a Philadelphia firm to build the press for him.[24] This press included a cast iron screw instead of the wooden one in the Greenleaf press. After it was delivered to Dunbar in 1802, he assembled the press on his plantation, and it was a sight to behold. The press, with all of its working parts, was quite expensive to manufacture. Dunbar paid for it by shipping seven bales of cotton worth a minimum of $1,000 to the Philadelphia manufacturer.[25] His original intention was to use it to press his cotton bales into a small rectangular shape that would need no further compressing at any seaport. Dunbar also hoped to recoup its cost by using the press to crush cottonseeds and selling the oil extracted. Dunbar's press could pack up to fifty bales of cotton a day—revolutionizing the baling process as practiced throughout the South.[26] The press, however, was never popular in the Natchez region, most likely because of its high cost compared to Greenfield's wooden press and others like it, and also because of the difficulty of manufacturing a similar press locally. It simply could not be done in the early nineteenth century. Large cast iron screw presses were not common until 1840; once again, Dunbar was ahead of his time.

In no other arena did William Dunbar make more of a contribution to the territory and the nation than in agricultural experimentation. Only later did people realize that his prognostications were correct and his examples worthy of serious consideration, even emulation. His horizontal plowing innovations and farm tools were given only a cursory nod during his lifetime. Some adopted his practices; most did not. It is true that Dunbar led the territory into cotton planting and made it the primary crop based on his knowledge of the hunger for cotton in Britain and his adaptation of the Mexican hybrid cottonseed. Yet the improvements he offered in the important area of baling cotton were passed over by local planters as too costly to manufacture and maintain locally; just as important, his improvements were known only locally because of the absence of agricultural publications, farm equipment companies and stores, and trade shows where the Dunbar press could have been explained to a wider southern audience. If Dunbar's fellow planters had known of the press and tinkered with it to bring down the cost, it might have become widely used, for it was efficient and productive beyond any other baling processes at the time. Mississippi Territory mechanics and blacksmiths were quite remarkable and inventive; they might well have turned a costly press into an affordable one.

In no area of experimentation was Dunbar more ignored than in his recommendations for uses for the cottonseeds most planters destroyed. He knew that cottonseeds were almost as valuable as the raw cotton itself, but he was never able to convince fellow planters and farmers to use the seeds for economic purposes. They simply hauled the seeds to an isolated corner of the plantation, or to a bayou, and disposed of them as an unwanted by-product of a major economic endeavor. In fact, Dunbar's friends and neighbors got tired of hearing him extol the virtues of something they considered waste.[27]

The possibility of using cottonseeds for something useful was discovered by a Dr. Otts of Bethlehem, Pennsylvania, in 1768.[28] He sent a sample of the oil extracted from the seeds to the American Philosophical Society for examination. There is no evidence that Dunbar knew of Otts's work, but as a cotton planter extracting seeds from fiber, he began wondering and experimenting in 1800, trying to determine whether there was some good use for those seeds.[29] The screw press he designed for manufacture in Philadelphia included mechanical parts that helped press oil from cottonseeds as well as other parts for baling cotton. The press's dual purpose inflated its cost—a fact he tried to explain to neighbors. Universally, cottonseeds were considered a disposal problem.[30] Dunbar knew better, and he accumulated evidence for the seed's multiple uses. He knew that it was excellent for cooking because it was as pure as any oil he ever used. Indeed, he found it was good for everything from lighting lamps to lubricating farm equipment and household goods. But he continually asked, "Where shall we find a market for such oil?"[31]

Dunbar also experimented with using the crushed hulls as part of the feed he gave cattle, and that experiment was quite successful. Then he started using the hulls as fertilizer for his fields, and he noticed improvement in his gardens, orchards, and vegetable fields.[32] Historian Franklin Riley wrote that Dunbar's was "the first suggestion of that product which has now become a great article of commerce, or indeed of utilizing cotton seed at all. At that period it was not dreamed of as a fertilizer, nor fed, in any shape, to stock. It was usually burnt or hauled to a strong enclosure, at a remote part of the farm to decompose."[33]

It was not until the 1870s that cottonseed oil finally became an important industry, with factories in Jackson and Meridian, Mississippi, devoted to turning "cottonseed . . . into meal and hulls for feeding animals and into oil for a number of purposes, including cooking."[34] But articles had appeared as early as 1818 damning the "useless and wanton waste of wealth" of throwing away cottonseeds. Some opponents claimed that too many seeds were needed to produce a small amount of oil. As one magazine pointed out, however, America produced 125 million pounds of ginned cotton in 1816. Since gins used only about one-fourth of the mass for baling and shipping, 375 million pounds of cottonseeds were wasted—enough to produce 3.75 million gallons of oil. At twelve cents a gallon, the oil would have been worth $468,750. The article concluded, "There is no other wealth than human labor, and its products are too painfully obtained to justify or excuse their willful loss."[35] In 1818, experiments were under way in New Orleans to sell the oil for use in lamps. In 1823, Professor Frederick Olmsted of the University of North Carolina noted that cottonseed oil had a brisk market in lamp oil. In 1857, refined cottonseed oil entered the New Orleans marketplace for both illuminating and lubricating purposes. At approximately the same time, several cottonseed oil mills were operating in New Orleans, Memphis, St. Louis, and even Providence, Rhode Island.[36] In 1904, an article about the cotton oil industry stated that "cotton seeds yield a considerable portion of valuable oil."[37]

Like many experimenters in myriad fields, William Dunbar was ahead of his time. His failure to generate interest in his cast iron screw press and cottonseed oil in no way diminishes the Dunbar legacy forged during almost forty years in America. During his lifetime, he was recognized for the foresight he showed in so many fields. In 1808, he received a most welcome letter informing him of his election on March 8 as an honorary member of the Philadelphia Society for Promoting Agriculture. The letter stated, "Your assistance in forwarding the objects of its institution will be acceptable to the Society, and beneficial to the interests of agriculture, so essential to the welfare and prosperity of our country."[38]

Portrait of William Dunbar

Portrait of William's wife,
Dinah Dunbar

All illustrations courtesy of the Mississippi Department of Archives and History, Jackson.

Pencil drawing of the Forest, the Dunbars' home near Natchez, Mississippi

The Forest church on Dunbar's plantation, across the street from the Forest

Thunderton House, the Dunbar family home, Elgin, Scotland

Manuel de Gayoso, Spanish governor of West Florida and close friend of Dunbar

Winthrop Sargent (1798–1801)

William C. C. Claiborne (1801–5)

The four governors who served Mississippi Territory

Robert Williams (1805–9)

David Holmes (1809–17)

Anthony Hutchins, Democratic-Republican adversary of Dunbar and Governor Gayoso

Bernardo de Gálvez, Spanish governor of West Florida

The colony of
Georgia running
from the Atlantic
Ocean on the
east to its western
boundary, the
Mississippi River

Jefferson College, Washington, Mississippi

Benjamin L. C. Wailes, author of *A Report on the Agriculture and Geology of Mississippi* (1854)

An early map of Mississippi showing growth from Natchez outward and noting lands occupied by Choctaw and Chicksaw tribes

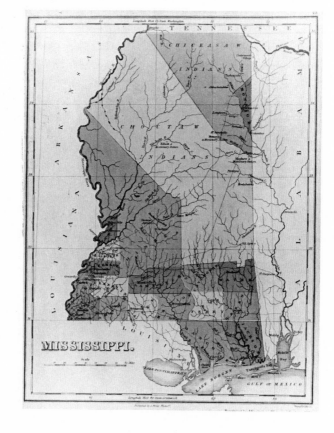

Extract from the 𝕸𝖊𝖘𝖘𝖆𝖌𝖊 from the *President* of the UNITED STATES, read in Congress, February 19, 1806.

"HAVING been disappointed, after considerable preparation, in the purpose of sending an exploring party up that river, in the summer of one thousand eight hundred and four, it was thought best to employ the autumn of that year in procuring a knowledge of an interesting branch of the [Red] river called the Washita. This was undertaken under the direction of Mr. Dunbar, of Natchez, a citizen of distinguished science, who had aided, and continues to aid us, with his disinterested and valuable services in the prosecution of these enterprises. He ascended the river to the remarkable hot springs near it, in latitude 34° 31' 4".16, longitude 92° 50' 45" west from Greenwich, taking its courses and distances, and correcting them by frequent celestial observations. Extracts from his observations, and copies of his map of the river, from its mouth to the hot springs, make part of the present communications. The examination of the Red river itself, is but now commencing.

TH: JEFFERSON.

February 19, 1806.

President Jefferson's comments to Congress when presenting Dunbar's report on the Ouachita–hot springs expedition

12

An Invitation to Serve

The years 1803 and 1804 were exciting ones for the United States. In 1803, an area that almost doubled the size of the country was transferred, without a war or dire threats of one, from Spain to France and, then, to the United States. How this happened, and why, is an interesting and complicated chapter in the history of the old Southwest—a region whose evolution involved many countries and Indian tribes and was as unpredictable as the mighty river all tried to control and use to their advantage—but only ancillary as a chapter in the William Dunbar story. The United States was offered a golden opportunity in 1803: the opportunity to purchase Louisiana from France for three cents an acre and become the beneficiary of the greatest real estate bargain in U.S. history. In the Napoleonic wars, France had defeated Spain and taken Louisiana. Because Spain had recently withdrawn the privilege of free deposits in New Orleans, Jefferson, anxious to champion the needs of frontier supporters, sought to purchase the port and its environs from France. France was committed to a European conflict on many fronts, and it was nearly impossible for Napoleon to take control of the entire Louisiana region and administer and protect it with soldiers badly needed elsewhere. Robert Livingston, the American minister in Paris, had been talking with the French minister of finance, Talleyrand, and other officials about President Jefferson's concern for fair and proper import and export regulations governing American shippers using the port of New Orleans. On April 11, 1803, surprisingly, Talleyrand asked Livingston if the United States would be interested in purchasing all of Louisiana. A flabbergasted Livingston begged President Jefferson to take the offer seriously and to allow him and others to negotiate for a purchase, despite that Jefferson and his strict constructionist followers believed that doing so would be unconstitutional. The Constitution gave the president certain powers;

purchasing land to be added to the nation was not one of them. Yet, constitutional or not, a good deal is a good deal, and on April 30, the United States purchased 828,000 square miles of territory for $15 million.

Americans believed the deal was a good one but honestly did not know what the nation was getting for its $15 million other than the much-desired port of New Orleans. Jefferson had believed since his youth that there must be an all-water route from the Atlantic to the Pacific Ocean, and as a student of geology and cartography he believed that the Mississippi and Missouri rivers held the key to that possibility. To test his belief, he persuaded Congress to appropriate up to $12,000 and allow him to commission Meriwether Lewis and William Clark in November 1803 to lead an expedition to Oregon via the Missouri River and its headwaters. Jefferson wrote to Lewis on November 16, 1803, "The object of your mission is single, the direct water communication from sea to sea formed by the bed of the Missouri."[1]

Maybe it was because of his emerging friendship with Dunbar—and his new friend's growing number of important and respected scientific publications in the *Transactions of the American Philosophical Society*—that Jefferson became keenly interested in exploring "Dunbar's region" at the same time Lewis and Clark were heading for the headwaters of the Missouri River. As an amateur cartographer, Jefferson realized the importance of New Orleans at the mouth of the Mississippi River, and he had at least a passing acquaintance with southwestern rivers that emptied into the Mississippi or flowed westward. Perhaps the Red River flowed to the Pacific Ocean. It was worth exploring. Jefferson knew that rivers were plentiful in the region and that rivers attracted settlers and led to the growth of the nation. As one who favored land for yeoman farmers over industry for cities, he developed an expansionist mentality. Even more, Jefferson's scientific bent fostered a desire to know about minerals, flora, and fauna and their locations in the region recently purchased for a nation not yet knowledgeable about the treasures contained in the country west of the Mississippi River.

During 1803 and early 1804, Jefferson and Dunbar corresponded much about southern Louisiana lands and what they might contain. Since Dunbar had lived in the region for thirty years, Jefferson depended upon him over others for such information.[2] Dunbar, even before Louisiana was purchased in April 1803, wondered about the "future fate of our neighbouring province of Louisiana" and expressed concern about a possible cession of Louisiana from Spain to France. Such a change, he believed, would make it "impossible to predict what embarrassments may be placed upon the navigation & commerce of this river."[3]

Dunbar's concerns were practical ones, such as how transfer of power might affect his imports and exports through New Orleans. Jefferson's concerns were more general, having to do with the correct boundary between Louisiana and Spanish Texas after the purchase.[4] Jefferson was curious about what the land was like and what minerals lower Louisiana contained, and he wondered about the disposition of current inhabitants regarding the transfer of their lands from Spain to France to the United States in one year's time.[5] They could hardly be happy about these international land transfers that, clearly, affected their lives more than others'. Dunbar was a good person for Jefferson to lean on during 1803 and 1804 because, as a resident in a territorial district transferred from Spain to the United States a few years earlier, he knew how transfer of power and the inevitable new rules and regulations affected land titles and individual and family allegiances.

As Dunbar and Jefferson corresponded, it became obvious that certain waterways interested them more than others. Jefferson sent Lewis and Clark forth to examine the Missouri, Yellowstone, and other northwestern rivers and, at the same time, discussed exploration of the Red, Arkansas, and Ouachita (or Washita) rivers with Dunbar.[6] Jefferson's interest in the Red and Arkansas rivers is understandable, for both were known to be important Southwest waterways, but the Ouachita River was different. It was not a major waterway, except that it traversed southwestern Arkansas to the now-famous hot springs, a scientific wonder that would whet the interest of men like Jefferson and Dunbar. If an expedition were sent up the Arkansas River to its headwaters and then west overland to the headwaters of the Red River, returning home down the Red to the Mississippi River, or if it went in the opposite direction, how could it include the Ouachita River? True, the Ouachita emptied into the Arkansas River, but if one were going up or down the Arkansas River, one would not be traveling near the Ouachita River. The Ouachita appeared often in Jefferson's and Dunbar's letters, but it is not clear whether they thought the Ouachita could actually be included in an expedition or were considering a separate, smaller expedition.

In 1803, the Ouachita District was home to about five hundred people, sixty of whom were slaves. Settlers lived mainly on the west bank of the river and were scattered over approximately fifty miles. The population was fairly heterogeneous; early arrivals were Canadian hunters, and later, Spanish settlers arrived from Mexico and Irish and Americans from Natchez. It was from the latter group that Dunbar learned about the Ouachita River and the hot springs. The settlers cultivated a bit of cotton and corn, but they were mainly occupied raising cattle, hogs, and horses. The Canadians attempted to farm, but as hunters they were nomadic and "unfit for steady work."

They did much gambling and drinking, and they talked a great deal about things they could not explain in and around those hot springs.[7]

As the president asked questions, Dunbar shared comments on matters he knew about solely through living in the old Southwest, in particular matters currently being discussed in the area. He told Jefferson that both the "substantial settlers" and the Indians living on Louisiana Purchase lands were fearful and unhappy because of the double land transfer in one year.[8] That news did not take the president by surprise. Dunbar also noted that Louisiana was filled with traders, smugglers, squatters, Indian hunters, and a goodly number of scamps. He told President Jefferson that Governor Salcedo had already heard about the Lewis and Clark expedition into northern Louisiana lands, and Salcedo later received a letter from the Marquis de Casa Calvo in New Orleans informing him of a possible Red River expedition as well. Both Casa Calvo and Salcedo, along with most Spaniards in the old Southwest, felt that Napoleon had betrayed them by acquiring Louisiana and then selling it for a pittance to the feisty, aggressive Americans. The transfer to the United States was negotiated so quickly that Spain still had administrators in Louisiana, along with as many as ten thousand soldiers. Casa Calvo told Salcedo that so far as he was concerned they should preserve "the vast dominions of His Majesty" and that Salcedo should immediately arrest any and all Americans who tried to ascend or descend the Red River. The boundary between Louisiana and Texas had not yet been run by surveyors representing both sides, and until that was completed, Spanish soldiers should protect what Spanish administrators thought was theirs. Dunbar believed this information, since it was passed along to him by a close friend and trusted Spanish official with whom he labored running the thirty-first parallel boundary line—Major Stephen Minor.[9] Dunbar relayed the message to the president as probable fact.

On January 24, 1804, Lewis and Clark arrived in Natchez on their way up the Mississippi River, heading for St. Louis. They stayed six days and left behind impressed Natchez citizens, including William Dunbar. Dunbar noted that the gentlemen appeared to be well qualified for the enterprise. He commented on their good health and spirits and noted that they seemed to have thought through every difficulty they might encounter along the way. They were well prepared and highly motivated, and Dunbar wished them well on the long journey before them. Of course, he would have liked to join them on the great adventure as a scientific observer, but he knew that his age and recurring health problems made that dream impossible. He admired Jefferson's choice of young, talented military officers for expedition leadership roles.[10] Little did he know, as Lewis and Clark departed on January 30, that in less than six weeks he would be asked to lead a second major foray into Louisiana Purchase lands.

Jefferson and Dunbar continued their correspondence about a possible second expedition and decided that it should go up the Red River to its source, overland to the source of the Arkansas River, down that major waterway to the Mississippi River, and back to Natchez. On March 13, 1804, Jefferson wrote to Dunbar that he had asked Congress for $12,000 to fund two expeditions—one that would follow the Panis (Platte) River to its source, the other, the Red and Arkansas rivers to their sources. The leaders of both expeditions would be required to keep journals of minerals, flora, and fauna and to take astronomical observations and make correct notations of latitude and longitude. "These several surveys," Jefferson wrote, "will enable us to prepare a map of La., which in its contour and main waters will be perfectly correct & will give us a skeleton to be filled up with details hereafter." Then Jefferson dropped the bombshell. He wrote that since Dunbar lived "so near the point of departure" of the Red River expedition, "I have thought that if Congress should authorize the enterprise to propose to you the unprofitable trouble of directing it." For the party, Jefferson recommended ten to twelve soldiers, an officer, volunteers, and one or two aides qualified to assist Dunbar in all scientific activities.[11] Jefferson would want one of the assisting scientists to know much about botany, natural history, and mineralogy—all of which were scientific strengths possessed by Dunbar.

Dunbar could not believe what he was reading. He was fifty-four years old and, if one believed him, had experienced just about every malady known to man. He wrote to Jefferson so often about his ailments that the president correctly assumed that his friend was a bit of a hypochondriac. Even so, Dunbar was not physically strong, having spent much of his free time in a laboratory, but Jefferson did not give him time to think about the offer. In a second letter written the same day, Jefferson told Dunbar he was free to choose the two scientific associates but suggested that he consider a Mr. Walker in Natchez and a Mr. Gillespie in North Carolina, both of whom seemed to possess solid qualifications. They would be paid $1,000 a year, plus subsistence. Jefferson was concerned about Spanish reluctance to allow Americans to ascend or descend the Red River before a firm Texas-Louisiana border had been run and accepted by both sides. The president suggested in passing that Dunbar was the perfect leader for this expedition because for decades he had lived in the lower Mississippi region among the Spanish and had earned the admiration and friendship of Spanish. In addition, Dunbar still had important Spanish friends such as Stephen Minor, with whom he often communicated. If anyone could secure Spanish permission to journey up the Red River, passing Natchitoches, Louisiana, on the way to the source of that river, Dunbar could. Jefferson also asked Dunbar if he would recommend to Spanish officials that he, William Dunbar, be the American, Spanish, or joint lead commissioner to delineate the Louisiana-Texas border while he was in the neighborhood with an expedition party—a recommendation Dunbar never did pass along.[12]

Before Dunbar could respond to Jefferson's assumptions, suggestions, and flattery, he received an April 15 letter from the president informing him that Congress had accepted his request for two more expeditions but had appropriated only $3,000 for both efforts. That was hardly enough money for one expedition, so Jefferson decided to place the Panis River expedition on hold and to move forward with the Red-Arkansas rivers expedition, with Dunbar as its leader. He apologized for not allowing Dunbar time to think about the invitation, blaming the need to move quickly for his impertinence in assuming that Dunbar would accept the assignment. He then played to Dunbar's ego by adding, "Presuming on your attachment to science, & attainments in it, and the dispositions to aid it necessarily flowing from these, I have made out the instructions now inclosed." One part of the letter did please Dunbar. He had been unhappy with Jefferson's original suggestion that Dunbar pick the scientists to help him maintain journals and undertake scientific inquiries, because he lived so far away from the centers of scientific inquiry that he knew only local scientists—who were few and lacking in training or talent. He knew a little about Mr. Walker of Natchez (one of the two Jefferson had suggested earlier), and Dunbar considered him a lightweight. If Mr. Gillespie (the other one recommended) was as pedestrian a scientist, the expedition would be in trouble. Jefferson cheered Dunbar somewhat by informing him that he had appointed Dr. George Hunter of Philadelphia to serve as both a scientist and Dunbar's assistant on the expedition.[13] Thereafter, the venture would be known as the Dunbar-Hunter expedition.

George Hunter was a fellow Scot born in Edinburgh in 1755. His family came to America in 1774; during the Revolution, he served in an army hospital, was captured, and served time on a British prison ship off the coast of New York. After the war, Hunter moved from business to business, seeking his niche in this new country. He was part owner of a distillery and then a coach maker with his brother and stepfather until 1792. At that time, he entered the drug business and "built a reputation as a chemist," as Jefferson wrote to Dunbar. Later in life, Hunter became an original member of the prestigious Society of the Cincinnati. Though Jefferson testified to his talents, Hunter was also known to be greedy, slow moving, and opportunistic.

He was a practitioner of the "what's in it for me" philosophy. Jefferson saw Hunter, who was forty-nine, as a younger man who would serve as Dunbar's assistant. He made it clear to Dunbar on many occasions that "the ultimate direction of the expedition is left to yourself."[14]

In his April 13 letter to Dunbar, Jefferson laid out his instructions for the Red-Arkansas rivers expedition. The party would embark at Natchez and travel to the headwaters of the Red River and "thence to the highlands dividing the waters of this stream from those of the Bravo [Rio Grande] and the Pacific." After carefully studying that highland, the party was to descend the Arkansas River to the Mississippi, then continue home to Natchez. Along the way, they were to note everything possible—Indian tribes, Spanish soldiers, land formations, all of the rivers entering the Red and Arkansas rivers, flora and fauna, and chemicals, all the while taking countless astronomical observations. Dunbar should offer the Indians presents and tell them that the Spanish were leaving the region and that Indian people would find the Americans kind and fast friends—and much more generous as traders. Jefferson worried about unhappy Spanish officials who might be encountered along the way, and he told Dunbar to avoid confrontation, for "the lives of the members of the expedition are too valuable to be exposed to probable destruction." What Jefferson wanted most from this expedition was scientific information that would be placed on new maps of lower Louisiana lands so that the government and future expeditions and settlers could start out with accurate knowledge of the region.[15]

Since Hunter was still in the East, Dunbar was the one with whom Secretary of War Henry Dearborn negotiated in making preparations for the trip. He was not one of Dunbar's favorite people; in fact, Dunbar often cursed his skinflint demands. The secretary authorized the expenditure of $1,460 for two-thirds of a year's pay for the two scientists to be hired; $500 for necessary instruments; $300 for outfits; $600 for Indian presents; and $140 in cash for Dunbar to use for unforeseen purchases. Dearborn was particularly concerned about the quality of Indian trinkets, for Jefferson wanted to avoid confrontation with tribes as much as possible. Since Hunter lived in the East, where Indian gifts would be purchased, he was authorized to purchase $500 worth of trinkets and was instructed to store them in small kegs and boxes that might cost $50 and to ship all to Pittsburgh, where the instruments and all other expedition goods were being stored for the trip down the Ohio and Mississippi rivers to Natchez.[16]

Despite that Jefferson had told Dunbar that Congress had authorized only $3,000 for this important venture, Dunbar was furious when he learned from Dearborn the actual amounts allocated in each of the categories. Dunbar wrote heatedly on May 13 that $500 for important scientific instruments was ridiculously inadequate, as was the pay for gifted scientists. He sarcastically suggested that he might not get quality work out of scientists who, at that pay, would be "making fortunes," and whose object might be an "all devouring passion of gain." In selecting soldiers, Dunbar recommended that Dearborn pay extra for the ten or twelve hired so "that they will be more obedient & think themselves more responsible" than those not selected and volunteers who simply signed on for adventure. And Dunbar literally begged for a "young meritorious commissioned officer" who possessed the passion for discovery of a William Clark or Meriwether Lewis.[17] To Dunbar's credit, he seldom carried the fight for more dollars to Jefferson, but he did so on May 13. Dunbar closed a passionate letter by stating that important endeavors requiring courage, patriotism, and skill "cannot be accomplished without great sacrifices of precious time and when a great Empire talks of compensation, this ought to be adequate to the importance of the service and honorable both to Gov. & to the selected individuals."[18]

It was not inadequate funding that doomed this expedition, however; more than anything else, it was enraged Indians and Spaniards who refused to allow passage until a clearly defined western boundary for Louisiana had been accepted by both nations. Dunbar informed Jefferson that Stephen Minor had informed him that the only way Dunbar could get the Marquis de Casa Calvo to budge was to flatter him. He was "proud & highspirited," but Dunbar doubted that flattery would work. It did not. Spanish officials and settlers simply did not believe that the western part of West Florida was included in the Louisiana Purchase lands. Until proven wrong, Spanish officials were not going to allow an expedition to ascend the Red River in the disputed territory. Dunbar then suggested an interesting change of plans. He wrote the president, "We might go up the Arkansas river & come down the red river without any great probability of the Spaniards obtaining a knowledge of the expedition." He added sadly, however, that if they reversed the direction of the expedition, they might make little if any progress. Doing so would require the party, early in its journey, to meet Indian tribesmen, especially the powerful Osages, who appeared unhappy with all whites—Spanish, French, and American—who had disrupted life, especially trade, by ceding Indian land in America to each other without even informing the affected Indian nations.[19] It seemed to Dunbar that beginning an expedition by ascending the Red or Arkansas was equally dangerous, given Indian unrest and an uncertain western Louisiana boundary. This dual problem would, in the end, doom this expedition until later in the decade and rob Dunbar of his day in the sun.

An additional frustration for Dunbar was the lackadaisical attitude of George Hunter. April, May, June, and July were history before Hunter carried out his few duties of gathering equipment and trinkets and floating from Pittsburgh to Natchez—in a boat inappropriate for the expedition. First, Hunter spent more than a month trying to convince Secretary Dearborn to allow his son to become a member of the expedition. A frustrated secretary told Hunter he could take his son along but that Dunbar would be the one to determine if the young man would be compensated for any work he did. No more money was appropriated, which left the young man unpaid. Dearborn wrote Hunter on May 21 pleading with him "not to delay your departure . . . longer than is absolutely necessary."[20] But Hunter would not be rushed. He had sent the presents, medicine, chests, tools, and mathematical instruments to Pittsburgh, and on May 27, he and his son finally rode out of Philadelphia, crossed Pennsylvania in eight days (visiting along the way), and arrived in Pittsburgh on June 4. Not having inquired ahead, Hunter could not find a boat to take them and their goods to Natchez, so without authority he directed the building of a new boat for the journey. The boat that emerged was made for floating down a river needing only five to ten inches of water to pass; it was not made for an expedition with men, equipment, and specimens needing twelve or more inches of water to pass safely up and down western rivers not yet explored. Apparently Hunter never considered the need for the boat to do double duty. The construction cost was $159.20 without hands to man the boat, so he hired three and billed the boat's construction cost and pay for the hands to Dunbar.[21]

While Hunter was tarrying in Pennsylvania, Dunbar asked traders and other observers about what he might find in the Red River area. He asked about water quality and depth, vegetation, minerals, navigable creeks, soil, tribes, and much more.[22] He also instructed the American commander Lieutenant Colonel Thomas Freeman, who was selecting men for the expedition, about the types of soldiers he wanted. "Those who are chosen," he wrote, "ought to be all men of general good health & if possible robust temperaments." The officers chosen "should possess a persevering disposition, an equanimity of temper & agreeable manners."[23] And, in letters to Secretary Dearborn, Dunbar sought money for an Indian interpreter-hunter, a botanist, and better equipment.[24] To ensure success, Dunbar would not accept a dime in salary, and he planned to spend some of his own money to hire helpers he believed necessary for success.

It was almost August before Hunter and his son arrived in Natchez. Dunbar inspected the vessel and expressed strong doubts about its suitability for the trip ahead to the Arkansas River. He told Hunter to continue to

New Orleans to meet with Freeman to determine whether he could swap this boat for a more suitable one—and, if not, to ask Freeman to rework the current boat by incorporating specifications Dunbar gave to Hunter. They removed all the goods from the boat, stored them in Dunbar's warehouse at St. Catherine's Creek below Natchez, and reloaded the boat with twenty-seven bales of Dunbar's cotton (there was no need to waste free cotton transportation to the port of New Orleans). Hunter departed on July 31, ran the boat day and night, and arrived in New Orleans on August 7—almost four months after Jefferson appointed Dunbar as the expedition's leader and urged him to embark as quickly as possible.[25]

Freeman searched for another boat, but there was not one to be found. A week was wasted searching and then caulking the bottom of the inadequate boat. Freeman did understand the urgency of getting the party off before bad weather set in, and he was "occupied from morning to night in superintending the work done to the boat," which was completely fitted out by August 25. That same day Hunter received a letter from Dunbar informing him that Dunbar had received notification from the president that the expedition's departure was postponed until the following spring.[26] In truth, the delay in Mississippi Territory had caused Congress to rethink the expedition. Congressional leaders decided that it was too large an undertaking for the $3,000 they had provided to the president, so Congress cancelled the major expedition for the time being, but it did grant the president permission to spend the $3,000 on a smaller, less ambitious expedition. In hindsight, the delay caused by Hunter's inaction was the main reason that the expedition was not launched earlier, and that inaction may well have saved the lives of Dunbar, Hunter, and the rest of the crew: angry Spanish soldiers and renegade Osage tribesmen were not to be trifled with on the Red and Arkansas rivers in late 1804.

Between June and early August, many letters were exchanged between Dunbar, Jefferson, Freeman, and Dearborn analyzing the possibilities for success if the party ascended the Red River and then descended the Arkansas to the Mississippi. Intelligence verified both the anger of Spanish officials and traders and America's inability to reason with Arkansas and Louisiana Indians who were well aware of the manner in which Americans were confiscating Choctaw land in Mississippi Territory through one treaty after another.[27] America's image among Indians seldom was as low as it was during the early nineteenth century. The more Jefferson and Dunbar learned about the hazards that awaited the expedition party, the more they questioned the wisdom of going in 1804. Still they continued planning to do so later.[28]

As it turned out, the Osage problem was really an internal squabble, and not a united tribe willing to fight hostile Americans; a deep schism had festered and grown over time within the tribe. Two years earlier, approximately four hundred warriors and their families, led by a disgruntled chief, deserted the main tribe and settled on the Arkansas River. That group, Jefferson noted, "will undoubtedly oppose the passage of our party and perhaps do worse." To attempt to heal the tribal breach, Pierre Chouteau of St. Louis had, at Jefferson's invitation, brought twelve Osage chiefs to visit with the president in Washington. When Jefferson mentioned to the head chief the possibility of an expedition up the Arkansas River, he was told that the Arkansas branch of the tribe would oppose passage through their lands. This news sealed the fate of the expedition for Jefferson, and he wrote Dunbar on July 17 about the Washington meeting and his unwillingness to endanger an expedition that surely would be opposed on the Arkansas River.[29]

Earlier, on June 9, Jefferson had received a letter from Dunbar praising the Ouachita River and hot springs as a destination for a smaller expedition. Dunbar noted that the river was supposed "to offer many curious objects" and might be more scientifically interesting than the Arkansas River into which the Ouachita flowed. The letter extolled the scientific wonders that the river and surrounding countryside might hold, from boiling springs and fountains to minerals not yet discovered.[30] The letter was filled with enthusiasm—unusual for a Dunbar letter—and suggested that Dunbar would go there some day, even if he went on his own. Jefferson, the scientist, became excited too, and on July 17, he combined Dunbar's enthusiasm for the Ouachita and the distressing news he heard from Osage chiefs and authorized Dunbar to use the soldiers, volunteers, presents, equipment, and boat to lead an expedition to the hot springs.[31] In so doing, he placed the longer, more treacherous Arkansas-Red rivers expedition on hold. Most friends in Natchez agreed with the change in plans, if only because they feared the worst on both the Arkansas and Red rivers. The Ouachita–hot springs trip would be both interesting and safer for their friend.

In New Orleans, working with Freeman in selecting soldiers and reworking the boat, Hunter learned from Dunbar that the president was postponing the major expedition in favor of the smaller Ouachita one. The news did not please Hunter, who was dreaming of being a key part of a major expedition that would guarantee his place in American history books. Later, however, he became excited about the scientific curiosities, including minerals, awaiting them in and around the hot springs.[32] Dunbar had hoped Jefferson might relieve him from expedition leadership duties and appoint Freeman or another younger military man in his place, thereby allowing him to be an expedition member, but only as a scientist. In this case, Dunbar's wishes did not prevail; Jefferson would not hear of another person's leading this exciting venture that might fulfill a scientist's dreams.

Once the change in destination was determined, Dunbar spent his time changing the preparations from a large expedition to a smaller one.[33] He had not yet hired a second scientist, so he ended that search; he and Hunter would do all of the scientific observations. Dunbar wrote Jefferson that he had contacted Colonel Freeman and told him to stop refitting Hunter's boat and "provide only a good strong flat bottomed broad & safe canoe fitted up in the plainest manner, & such as may be impelled rapidly against the stream by six oars & which I have requested . . . dispatched with all convenient speed manned by a discreet non com officer & privates with 3 months rations."[34] He put his New Orleans agent, Chew and Relf, to work gathering the supplies needed for the expedition. For a three-month expedition undertaken by up to twenty people, they took along one barrel of brown sugar, forty pounds of chocolate, six pounds of Hyson tea and one tin canister, fifty pounds of coffee, sixty pounds of lump sugar, one dozen bottles of Madeira wine, one pound of pepper, six bottles of mustard, three boxes of herrings, four nutmegs, one case of gin, one box of split peas, one barrel of rice, one barrel of brandy (seventeen gallons), four ounces of cloves, two bottles of cucumbers, twelve bottles of anchovies, one barrel of molasses (thirty gallons), and six empty barrels for delivery. The total cost of these goods was $186.[35]

The expedition left for the Ouachita River and the hot springs of Arkansas on October 16, 1804. Preparations had not gone smoothly, and the final days were hectic; from mid-August to mid-October crisis after crisis had to be faced and resolved. For example, Colonel Freeman was unable to find the kind of boat Dunbar wanted, so he returned to the original large boat and began making alterations to come as close as possible to meeting Dunbar's specifications. Freeman made places for twelve oars on the boat so that all the privates might row.[36] Dunbar wanted an officer, but the best Freeman could do was to provide a noncommissioned officer for the trip and an officer to escort the boat, men, and goods to the point of embarkation near Natchez. Dunbar grumbled but took solace in the fact that twelve privates were provided instead of the ten some had suggested.[37] He was also unhappy that some people in the lower Louisiana territory, opposed to any expedition into what had been Spanish territory a short time ago, had petitioned Congress to halt the expedition. Add to the list of concerns an initially disappointed George Hunter; extremely bad weather in early October, with constant rain and "contrary winds"; ill health that kept Dunbar in bed and prevented departure for five days; and Dunbar's constant grousing about the quality of the privates, of the instruments provided, and of the boat. None of this suggests an auspicious beginning for an exciting adventure.[38] Dunbar spent the last few preexpedition days catching up on correspondence, completing important business transactions, and making sure his estate was in order in case he did not return.[39] Both his irritation with bureaucratic impediments and the excitement in the tone of his journal entries suggest that as he and his expedition party embarked on the morning of October 16, he believed that this moment was among the happiest of a full and successful life. Dunbar was now rising above economic security and high society. He was going where few had been before, and he was going to record what was to be seen.

13

One Hundred Three Days

A s the Ouachita–hot springs expedition left St. Catherine's landing on the morning of October 16, 1804, in a boat totally unfit for the journey ahead, there were aboard seventeen men participating in the adventure of a lifetime: Dunbar, one of his slaves, George Hunter, Hunter's son George Jr., a sergeant, and twelve enlisted men garrisoned in New Orleans (a pilot-guide would be added at Fort Miro). Dunbar bade good-bye to family and home and, when he saw his beloved cliffs, nearly two hundred feet high, fade into the distance, he must have wondered whether he would ever again see home and family.[1] At this point in his life, William Dunbar was one of the leading citizens of Mississippi Territory, probably the entire old Southwest. He had done more than any other, on and off his four plantations, to earn a quiet, respected old age surrounded by Dinah and their children, books, his beloved laboratory, and a growing correspondence with scientific colleagues the country over seeking answers to questions that plagued them all. Yet here he was challenging the unknown and facing possible death on an expedition thrust upon him by fellow scientist Thomas Jefferson.

The expedition headed a short distance down the Mississippi to the mouth of the Red River on its way to the Ouachita River and the hot springs that had become legendary as tales of their wonders were passed from person to person who had seen and used them. The men traveled only seven miles that first day and spent the night on an island, but it was the getting away that was important. They would be gone 103 days, travel a total of one thousand miles during the late fall and winter, and endure hardships probably not anticipated—at least in their severity—during the planning stage. Many of the problems they encountered were caused by a boat that was ill suited for the waters of the Red, Black, and Ouachita rivers. The craft had six oarsmen on each side who could move it along smartly in water deep enough to accommodate it, but it needed a minimum of twenty-five inches of water to pass freely over shoals, sandbars, submerged logs, and rock formations. Dunbar and his companions should have had a boat that needed no more than twelve inches of water to pass by unobstructed.[2] Until they exchanged their boat for a flatboat at Fort Miro on day twenty-six, they were constantly unloading and reloading as the depth of the water demanded so that the boat could float or be inched forward by men pulling ropes on a bank or through the freezing water ahead. It took them twenty-two days to reach Fort Miro; they should have made that trip in half the time. (Fort Miro, often simply called the Ouachita post, would later become the thriving Louisiana city of Monroe.)

They left the island on October 17, passed Fort Adams, and reached the mouth of the Red River—fifteen miles from St. Catherine's landing—where they encamped and began recording their observations.[3] Dunbar and Hunter penned notes later to be entered into day-by-day journals. The journal the former kept was pure William Dunbar; his observations were limitless. He explained why the Red River was red and recorded the width of the river at its mouth (and all along the route), the speed of currents, the birds thereabouts, the variety of trees, the kinds of grasses found, latitude and longitude, the miscellaneous animals encountered, the extremes of temperature during the day, the fertility and components of soil, and—maybe most important—the streams that flowed into rivers and the rivers that became part of larger rivers. To read his journal is to accompany him on the journey. Dunbar was, indeed, gathering the information President Jefferson wanted for an accurate map of what would become the states of Louisiana and Arkansas. Even though the exhausted, cursing soldiers pulling the boat might disagree, the snail's pace at which the expedition often had to proceed was a plus because it gave Dunbar and Hunter time to go ashore, observe, and gather specimens—which of course made the boat heavier, thereby necessitating deeper water. The specimens ranged from bark to stones, from leaves to soil and plants. Seemingly nothing eluded Dunbar's eyes and journal. He ended each day's entry by recording how many miles they had traveled that day, and he was precise in doing so. On the third day they went 12 11/12 miles.[4]

Since the format of Dunbar's journal was consistent, a few excerpts from days four and five—typical days—will demonstrate the flavor and breadth of his comments. Dunbar wrote,

> Continued our rout up the river; having given the Soldiers this morning a few words of advice and encouragement; they improved

considerably in activity and cheerfulness. . . . [F]ound we went 3 perches per half minute, the current yet continues so moderate as to offer no impediment to our rowing along shore therefore not worth estimating: landed before 12 to observe and for dinner. Latitude 31 14' 59" 1. After dinner caught a runaway negro; proceeded on to the confluence of red and black river in latitude 31 15' 48" which by our reckoning appears to be 26 1/3 miles from the Mississippi, the Contrast of the two rivers is great, the red river being charged with red marly earth and the other a clear river gives it by comparison a dark appearance hence the name of black river—Each river is about 150 yards and when united about 200 yards wide. Sounded in the black river and found 20 feet black sand. The water of the black river is rather clearer than that of the Ohio and of a warm temperature, probably owing to the waters which flow into it from the valley of the Mississippi particularly from the Catahoola. Made 15 miles 102 perches.[5]

The next day Dunbar wrote,

Continued ascending the river; Thermometer 47 Temperature of the water 73 a spring issuing from the river bank 66. Forest trees on the bank chiefly red and black oak interspersed with ash, paccawn, hickory, some elms, pirsimon etc.; several kinds of grass and many humble plants in flower, so that even at this season our country affords employment for a Botanist. Great luxuriance of vegetation along the shore, grass very rank, and a thick curtain of shrubbery of a deep green; the soil black marl mixed with a moderate proportion of sand, resembling much the soil on the Mississippi banks, yet the forest trees are not leafy like to those on the margin of the great river, but resembling the growth on the red river. I omitted mentioning in its proper place, that the last single inundation of the red river appears to have deposited on the high bank a stratum of red marl about 1/3 inch thick now dry; some specimens were taken. Took a meridian altitude of the Sun, from which the Latitude deduced was 31 22' 46" 6—observed Canes growing on several parts of the right bank, a proof that the land is not deeply overflowed, perhaps from 1 to 3 feet: the banks have the appearance of stability, very little willow or other productions of a newly formed soil being seen on either side: the solid high bank being deeply shaded by vegetation from the humble creeping plant to the spreading oak.

Encamped at sunset. Sounded; 5 fathoms—black sand—Extremes of the Thermometer 47–80. Made this day 13 miles 40 perches.[6]

On the sixth day, the party happened upon a small island. While investigating, they noticed a settlement on the left bank of the Black River started by a man and his wife, who lived in a covered frame hut with rough poles and no walls. The couple tilled a couple of acres of corn that they used to make their yearly supply of bread, and they lived off the forest and river, which supplied venison, bear, turkey, other fowl, and fish. When asked why they lived that way, they answered that independence meant more to them than anything else in life. They took meat and hides to market, bought necessary articles, then returned to the forest. Dunbar wrote, "How happy the contrast, when we compare the fortune of the new settler in the U.S. with the misery of the half starving, oppressed and degraded peasant of Europe." The couple told them much about the land and animals thereabouts, and Dunbar duly recorded their comments in his journal.[7] Dunbar made similar notes several times on the journey as he met, communicated with, and befriended individuals who could illuminate life along those rivers.

As they traveled, Dunbar noted with enthusiasm every creek and river and took a fix at the spot to record accurate location. On October 23, he found the mouth of the Boeuf River, noted it, and met with a Frenchman who had settled there on a land grant made by Spanish officials. The man ran a ferry that allowed people and horses traveling north to the Ouachita River or south to the Mississippi River to cross safely. Dunbar noted that the settler lived on an Indian mound surrounded by several other mounds. All were equal in quality and size to those built by the Indians in Mississippi Territory, he noted. The party also reached the mouth of the Ouachita River that day; Dunbar estimated that they had traveled thirty miles from the mouth of the Red River to the mouth of the Black River and that it would be sixty-six more miles from that location to Fort Miro, north on the Ouachita River. Unfortunately, Dunbar also noted on day eight, the boat was requiring thirty inches of water for navigation—specimens and game killed weighed it down—and, because of a lack of rain, the water ahead was only twenty-two inches deep.[8] The easy part of the trip was over.

From day ten to day twenty-two—the day they arrived at the Ouachita post—the trip was almost impossibly torturous. The boat needed more water depth than the river provided, so soldiers pulled it from one sandbar to another, over shoals, log jams, and rocky bottoms. On the tenth day, Dunbar ominously noted that the "boat got hung up in shallow water," and from that point on the journal is filled with notations such as "commenced digging a canal which was required to be about 100 feet long, this business went on heavily & slowly."[9] One day the soldiers had "to use their exertions in getting the boat over a shoal . . . exerting themselves to my entire satisfaction." After dinner that same day they pushed on, only to find "a ledge of rocks across the entire bed of the river. . . . [W]e got over into deep water after grounding and rubbing two or three times."[10] Dunbar made frequent notations such as "channel was very narrow," "sandbars at every point extending so far into the bend," and "a shoal upon which there is 18 inches of water in the deepest place, we prepared, & unloading part of our Cargo, to cross it."[11] On the eighteenth day, Dunbar wrote about "immense sand bars in view at every point. . . . [W]e suffered much detention this day, being twice fast upon a sunken log under water, and our boat being so unwieldy & heavy, there was no getting her off by any exertion of poles which could be made on board, a rope was carried ashore from the stern & by that means she was hove backwards & cleared of the log."[12] It was now November, and the weather was getting colder.

On November 6, the twenty-second day of the expedition, the party arrived at the Ouachita post. They were well received by post commander Lieutenant Bowar, who offered hospitality to all the men and rooms in his home to Dunbar and Hunter.[13] The post numbered approximately five hundred persons of all ages who were served by three merchants who had settled there and supplied the needs of the settlers "at very exorbitant prices." The settlers had been enticed to that location by Baron de Bastrop, who had secured a large parcel of land for settlement from Spanish officials.[14] Dunbar reported seeing excellent land in the vicinity of the post watered by several creeks running into the Ouachita River. Great hunting in the area gained the attention of the men year-round, thereby allowing fields of corn to go unattended. Those who gave their attention to agriculture and used hunting to supplement that pursuit, rather than the other way around, lived quite comfortably in the region.

While at the post, however, Dunbar had other things on his mind; for the rest of the trip to the hot springs, he wanted to get rid of the deep-drawing boat they all hated. He spent November 7–12 searching for a boat suitable for the waters ahead—one that would draw not more than twelve inches of water.[15] In a letter to President Jefferson, Dunbar described what he was looking for,[16] but the best he could do was to rent a barge at $1.25 per day. The barge was 8 1/2 feet wide, which was adequate, but it was 50 feet long—too long for sharp turns in the Ouachita River. Still, the barge was the best vessel available, so Dunbar contracted for it on November 9, pulled it out of the river on November 10, recaulked it, added a change here and there, and packed belongings on it, while storing specimens at the post. The expedition left for the hot springs on November 12, the twenty-sixth day of the journey. The wisest thing Dunbar did at the post was to hire a guide, Samuel Glazier, to lead the way for the remainder of the journey, making it far more likely they would safely reach the hot springs.[17]

The barge was a great improvement over the deep-drawing boat. It drew right at twelve inches of water, and it could cover up to three miles an hour "when the men use a little exertion," Dunbar wrote.[18] They stopped often along the way, visited with settlers, and other than too much rain had little about which to complain.[19] The men hunted with great success. On November 15 they crossed the present-day Louisiana-Arkansas border.[20] Signs of former Indian occupancy were all around them, from carvings on trees and rocks to abandoned settlements, and they knew outlaw bands of Osages were roaming in the neighborhood, but on the entire trip the party did not once meet an Indian party.

A near-fatal accident occurred on November 15 near a settlement that is today Camden, Arkansas. Hunter was ramming a ball down a pistol he held between his knees when it accidentally discharged. Even though the ball passed through fingers and thumb on the right hand, luck was with him: it went through the bill of his cap less than an inch from his forehead. Dunbar cleaned and dressed the good doctor's wounds and noted that Hunter "felt great pain and debility but after some repose felt better in the evening." The flash rendered his eyesight cloudy for the next two weeks, and he was of little use to Dunbar in making astronomical observations and recording what he saw in his journal.[21]

Dunbar noted many things that he wanted to examine more carefully on the return trip. He found the Island of Malley, at the future border of Louisiana and Arkansas. It was an island well known to hunters but little known to explorers. Dunbar marked the latitude and promised to study the whole island carefully when they returned from the hot springs.[22] He found creeks and small rivers and marked them too, hoping to return to study all more carefully. Despite that his feet were always wet and cold and the weather was daily growing colder, forcing him often to take to his sickbed, well into the expedition Dunbar was still as excited about flora and fauna, waterways, soil, and all around him as he was when they left St. Catherine's landing a month earlier.[23] He noted that they were in fast-changing country, not only because of hills and rocks but also because of changing trees, bushes, grasses, and weather. As always, he commented on all he saw. On November 17, he noted hunters, deer, an alligator, and a particular bear looking at them from shore. "The bear," he wrote, "is now in his prime with regard to the quality of his fur and the quantity of fat or oil which he yields, he has been feeding luxuriously for some time upon the autumnal fruits of the forest. . . . It is, however, well known that the bear does not confine himself to vegetable food, the planters have ample experience of his carnivorous disposition."[24]

The party moved forward and stopped often to take numerous astronomical observations and to gather specimens. When Dunbar saw signs of iron ore, he marked the location so that Hunter could examine the region when his health returned. Stones caught his eye, particularly those in and on the banks of the river. He promised in his journal to select a few to take home on his return trip.[25] Again the expedition passed the homes of Indian tribes but did not see any tribesmen. Dunbar found a substance that looked like coal but was not. He caught and examined butterflies and identified more than fifteen species of trees.[26] Often Hunter (mended by month's end), a number of soldiers, and the pilot went off on mineral-hunting excursions, but other than iron they found nothing.

By November 27, the forty-third day, Dunbar was supplementing his observations about geese and trees with comments about the increased swiftness of the river. He noted that the "river has risen at least 30 inches, & flows fast." The party began "catching hold of the willows etc. & hauling up along shore, oars and poles being insufficient to stem the violence of the torrent."[27] Despite fighting currents, they kept up their scientific observations and land trips. On November 29, Hunter went with a small party and a local duck hunter to gather saline known to be in the area, and he returned with a jar of it.[28] The pilot made sure they were careful on the river, hugging the shore as they made their way toward the famous and treacherous chutes. Hills were getting higher, and Dunbar observed that the country and soil would be excellent for growing grapes for wine. They studied salt licks, different grades of iron, and quarries, all the while hearing the roar of water getting louder and louder.[29]

On the forty-ninth day, December 3, 1804, they reached the chutes. They found a high, breathtaking waterfall whose torrents of water cascaded through breaches in the rocks. Since the width of the boat was 8 1/2 feet, they looked for a breach at least 9 feet wide through which the boat could be hauled upward and over the chutes. Most of the crew searched for such a breach while two of them were sent by canoe to creep along the shore and to maneuver above the falls. Having accomplished that slow and difficult feat, the men tied a strong rope to a tree and let themselves back down by that rope, which was then tied to the bow of the boat. The idea was to send several men above the falls and engage them in what appeared to be a nigh-on impossible task—hauling the boat up through a wide enough breach. All attempts failed. They needed to remove, from the mouth of a fairly wide breach, several pointed rocks that did not allow for proper positioning of the boat. The problem taxed the strength of all the men above and below and challenged Dunbar's ingenuity as well. At last, with many rocks removed, they tried to force the barge into a breach that led to a strait just wide enough to enter. The men pulled but the boat became wedged between rocks, as they tried again and again without success to pull the barge up and over the falls. All the while, daytime was giving way to dusk and the air and water were cooling, making misery for men already soaking wet and cold. Dunbar wrote in his journal, "Now sorry we tried." He ordered the men "to lighten the barge, take stuff ashore on rope, others to pull bow up." After lightening the vessel, they discovered that one of the three rope strands had broken; the whole exercise was in danger of failing, and the party would surely lose its boat and some of its belongings—including precious specimens—if the rope broke. A new rope was tied to the bow of the boat and the tree above the falls to supplement the damaged one. Dunbar continued, "We now sent the other men on shore as had been intended, who gaining a firm footing and exerting themselves with great vigor soon extricated us and drew us safely ashore, greatly rejoicing to find ourselves without accident above the chutes."[30]

The next day they faced water cascading down rocks in the Ouachita River heading toward the chutes, and they began again pulling the barge toward the hot springs. Water flowing fast down a waterway that seemed to offer only sharp rocks over which to pull the boat left Dunbar to write that what they were attempting that day was "much more difficult & dangerous than chutes."[31] The soldiers could not keep the boat in the middle of the river, where the water was deep enough to paddle, because that water was too swift. So they again hugged the shore and with ropes pulled the barge up the river. They encamped that night at the top of the major rapids they had conquered, but a second rapids awaited them on the morrow—thankfully, a shorter and less violent one.[32]

On December 6, 1804, on the fifty-second day of their journey, Dunbar could write in his journal that they were nearing Caulker's Creek, "where we terminate our navigation & encamp." At Ellis Camp, just below Caulker's Creek, he noted, "Here ends our voyage on river upwards for present."[33] The men rejoiced, thinking their exertions over the past six weeks would now be repaid with some time to relax and enjoy the beauty of the hot springs area. Those hopes were dashed, however, when the pilot told them that they were still nine miles from the springs—six miles to the west and three to the north—and they would have to carry most of their baggage, including all instruments, essentials, blankets, and clothing, overland to a base camp yet to be established at the hot springs. The task was a laborious one, requiring the soldiers to return to the boat for a second and even a third load.[34] The weather was cold, dipping to ten degrees Fahrenheit on December 8. The pilot led the soldiers with baggage and some provisions to the hot springs, hoping to find a cabin or two there to house most if not all in the party. The sergeant and one soldier were left behind at Ellis Camp to guard and protect provisions and specimens not taken to the springs; the rest of the party would be at the hot springs December 7–28 (days fifty-three to seventy-four). At the site, they did find a badly maintained hunter's cabin and abandoned huts. The huts were open; the cabin had cracks in the walls so wide one could easily look in or out.[35] They established camp and repaired the walls as best they could, though the cracks were still wide enough to look through. Dunbar sent most of the men back to Ellis Camp the next morning to bring more provisions and all of the scientific instruments.

It did not take Dunbar long to realize that their original expedition planned for the Red and Arkansas rivers would have been a disaster. In their planning, Dunbar and Jefferson thought only about angry Spaniards and Osages obstructing progress, not about overland walking distances. Now, as he observed the difficulties his men were experiencing moving goods (and not even having to carry a boat) nine miles from the Ouachita River to the hot springs, Dunbar realized the magnitude of the problem they would have encountered between the Red and Arkansas rivers, a much greater distance apart over even more rugged terrain. He wrote notes to himself on the topic to share with President Jefferson upon his return. He figured that if fifteen soldiers had been employed on their proposed journey, and if each soldier carried fifty pounds at a time for a distance of fifty miles from the headwaters of one river to the headwaters of another, and if planners added a factor for bad weather, the portage alone would have taken fifty days. "If the expedition is to be carried on by soldiers," he wrote, "who cannot travel without their rations, tents, baggage, above all their whiskey," they would spend as much time moving goods as in investigating rivers, and the party would be dangerously vulnerable in doing so.[36] This realization was one of the important results of the Ouachita–hot springs expedition. Because of Dunbar's portage experience in Arkansas, all future expeditions took river-to-land needs into consideration.

During the weeks spent at the springs, Hunter led many small parties on overnight excursions seeking the locations of salt licks and minerals. While the men were "complaining of length of walk & loads carried," Dunbar and Hunter separately explored the region. Dunbar spent much of his time studying trees, determining latitude, and recording the abundance of swans, turkeys, and deer. He noted often the beauty of the area: mountains clothed with trees and valleys with land that "lies very handsomely for cultivation."[37] From the moment of arrival, Dunbar knew that most of the examinations of soil, grasses and other foliage, minerals (if any of note), and rocks would have to be done in his laboratory at the Forest from samples he gathered now and brought down the river after their time at the hot springs was over. The weather was terrible: raining, sleeting, and even snowing much of the time. Temperatures did rise to the high thirties but went as low as nine degrees as well. Dunbar had no good place to write because he was housed in an uninsulated cabin without a fireplace and with constant drafts coming through walls and floor. It might have been adequate for hunters or trappers in the summertime and early fall, but not for explorers in December. In short, Dunbar became a gatherer, while shooting fixes, noting locations, and investigating the hot springs. While the men took specimens back to Ellis Camp and even busied themselves building a log chimney at the end of the cabin,[38] Hunter and the guide, Sam Glazier, and sometimes Dunbar, made excursions into the hinterland seeking mineral specimens, which they shared with each other and then packed for the return trip to Mississippi Territory.

On December 10, Dunbar ascended the hill to the hot springs. He noted that the hill was conical and that, at the top of the hill, the springs were twenty-five feet in diameter. "The rock which delivers hot water is composed of hard siliceous stones penetrated & cemented together by lime," he noted, "encrustations of iron ore also found probably deposited by water." As he ascended the hill, Dunbar noticed patches of rich black earth that Hunter believed was formed by decomposed limestone. About two hundred feet up the hill, he found a hot spring whose temperature was 140 degrees, and as he continued ascending he noted that the soil became quite rocky. He wrote about trees and vines on the hill, and he studied the soil carefully, selecting a sample here and another there.[39] The hot springs fascinated him; what he found made the exhausting trip worthwhile.

Day after day Dunbar returned to the springs. He studied the four major springs and took notes of their daily temperatures. On December 12, he wrote, "No. one 150, No. two 145, No. three 136, No. four 132."[40] When not studying the hot waters in the springs and the foliage and land thereabouts, Dunbar was working on his journals, recording observations, and asking himself questions, the answers to which he hoped to find through his laboratory back home. Now and again, when his infirmities did not restrict him, Dunbar did make longer trips around the region. On December 12 and 13, he "made excursion of neighbouring western mountains, visited many hills." He noted that the rugged mountains separated the Ouachita from the Arkansas River. He commented, probably with relief, that the mountains kept the Osages from visiting the Ouachita region. If they did visit, white people could not explore in and around the hot springs, Dunbar suggested. As he roamed, he made discoveries and observations. He wrote that approximately fifty miles to the southwest was a level ridge that he believed was the high plains of the Red River. "What surprised us most," Dunbar wrote, "is growing on ridge a species of cabbage, plants grew with expanding leaves on ground, deep green with shade of purple, taste like raddish, tap roots taste like horse raddish but milder, quantity brought to camp & dressed, palatable & mild; Highly improbable any cabbage seed ever spread on this ledge, must therefore consider this cabbage as indigenous to here."[41] He also found other plants, gathered some, and wrote a bit about each.

Despite constant overcast, sleet, and cold, the groups continued to undertake successful excursions to observe and study various aspects of the region. Yet what fascinated Hunter and Dunbar the most were the hot springs; they tested, cooled, drank, and bottled the water for further study.[42] What they wanted most, however, was to determine accurately how and why the water was heated—but they never could. That frustrated Dunbar, but it did not discourage him. He had spent his scientific life unraveling mysteries. He was a product of eighteenth-century Scotland and its intellectual renaissance, and as he sought natural laws he respected the deity that had hidden them from mortals. On Christmas Eve, less than a week before leaving the springs, he wrote, "The question of what causes the perpetual fire which keeps up without change the high temperature of the springs. Nothing around us but an immense bed of blue or black scystous; bottom or bed of creek is composed of nothing else; I have taken pieces of the stone, which was soft by decomposition, possessing a very strong aluminous taste; This scystous around here & in hills. Known to chemists that aluminous being moistened in due degree by water, generates in progress of decomposition a very great degree of heat. I leave it to scientific men to decide whether this cause may be sufficient to account for heat."[43]

During the three weeks at the hot springs, there was little complaining about the rain and cold and the inadequacy of open huts and a drafty cabin. The men did complete the log fireplace in the cabin, and Dunbar once noted, "The bad state of our mansion calling for further repairs in the present severe weather, we employed some of our people in shutting up the cracks." Nevertheless, none of the repairs were really adequate to keep out wind and cold. Party members went about individual tasks knowing that their days at the springs were limited and, more important, that they were achieving all of the expedition's goals. They observed and hunted; they gathered specimens and updated journals; they got sick and they recovered. Then it was Christmas. Not being particularly religious, Dunbar continued taking astronomical observations. He did, however, note that it was Christmas Day and that "we were obliged to indulge the men with a holy day for which purpose they had hoarded up their ration whiskey to be expended on this day; a great deal of frollick was the consequence; but perfectly innocent." There were dancing, singing, and volleys from rifles wishing all a merry Christmas from the hot springs. For a day, illnesses and hard work were forgotten.[44]

For the next three days, Dunbar continued gathering and arranging specimens. He announced that some of the soldiers could begin moving their belongings and all of their specimens to Ellis Camp so the party could begin its descent of the river by year's end, weather permitting.[45] Hunter was planning a three- to four-day mineral-seeking excursion into the mountains, but bad weather had delayed his departure for days. Finally, on December 27, Hunter and three others left while Dunbar remained behind, taking astronomical observations to determine the exact location of the hot springs. From December 27 to December 30, the men took turns transporting supplies and baggage to the Ouachita River while Dunbar "fooled around with the hot springs waters again."[46] Clearly, he hated to leave.

On December 28, Dunbar, George Hunter Jr., and two others "set out on a geological survey round hill of hot spring." Although they found no new, yet-undocumented springs, Dunbar noted that every time he studied the hot springs he learned something new. Most of the springs were located on the most elevated parts of the hill, but he was certain that the heat came from deep within the ground. On the excursion, Dunbar found on some green matter a tiny shelled animal shaped like a kidney. He used his microscope to study the animal, which was no larger than a grain of sand and was purplish brown. When Dunbar opened the shell, he found two sharp clawed feet near the head and behind. They allowed the animal to attach itself to the green matter and feed. He carefully wrapped a number of the creatures and took them home for further study with more sophisticated equipment.[47] Dunbar moved to Ellis Camp on December 29, and the next day a number of the men returned once more to the hot springs to await the return of Hunter and his party so they could escort them—baggage and all—to the Ouachita camp. Dunbar noted that December 30 was the coldest day of the trip, with a high temperature of nine degrees.[48]

The expedition party had hoped to break camp on December 31 and begin descending the Ouachita River on January 1, the seventy-eighth day of the expedition. But cold weather, drizzle, sleet, and snow, plus a river too low to float the loaded barge, kept the party in camp for nine more days. Dunbar put the waiting period to good use by working "to bring up & arrange my Journals. . . . We continued here as prisoners waiting for what is usually called bad weather, to bear us away from this place."[49] By January 6 the river was rising, and on the morning of January 8, 1805, the eighty-fifth day, the party began the journey back down the Ouachita River—heading south with the fast-moving flow of a waterway that had fought them inch by inch on the way up.

They waited until there was considerably more water in the river than the twelve inches they longed for in November because of the weight of all the fresh game they had killed and of their ever-growing number of specimens. They stopped along the way to retrieve specimens they had left in marked locations on the trip up the river, thereby adding even more weight to an already heavily loaded barge. In addition, Dunbar had marked several places he wanted to examine more closely on the way home, adding even more time and specimens. They moved swiftly down the river, "got over the great Chutes at 1 o'clock having lost 2 oars by brushing thro the willows with prodigious velocity." They stopped the barge, sent two soldiers and the canoe back up the river, and luckily recovered both oars.[50] Dunbar made the party stop often to study rocks and the terrain, always noting the latitude of those places of particular interest.

That first night, January 8, they disembarked in the rain and quickly set up tents, leaving most of their baggage and food on the barge and taking to camp only that which was needed for one night. The next morning they began a stop-and-go descent that irritated soldiers anxious to get home but satisfied Dunbar's interest about things identified earlier and marked in his journal. They no longer had to worry about sandbars and sunken logs because the river was high and the current swift, so he had the luxury of stopping whenever he wanted to. That morning they traveled two miles, examined some free stone and blue slate, took some specimens, and embarked again. They stopped briefly at least seven times that day, even once to view fowls and animals; yet the party had covered almost sixty miles by 5 P.M.[51] It took them only eight days to return to the Ouachita post, where they arrived around noon on January 16. In the meantime, they stopped at the camp of a Mr. LeFevre to listen to his observations, particularly about Indians. LeFevre was originally from Illinois, and he came to Arkansas to hunt, along with a few Delaware Indians he hired. He told Dunbar that they had been lucky not to meet a number of renegade Osages along the way. "He told of a large party of Osages from Arkansas river who made excursion round by prairie toward Red River & down Little Missouri where met small party of Cherokees, killed 6 & 4 more missing. 4 Americans & 10 Chickasaws were hunting into that quarter, they are in danger." LeFevre had considerable knowledge of the interior of Arkansas and Louisiana, and he spent much of the night of January 10 sharing that information with members of Dunbar's party.[52] Dunbar located other rivers and creeks and pinpointed the location of most area Indian tribes. The party even spent one night observing and recording an eclipse of the moon, with Dunbar explaining exactly what was happening.[53]

At the post, they returned the barge, paid for its use, and packed all of their supplies, specimens, instruments, and equipment on their own, deep-drawing boat.[54] They secured a new mast and additional oars for the boat. Dunbar wanted to buy three horses and set out overland with a soldier and his manservant, but no horses were available, so he took the canoe and said goodbye after sharing a drink with the rest of the party, now fast friends.[55] At daylight on January 20, the ninety-seventh day, Dunbar, his slave, and a soldier pushed off in the canoe, and they traveled ninety miles that day to the lower settlement. Dunbar called on the old hunter he had befriended on the journey north to the post, who told him a good deal about the Little Missouri River, which emptied into the Ouachita. The hunter told tales about gold, silver, and precious stones—probably pyrites, Dunbar reasoned, though he did admit that it was generally thought that there was silver in those parts. The old man showed Dunbar trees with fruit still on them, and Dunbar took samples and cuttings with him to Natchez, including bark from a tree that Dunbar thought beautiful.[56]

The next day, January 21, Dunbar and his small party bade his new friend good-bye, and during the next two days they canoed to Catahoula, 150 miles south of the Ouachita post. Dunbar wanted horses to complete his trip home to Natchez and was directed to the home of a Mr. Hebrard, who told Dunbar his horses were roaming around in the woods and he would catch three for them the next day. It was not until January 25, however, that Hebrard was able to run down three horses, and at 9 A.M. that day, the 102nd day of the expedition, the three left Catahoula for Crocodile Bayou, fifteen miles from the Mississippi River. They arrived at the bayou at 2 P.M., made a raft in two hours, crossed the bayou, and rode the final fifteen miles to the Mississippi River knowing that they would arrive too late in the day to cross the river. The thought of spending the night in the woods without even a fire disheartened them. Fortunately, at 9 P.M., still four miles short of the Mississippi River, the three found a house "where we were hospitably entertained with good homely fare."[57]

The last entry in Dunbar's journal simply stated, "Set out in the morning, very cold freezing air, crossed the river, breakfasted in Natchez and arrived at my own house at 10 o'clock A.M., found my family all well."[58]

14

Moments of Success
and Disappointment

The praise that accompanies success can be momentary or permanent. It was permanent for Lewis and Clark; it was momentary for William Dunbar, even though President Jefferson believed Dunbar's contributions to be significant. Though Lewis and Clark spent a considerable amount of time in Louisiana Purchase lands, they did not find an all-water route to the Pacific, nor were their scientific observations as diversified and thorough as Dunbar's. Dunbar was a scientist; Lewis and Clark were not. Yet the mention of Dunbar's Ouachita–hot springs expedition—the first completed in purchased Louisiana lands—brings forth an unknowing stare and the inevitable question, "Who was William Dunbar?" Perhaps this is because he lived in the southwestern corner of settled America, just east of the Mississippi River, and not on the East Coast, where a press and government could announce to the world important happenings whenever and wherever they took place, and where legends might well be born. Then again, that may not be the reason. Dr. George Hunter, Dunbar's Philadelphia associate on the hot springs journey, lived a quiet, uneventful East Coast life after 1805 and died in relative obscurity in 1824. Maybe it was Dunbar's failure to follow his expedition with a longer, more grandiose one.

Dunbar did enjoy some popularity at the time. From the moment he wrote to Jefferson, "I have the satisfaction to inform you . . . Dr. Hunter and myself are just returned from the Ouachita,"[1] many, especially in the region, applauded. Even among Spanish officials still in West Florida, there was a belief that the hardships suffered and the information gained were of significance to a developing nation.[2] The reports that Dunbar sent to Jefferson throughout 1805 pleased the president, and Jefferson submitted excerpts to

Congress, usually accompanied with requests for more exploration funding. Dunbar's specimens were shared with scientific scholars in many fields, and Dunbar's journals would lead to books, scientific articles, and offerings published in the *Transactions of the American Philosophical Society.*

One of the immediate results of the expedition was the institutionalizing of four recommendations Dunbar offered to the president. First, all boats used on expeditions should be specially constructed to meet the known needs of that particular expedition; second, at least one commissioned officer should accompany each expedition, because noncommissioned officers could not discipline unruly soldiers experiencing hardships along the way; third, expeditions should avoid having to move baggage from one river to another, for doing so was difficult and dangerous; and, fourth, scientists—as many as possible—should accompany all expeditions.[3] The quality of Dunbar's reports made implementing all recommendations most valuable as the government organized expeditions from that date forward. Carrying out the fourth recommendation, however, proved to be difficult. After working hard at doing so, Jefferson wrote, "These expeditions are so laborious and hazardous, that men of science, used to the temperature & inactivity of their closet, cannot be induced to undertake them."[4]

In the meantime, at least for a few months, Dunbar basked in the sunlight of approval. On February 13, 1805, after being home less than three weeks, he apologized to the president for having delayed working on his journals and sending him specimens for examination. He explained, "I have been much retarded in my progress by the almost perpetual interruptions of friends & acquaintances curious to inquire news of the western country."[5] But no one could call William Dunbar a procrastinator. As a scientist, he knew that the longer one delayed doing something, the more likely it was that one might forget something already known or discovered. He meant to work on his journals, maps, and charts the moment he returned home, and so he did, his apology to the president notwithstanding. Indeed, as early as February 12, 1805, he had written to President Jefferson informing him what he would be submitting, and in what order.[6]

Dunbar began the reporting process by sending a large variety of specimens for Jefferson to study and share with eminent scientists. Dunbar mentioned that most were "not of very high importance," but he tried to show what was to be found in Ouachita country. He wrote a good deal about the hot springs, which he termed a "very great natural curiosity." He analyzed their waters and found they contained a little carbonic acid, lime, and some iron. He wanted verification from other scientists regarding this conclusion as well as all other scientific observations he offered. He sent water from the various rivers and vegetable and animal life, including the cabbage and radish he found so fascinating on the journey. Dunbar mentioned that fall-winter expeditions should be rethought because "the season was unfavorable for botanical researches."[7] Jefferson examined all that Dunbar sent to him before sharing specimens with some of the finest scientists in the land; for example, he shared all botanical specimens with Benjamin Smith Barton, the leading botanist in the country.[8]

Dunbar then worked on a preliminary geometrical survey, "a record of course and distances as well as a thermometrical log" that would be followed by the details of all astronomical observations.[9] He noted that "the latitude was ascertained every favorable day" and that observations for longitude were occasionally made.[10] Dunbar was proud of those observations, likely believing that they were the most significant accomplishment of the journey. He noted that the Ouachita post was at the most easterly point of the Ouachita River and that it was nearly on the same meridian as Natchez; the hot springs were the most westerly point they visited.[11]

In the meantime, George Hunter delivered to Dunbar everything he did not need for his own report and all possessions on the boat; he drew ten days' rations, visited with friends in Natchez, and spent a night with Dunbar and his family at the Forest. Then, at 3 P.M. on February 14, he left for New Orleans with his son to deliver the expedition boat to Colonel Freeman. Always gregarious and in need of attention, Hunter arranged to have dinner with Governor Claiborne and granted an interview to reporters from the *Orleans Gazette* in which he relived the trip and offered generally correct observations about the countryside, the hot springs, and of course his place in the successful venture. Hunter noted that the country they traveled led him "to believe that there are few parts of La. that hold out greater temptations to emigrants."[12]

True to his promise, Dunbar spent more time in 1805 on journals and reports than he did on business affairs, family, or anything else. He wrote Jefferson on February 15, "I have . . . given my attention wholly to the transcribing of my journals and to calculating the longitudes."[13] Though his journal was often delayed, by February 23 he offered two more papers on the geographical survey of the Ouachita River—basic survey, mapping, and clarification of land conditions—along with more specimens.[14] On March 9, he wrote the president that he was sending along the conclusion of his journal on the geographical survey and preliminary comments on a journal he simply called "occurrences & remarks." Dunbar blamed some of the delays on the fact that the writer he had hired to help him with his work had been stolen away and hired as a local schoolmaster.[15]

In early March, Dunbar began receiving letters from Jefferson suggesting that it was time to put together the expedition they had discussed and dreamed about for two years—seeking the headwaters of both the Red and Arkansas rivers—and the president hinted broadly that Dunbar should lead the expedition as he would have in 1804. Jefferson proudly announced to Dunbar on March 14 that Congress, pleased with the results of the Ouachita–hot springs venture, had appropriated an additional $5,000 for such an expedition.[16] Jefferson offered this news on the eve of a short visit to Monticello to tend to personal business. His letter left no doubt that Dunbar was the man he wanted leading this major expedition. Dunbar received a letter from Secretary Dearborn shortly thereafter informing him that he was at liberty to select men for the pending expedition, and Dearborn added the hope that Hunter would once again join Dunbar. Dearborn also told Dunbar that he was directing the commanding officer at Fort Adams to select an officer and as many men as Dunbar required and to provide a craft to Dunbar's specifications "should you consent to accept."[17]

As before, Dunbar was flattered by the faith Jefferson had in him while also being astonished that Washington officials wanted in charge of such a major undertaking a fifty-five-year-old man, one who had just returned from another expedition two short months earlier. The compliment almost worked again, for exploring new lands and evaluating their potential for settlement had been in Dunbar's blood since leaving Scotland in 1771. He had been doing just that all of his life as he explored in and around Pittsburgh, the Manchac–Baton Rouge lands in West Florida, the Natchez region, the Red, Black, and Ouachita rivers, and the hot springs. In 1804, the major expedition was conceived as an effort to study scientifically the Arkansas and Red River regions, but Dunbar had been denied that opportunity by extenuating circumstances. Was the opportunity Jefferson offered him a second chance to realize that goal? Was the previous foray simply training for a bigger, more important one? Dearborn went so far as to write John Sibley in Natchitoches, Louisiana, requesting a report on the lands in Louisiana in general and the Red River region in particular. Sibley responded on April 2 by offering Dunbar a long, detailed report that demonstrated both the breadth of his knowledge of the area and his enthusiasm for an expedition to study the river all the way to its headwaters. Sibley wrote that for twenty-three years he had worked for the Spanish governor in San Antonio as an agent for peace with various tribes, and he had succeeded in that task. Sibley indicated also that he was currently a member of the West Florida Legislative Council and was departing soon for New Orleans, where he could be found until early August. If Dunbar needed any additional information, he could contact Sibley there.[18]

Despite Dunbar's strong temptation to accept Jefferson's invitation, his Scottish pragmatism, perhaps accompanied by Dinah's protestations about family obligations, forced him to turn down the opportunity. Dunbar pled age and infirmities, but he did offer to oversee the organization and management of either or both expeditions. Based on his experience in the Ouachita–hot springs trip, Dunbar offered to organize expeditions to the Red River and the Arkansas River separately, not as one trip, to avoid dangerous and difficult overland transportation. Jefferson accepted the offer with thanks and placed Dunbar in charge of selecting leaders, an officer, men, and scientists for the expeditions.[19] He was also authorized to outfit the expeditions—everything from boat specifications to scientific instruments. As late as May 24, Dearborn was still writing in the hope that Dunbar would accept the leadership of a combined expedition, despite Dunbar's objections. Dearborn had been trying to get young adventurers to sign on but was having no luck. "I am surprised," he wrote, "that young men of talent unencumbered by family affairs are not found in numbers with you who are solicitous to go upon so inviting an expedition."[20]

In the meantime, Dunbar recommended to Jefferson that only the expedition to the Red River source be conducted for the time being. It appeared prudent to Dunbar to concentrate on one effort when relations with Spanish authorities and regional Indian tribes were unsettled and congressional funding was inadequate to supply two ventures. The president accepted Dunbar's advice and directed Dearborn to write to Dunbar, informing him of the acceptance of that advice and putting him in charge of organizing the expedition. The president instructed Dearborn to write to Dunbar requesting that he contact Governor Claiborne in Louisiana, meet with the Marquis de Casa Calvo, and request of him a passport through the disputed terrain.[21] Claiborne was to emphasize again that the expedition up the Red River was strictly a scientific one under the control of a longtime, close Spanish ally, William Dunbar. Dearborn further informed Dunbar that the total amount of money at his disposal for the expedition, including the cost of a boat, was $5,000.[22]

As he contemplated spearheading an ambitious expedition to the source of the Red River, an enthusiastic Dunbar continued working on his journals, forwarding them to the president as they were completed. Dunbar and Jefferson discussed the upcoming trip, and both expressed excitement about what might be found along the Red River and at its source. On May 25, Jefferson informed Dunbar that he was receiving his journal installments as well as geographical survey information and that he was in the process "of putting the journal into the hands of a person properly qualified to extract the results of your observations." He would be sharing excerpts with Congress soon.[23]

Colonel Freeman, still believing that the expedition up the Arkansas River, then overland, and down the Red River was the current plan, gathered a detachment of forty men in New Orleans and secured a boat meeting Dunbar's specifications. Freeman left New Orleans for Natchez, only to learn upon his arrival that the joint rivers expedition had been scrapped in favor of one up the Red River alone. Freeman, greatly disappointed, stored most of the baggage for the expedition with Dunbar and returned to New Orleans with his men—promising that they would be ready for the Red River venture when new instructions were received.[24]

In the midst of all this activity, Governor Claiborne wrote to the Marquis de Casa Calvo, in the name of the president of the United States, requesting a passport for the Red River expedition and using William Dunbar's name liberally. He stressed that the mission would be under the "immediate direction of the Honorable William Dunbar . . . a gentleman whose life has been devoted to science." The president and Dunbar pledged, Claiborne wrote, that the "mission is merely geographical and scientific." Casa Calvo agreed to honor the request, but he reminded the president that even though the Red River emptied into the Mississippi River, the upper part of the Red ran through the province of Texas.[25] The passport would be issued to the person designated as expedition leader by Dunbar, a man Casa Calvo greatly admired.

Claiborne passed along the good news to Dunbar, who in July began in earnest putting together the Red River expedition. He enlisted the assistance of Isaac Briggs in helping find just the right person to lead the expedition. Secretary Dearborn recommended a scientist, George Davis, but after investigating him, Briggs and Dunbar deemed him "a very improper person." Davis was volatile and negative, a combination not geared to inspiring the harmony necessary on these strenuous ventures. Dunbar felt Davis was unfit to exercise authority. Others were recommended but also did not meet Dunbar's high standards for leadership. Eventually, Dunbar began thinking about Colonel Thomas Freeman as a possible expedition leader. "An officer of his rank & respectability will be of considerable advantage," Dunbar wrote to Jefferson on July 6.[26]

Several 1805 letters between Dunbar and Jefferson about the pending expedition included comments on Dunbar's Ouachita–hot springs journals, which the president was still receiving from Dunbar. Jefferson reflected positively on Dunbar's rock samples or observations and then offered his own explanations in response to Dunbar's questions. Jefferson also commented on the validity of certain scientific observations and means of conducting latitude and longitude measurements, and Dunbar replied with data he had found in his continuing studies. What emerged from these exchanges were gems of knowledge and insights that marked both men as bright, curious students of science matched by few Americans during the early national period.

Trying to keep four plantations operating in the black, make a family with very young children happy, and complete detailed maps and journals while putting together for the president and secretary of war a major expedition became too much for Dunbar. He fell behind in his self-imposed submission deadlines for 1805. On July 9, he wrote Jefferson from Natchez, "I should have by now, completed my sketch of the course of the Ouachita River, but I shall certainly get it prepared & forwarded long before the meeting of the Legislature."[27] On November 10, however, Dunbar had to report to Jefferson that "an apology is due for the late appearance of my sketch of the Ouachita River, and I have not a good one to offer. I was not aware that upwards of twelve hundred courses and distance would require so much time. . . . I think it better to send it in the present state than to delay another week fearing already that it may arrive later than it was your desire to receive it."[28]

Meanwhile, as in 1804, Dunbar and Dearborn began wrangling. They haggled over the number of men to be included, the officer, the scientists, the instruments, the boat, the equipment—everything. When Dunbar finally found the commissioned officer he wanted to oversee the work of the soldiers, a Captain Sparks, he shared that information with Dearborn, who admitted that Sparks was a fine woodsman and a brave and prudent officer. Dearborn gave his approval, but with the condition "that should he go, it would supersede the necessity of sending any more than one other person as a mathematician."[29] The decision infuriated Dunbar, who did not need Dearborn's approval to appoint anyone in the first place, and he demanded to know why the appointment of an officer to oversee men should deprive the expedition of a trained mathematician.[30] So the squabbling persisted, with Dunbar giving the secretary a list of instruments he needed and, as in 1804, Dearborn vetoing one or another on the list, or promising to secure a used instrument from Fort Adams or another military post. The wrangling continued and time elapsed. In March, Jefferson had written of an expedition to be undertaken in April or May, but as late as August several major decisions remained to be made.

By the close of July, Casa Calvo was wanting to know whose name should be on the Red River passport, but the person to head the expedition had yet to be chosen.[31] Finally, on October 9, Dunbar wrote to President Jefferson recommending the best person to head the expedition. Dunbar had hoped to get a scientist to accept the leadership position, but, unfortunately, he could not find any first-rate scientist to accept the post. The pay was too low, the dangers too real, and the instruments inadequate. Dunbar noted that the last complaint was a legitimate one—he had been forced to supply many of his own instruments on the previous expedition. Having failed to find a scientist to lead the major expedition, Dunbar recommended that they lower their sights a bit and seek someone who possessed leadership qualities and some scientific knowledge in at least one important field. He again recommended that Thomas Freeman—who possessed scientific knowledge in geography and whom Dunbar liked and admired—be appointed to lead the Red River expedition.[32] Dearborn agreed in mid-December.

In a December 17 letter to Jefferson, Dunbar announced that they were ready to begin the Red River expedition; he had acquired two boats twenty-five feet long and eight feet wide that were curved to his specifications. One boat had a perfectly flat bottom; the other had a slight elevation toward each side. The object of the construction and the use of two boats was "to draw as little water as possible, and at the same time to preserve a form of small resistance; they may be considered experimental boats."[33] Splitting the load of men and baggage into two boats allowed each to glide high on the river, flowing more smoothly over shoals and sunken logs.

Unfortunately, too much time had been wasted and too much enthusiasm lost during a year of wrangling; many others, including Casa Calvo, were disgusted. When Dearborn finally appointed Freeman to lead the expedition, and when Claiborne was ready to approach Casa Calvo with Freeman's name for the passport, the marquis had left on an annual excursion to visit Spanish forts and officials throughout West Florida. He would be gone for at least a month, probably six weeks, Claiborne was told.[34] In the meantime, a good scientist for the expedition, Peter Custis, had been found in Philadelphia, and he left for Natchez on January 17, 1806.[35] By that time, however, the expedition had been ten months in the making, and events on the horizon would further reduce its possibility of success.

In the meantime, Dunbar had completed and submitted all his Ouachita–hot springs journals, maps, charts, and specimens to President Jefferson, and he was reaping some of the benefits from the success of the hot springs journey. Samuel L. Mitchell, a Columbia College professor of natural history who in 1797 founded *Medical Depository*, the first scientific journal in the United States, became interested in the Dunbar-Hunter expedition. He published an article about the venture, reviewing their route and discussing hot water plants, animals, even the wild cabbage, in *Medical Repository*. The article, published in January 1806, offered a most favorable review of what Dunbar and Hunter had achieved.[36] That same year, several publications of the government and of various scientific societies included information on the expedition. In a February 1806 letter to Congress, President Jefferson wrote about the Ouachita–hot springs expedition and Dunbar's contributions: "This was undertaken under the direction of Mr. Dunbar, of Natchez, a citizen of distinguished science, who had aided and continues to aid us, with his disinterested and valuable services in the procurement of these enterprises."[37] Dunbar also contributed to a book, *Discoveries Made in Exploring the Missouri, Red River, and Washita by Captains Lewis and Clark, Doctor Sibley, and William Dunbar*, that provided a first-rate account of the trip. The volume included extensive lists of flowers, minerals, grasses, trees, shrubs, vines, and vegetables, along with a meteorological chart, which included wind, air, latitude, longitude, and weather. Dunbar also recorded all of the towns and villages encountered and listed distances one from the other. It was a handsome and popular book that was recognized by both the *Mississippi Herald and Natchez Gazette* and *Mississippi Messenger*. Exploration of new American territory to the west excited Americans in the more settled states east of the Mississippi River. The relatively unknown part of America that Dunbar, Hunter, and their party had explored had, indeed, captured the imagination of many American citizens.[38]

By the end of December 1805, with Freeman's appointment approved and Peter Custis soon to be on his way, Dunbar began to ponder a matter much on his mind since the end of the hot springs adventure. There were a number of interesting places on the Ouachita River that Dunbar had not adequately studied because of time constraints. He was most bothered by his failure to explore the Little Missouri River and the mines that he was told were there. Dunbar wrote President Jefferson, "Should you be of opinion that those merit a visit, I will just observe that altho my situation with a family & other concerns demanding my protection & care, prevent me from undertaking an expedition, such as the Red River . . . I might be able to find an interval of a month or two to be dedicated to a less distant object." If Jefferson wanted him to do so and could provide a corporal and four men to row a light boat, Dunbar would be willing to undertake such a venture, with high-quality instruments and a chronometer.[39] For health reasons, he never made the journey, but until the end of his life Dunbar was eager to undertake such a trip.

Time and timing were the enemies of the Red River expedition. At any time during 1805 and January 1806, the Marquis de Casa Calvo would have signed a passport submitted by Dunbar via Claiborne; the marquis had no objections to a scientific expedition through territory that was still being disputed by the two countries. Then, on February 6, 1806, President Jefferson turned a friend into an enemy by acting on a problem whose clock had begun ticking in 1803. When France and then the United States took over Louisiana, Spanish officials and soldiers should have evacuated all of West Florida. The Spanish, though, dragged their feet and lingered in American territory for the rest of 1803, all of 1804 and 1805, and into 1806. Seemingly, they had no plan to evacuate any of the territory until a Louisiana-Texas boundary had been negotiated and accepted by both countries. Jefferson waited and waited for Spanish movement. He did not push for withdrawal in 1804 or 1805 because of his desire to explore the Red River unimpeded by Spanish forces.

On February 8, 1806, Claiborne informed Casa Calvo that the Red River expedition was under the command of Colonel Thomas Freeman—a man well known to Spanish officials—and requested the passport in his name. Claiborne told Casa Calvo that the expedition would be leaving Natchez shortly, and he reminded Casa Calvo that it was a mission with scientific goals only. On the same day, Claiborne also informed Casa Calvo that the president of the United States had issued an executive order requiring "that your excellency & all other Persons holding commissions or retained in the service of His Catholic Majesty should quit the Territory of Orleans as soon as possible." He reiterated that their departure should not be delayed more than a few days. The marquis was insulted and refused to leave, whereupon Claiborne told him on February 11 that all Spanish officials were to leave the province because they had remained long beyond the time stipulated in the 1803 sale by France. He concluded flatly, "Without entering therefore into further discussion with your Excellency, on the Subject of the Orders of the President . . . , I shall proceed to execute them, and must require that you depart on or before the 15th day of the present month" and be followed by all persons "now in the Territory, who hold commissions, or are retained in the service of Spain."[40]

On February 12, 1806, Claiborne wrote Dunbar informing him of the inevitable: Casa Calvo had refused to issue a passport to Thomas Freeman.[41] Even if a passport had been issued earlier, however, the Spanish would not have honored it after the eviction order from President Jefferson. To suggest that national interests put a scientific expedition at risk would be an understatement. Dunbar knew not what to do. Should he send the expedition on its way come what may? Should he refuse to put a few men trying to find scientific information in harm's way? The decision was his to make; Jefferson and Dearborn made that crystal clear. If the party had been in place, and if all baggage and equipment were already stored on the two small boats, the decision to go, though difficult, would have been made immediately. As luck would have it, time wasted on loose ends forced changes in personnel to be made, particularly the second in command. Dunbar had selected a Lieutenant Gaines, who backed away in mid-February 1806. By the time Dunbar found his replacement, a Lieutenant Humphrey, put forward by Freeman because of his leadership potential and his geography background, mid-February became mid-March—giving Dunbar time to continue monitoring the confrontation between Jefferson's eviction notice and Spanish resistance.[42]

The situation became so dangerous that it appeared impossible to Dunbar that an American party could get past Spanish soldiers at Bayou Pierre. Therefore, he recommended to Dearborn that they change their course once again and ascend the Arkansas River and explore that region if the change could "be kept a profound secret." His recommendation was made on February 25, with the knowledge that by early March "water will begin to fall with coming of summer."[43] Jefferson's response to the suggestion reflected once again the faith he had in Dunbar's judgment. It was one thing to tell the Spaniards to get out; it was quite another to have in place the forces needed to carry out the order. Jefferson had no such soldiers in Louisiana, so he wrote Dunbar, "Whether our party had better go up the Red river or the Arkansas first you are the best able to judge."[44]

In March and April 1806, Dunbar weighed the Osage danger on the Arkansas River and the Spanish access problem around Natchitoches. The more he thought about the Arkansas River, the less he liked the option because the boats, instruments, baggage, and personnel were all geared to studying the Red River—a quite different situation from the Arkansas. Finally, with Freeman's agreement, Dunbar selected the Red River mission and, on April 28, watched the men cast off at Fort Adams. Before sending them on their way, he spent time with the group offering advice or, as Dunbar put it, "adding a few hints derived from my own experience."[45]

The expedition was ill fated. By late July, as they approached Natchitoches, six hundred miles distant from Fort Adams, the party encountered Spanish forces that outnumbered them many times over. There were 1,200 soldiers with 4,000 horses encamped thereabouts. The Spanish stopped Freeman and his party, and because Jefferson had told the party to avoid confrontation, they turned around and headed home.[46] Two years of plan-

ning and much expense went for naught. The expedition was an utter failure, and the net results were observations in a part of Louisiana already
investigated and evaluated.

Though the failure of the Red River expedition disappointed Dunbar, it
did not dampen his interest in the importance of discovery through formal,
sponsored expeditions. He continued to refine his journals in 1806 and
started planning an expedition to the Arkansas River region in 1807.[47] He
was saddened when Dearborn informed him that Congress had not appropriated any exploration dollars that year. He told Dunbar "to inform Mr.
Thomas Freeman that his services in exploring the line are at an end."[48] In
addressing Dunbar, the frustratingly frugal Dearborn wrote with kindness
and respect that "drafts made on account of the United States upon your
time and patriotism demand an apology, while your disinterested and highly useful services entitle you to the most grateful acknowledgments."[49] With
that sign of approbation, Dunbar's exploring days came to an end. Without
appropriated funds, President Jefferson cancelled all expeditions planned for
1807. Though rumors of expeditions abounded in 1808, Jefferson, in his
last year in office, did not press any of them. Dunbar spent his time making
sure that all government baggage and instruments stored on his property at
St. Catherine's landing were ready to be returned to the federal government
as soon as requested.[50]

Throughout its history, America has been blessed by the efforts of many
committed and talented explorers, some of whom have been fondly remembered as national heroes. Others, including William Dunbar, have been
forgotten, or nearly forgotten, for a variety of reasons. In Dunbar's case,
his observations drew praise, many of his recommendations were implemented, and his journals were recognized by the president, congressmen,
and fellow scientists.[51] He has been nearly forgotten because of unfortunate circumstances that kept him from commanding major explorations
of the headwaters of the Red and Arkansas rivers. Primary among those
circumstances were renegade Osages unhappy over internal tribal matters
and West Florida Spanish officials furious over Napoleon's sale of Louisiana
to the United States. Neither of these, of course, was of Dunbar's making,
but both forced him to lead a smaller, successful foray to the hot springs,
then fail two years hence to oversee a second effort commanded by Thomas
Freeman. The result relegated him to a footnote here and there rather than
giving him a chapter among the great American explorers. In fact, until a
few decades past, a pamphlet published by a U.S. government agency spoke
of the Dunbar-Hunter 103-day expedition as a part of the Lewis and Clark
expedition to the north.[52] This mistake was most unfortunate, for though

Lewis and Clark deserve a great deal of praise for their explorations, Dunbar had no part in them.

Whereas Lewis and Clark explored in the north and became household names saluted to this day by grateful fellow citizens, Dunbar's contribution to the development and understanding of the previously unknown lands and rivers of the southern Louisiana Purchase was forgotten by all but a few American historians. In his day, William Dunbar was one of a select group of explorers who ventured into new southern lands. The brilliance of his mind was widely acknowledged, as was the scope of his accomplishments, particularly his success as a pioneering explorer-scientist.

15

The Importance of Education

From childhood, the center of Dunbar's life was education; he was the product of a brilliant mother who taught him the wonder of learning and the magic of problem solving. In addition, Dunbar was born in the middle of Scotland's eighteenth-century educational renaissance, when its colleges and universities were without peer the world over, and he emerged from his youth and King's College as an educated youngster committed to continuing to learn for the rest of his life. And learn he did, becoming a trusted surveyor in Spanish West Florida and an architect in the old Southwest while gaining recognition for his work as a mathematician, planter, inventor, explorer, and businessman. Through all of that, Dunbar's greatest asset was his lifelong curiosity, knowing always the potential of a mind being used. In short, his education took; he was hooked on learning for life.

It seems fitting, then, that a biography centering on Dunbar's life and accomplishments should include a chapter on his beliefs and initiatives showing him as an advocate for learning as a way of life for a young nation seeking greatness. Since Dunbar rarely expressed his emotional commitments, a study of his life must focus on his efforts, accomplishments, and few failures, not his thoughtful or intimate family comments. There were occasions, however, when Dunbar did find it expedient to speak, advise, and wish another well. Such occasions usually come when one's progeny stand poised to leave the family nest, and Dunbar was no exception. His first occasion to speak in such a personal way was when their eldest son, William Jr., prepared to leave the family for prep school on the East Coast. Dunbar wanted for his children—female as well as male—education that enhanced their lives, and he made that point quite clear. On May 2, 1808, William Dunbar Sr. ceased for a moment being a strict parent and became a father filled with hope and high aspirations for his eldest son. On that day, young Dunbar left his home at age fourteen to travel to Philadelphia to enter a high school and, later, a university. He would live in the family home of Dunbar's son-in-law, Samuel Postlewaite, who was originally from Philadelphia. Many of today's students might not understand or appreciate the advice Dunbar gave his son, but he wrote of the basics of learning and discipline, terms he lived by every day of his life.

Dunbar's May 2, 1808, letter was addressed to John Vaughn, a wealthy Philadelphia merchant who would serve as a surrogate father to the young Dunbar during his days at Germantown Academy. He told Vaughn that William Jr. would be accompanied to Philadelphia by his eldest sister, Anne, her husband, Samuel Postlewaite (who had business in Philadelphia), and their daughter. Dunbar told Vaughn that he placed his son "under your protection." He thought Vaughn should know that young Dunbar had not had the "advantages of education in this Country which he ought to possess" as a fourteen-year-old student, but he was "tolerably grounded" in arithmetic and bookkeeping, knew a "smattering" of mathematics, had "some little notion" of botany, and had read widely on many subjects. "He is not deficient in natural talent and genius," Dunbar observed, and he hoped Vaughn would help "bestow upon him the education of a Gentleman and a man of Science."[1]

Dunbar let Vaughn know that he believed Americans were far too liberal in giving their school-aged children money and time to waste. He did not believe in "rigid confinement" when a student was not in class or laboratory or library, he wrote, but he urged Vaughn to see that a goodly part of his son's spare time was spent in "healthful & vigorous exercise. . . . I am an old advocate for strict discipline & necessary restraint during the hours of study . . . and physical improvement," Dunbar stated. Still, Dunbar admitted that he wanted his son to have as much pocket change as his peers.[2]

Dunbar completed the letter by telling Vaughn that it was time for him to stop writing in generalities and to offer specifics he wished to see inculcated into his son's curriculum. He wanted young Dunbar to have a "moderate knowledge" of Latin and Greek, both essential for a general education, and "genl. History and the Belles Lettres, Chemistry, Nat. history and Botany are not to get neglected." In the arena of personal accomplishments, "he should consider dancing, fencing, drawing, and music, and, of course, the French and Spanish languages ought . . . to have their share of attention." He ended the instructive letter by saying, "Take care of my son & make him mind you as a father."[3]

Young Dunbar arrived safely in Philadelphia and wrote his mother and father a short letter to that effect. Dunbar responded with a letter of advice that he probably could not have articulated face to face with his son. He wrote a bit about the quality of the Postlewaite family, particularly the father. Postlewaite might say things with which he did not agree, Dunbar wrote, but "conduct yourself with great modesty." Dunbar asked his son to respect age and wisdom at all times and to conduct himself in a "polite obliging and condescending manner, because, in doing so, you will earn their affection." He should never "dispute with an elderly person . . . even if you thought yourself right."[4]

Dunbar was pleased to learn that his son had met and liked John Vaughn. He warned William Jr. not to allow Vaughn "to make a fool of you by giving you too much pocket money." He acknowledged that the younger Dunbar was homesick and suggested that being "gloomy" was normal; he should not be at all concerned. It would pass, Dunbar advised. "Know that we, too—your family—are gloomy, but we want you to procure for yourself the education of a Gentleman and a man of Science." Dunbar expressed the belief that his son had the ability and the desire to succeed in school, "so take advantage of all before you and make us proud, as you make yourself proud."[5]

Dunbar then offered comments on the cotton crop just harvested and the overabundance of rain that summer and ended the letter with a mild bit of scolding. Dunbar reminded his son that the letter the boy had just written to the family covered only about one-half of the full sheet of paper he had used. There was a postage charge of fifty cents for a full sheet, but only twenty-five cents for a half sheet. He advised his son to fill a full sheet if he used one and to use a half sheet for a message of shorter length. He continued his waste-not lecture by saying, "Altho' a letter from you to mama or me will always be worth a great many dollars yet there is no reason to pay more than is necessary" (a guiding principle of Dunbar's adult life). Dunbar concluded by reiterating the expectation that his son write home at least once every fortnight.[6] This letter is the most poignant, the most human one in his entire collection. Dunbar did, indeed, love his family.

Learning was to Dunbar both an individual and a group activity. He was happiest working in his extensive library and state-of-the-art laboratory at the Forest and sharing information and possibilities with others by offering scholarly articles in the *Transactions of the American Philosophical Society*, hosting gatherings at the Forest to view a comet, or simply meeting or corresponding with others and exchanging ideas. As early as 1773, as we have seen, Dunbar found time to gather with other planters to talk about the world around them while sipping a glass of Madeira. They sometimes talked about slave problems, but they more often spoke of the difficulties of cultivating indigo, the effects of growing tobacco on the land, and natural phenomena that could not be explained. As Dunbar's scientific equipment increased in both quality and quantity, so did his experiments and the number of groups discussing what he and others were doing. He looked forward to those gatherings, as much for the intellectual exchanges as for the social interaction.

The need for intellectual interchange continued throughout Dunbar's life and led some to suggest that Mississippi Territory's "most fertile and stimulating mind was that of William Dunbar."[7] In 1803, Dunbar and eighteen other leading intellectuals in Mississippi Territory, including Governor W. C. C. Claiborne, Isaac Briggs, and David Lattimore—representing the spectrum of political thought at the time—petitioned the territorial legislature to create the Mississippi Society for the Acquirement and Dissemination of Useful Knowledge, patterned after formal agricultural societies formed in several states beginning in February 1785 with the Philadelphia Society for Promoting Agriculture. The legislature overwhelmingly approved the request.[8] The Mississippi society had a good number of privileges bestowed on it by the legislature, including the right to purchase, lease, or sell land, to make recommendations to the legislature, and most of all to meet often in "intellectual good fellowship."[9] For the remainder of his life, Dunbar looked forward to society meetings and the intellectual—especially scientific—exchanges offered by friends and colleagues at these meetings. They harkened back to the informal gatherings held by a professor at King's College during Dunbar's college days, and perhaps to tutorial discussions with mother and siblings as well. To discuss, to argue, and to listen became parts of Dunbar's intellectual arsenal throughout his life. Society members discussed new inventions, longitude modifications, cotton prices, explorations, and possible articles for publication based on research done by leading scientific scholars who lived in what easterners considered the backwater of America. Geographically the old Southwest may have been just that, but it was a region filled with bright friends and colleagues of Dunbar, all starved for intellectual discourse.

Mississippi Territory planters with the financial assets of a William Dunbar would always enroll their children in eastern prep schools and colleges, but Dunbar, Claiborne, and others yearned to make available in or around Natchez a college dedicated to the basic liberal arts for families who could not afford an East Coast education for their children. Therefore, on May 4, 1802, Governor Claiborne recommended that the territorial legislature create a public institution of higher learning for the territory.[10] Claiborne told legislators that a republican form of government must have as its cornerstone a place of learning where discussion and debate are welcomed. "People involved in mental darkness become fit subjects for despotic sway," he said. "When informed of their rights they will never fail to cause them to be respected by the public authority."[11] Nine days after Governor Claiborne's request, the legislature created Jefferson College.[12]

The legislation noted that it was fitting to name the institution for President Thomas Jefferson, the nation's leading advocate of learning and a fast friend of rural America. Thirty-three men were named as incorporators, and twenty-five would serve as trustees; Dunbar became both. The trustees were charged with selecting a site for the college; getting it built; hiring a president, professors, and a treasurer; examining the qualifications of student applicants; and conferring both baccalaureate and master's degrees. They were charged also with approving all rules and regulations of the college and soliciting support from the people of the territory, in part through a public lottery.[13]

Selecting a site proved to be difficult. Natchez was the most powerful town in Mississippi Territory, but it was extremely Federalist leaning, whereas much of the rest of the territory was Democratic-Republican. Many Federalists found education of the masses threatening and therefore did not want a college at all. Still, if there was to be one, they believed it should be in Natchez, where they could keep an eye on curriculum and student attitudes. So the fight began.[14] In his heart and mind, Dunbar was as much a conservative Federalist as anyone in the territory, but he was a passionate advocate of education as the chief means to regional and national progress. Thus the quality and relevance of Jefferson College became central to his life from 1802 on. There were two perfect sites for the college in downtown Natchez, but the city wanted those lots for something else, possibly a market house.[15] There were also thirty acres on the bluffs overlooking the Mississippi River that had been granted to Dunbar by Spanish governor Gayoso for the work he did in establishing the thirty-first parallel line, but the grant had been made after the final treaty date—the date all the land north of that line became part of the United States. The town council of Natchez claimed ownership of that land and wanted to use it as a public park.[16] Dunbar wanted to give the land to the new college to help it financially, not necessarily as a location for the school but possibly to sell at fair market value as income for the college's board to use in erecting buildings elsewhere. Natchez said no to both possibilities and turned for relief to David Lattimore, the territorial representative in the U.S. House of Representatives, to challenge the date of the grant to Dunbar. Dunbar filed a brief proving that the thirty acres legally belonged to him and that ownership had been accepted by the United States in 1798.

It would be hard to find a sorrier moment to chronicle in the nineteen-year history of Mississippi Territory. At the January 3, 1803, meeting of the college's board, a committee of five (including William Dunbar) was appointed to recommend a site for the new college.[17] This was an assignment that the usually nonpolitical Dunbar should have rejected, because the other four were partisans representing Federalist or Democratic-Republican aspirations, and the committee never agreed on anything unless one or more members happened to be absent from a meeting. Throughout the first half of 1803, the founding of a college was lost in the mist and gloom of raw partisan politics. Democratic-Republicans, led by the powerful Green family, wanted the college built away from conservative Natchez and argued for its location in the upcountry—Greenville was a prime contender. Natchez could not find a home for the college, but it certainly did not want it under the guidance of those liberal Democratic-Republicans in Greenville. At a meeting in Washington, Mississippi, on March 14, 1803, the full board of trustees received a committee report recommending Greenville; it was so ordered. That action infuriated the Adams County folk, who, at the next board meeting held in Greenville, packed the meeting and undid the decision. Finally, at a June 6 meeting in Selsertown, a new committee recommended Selsertown—a town twelve miles closer to Greenville than Washington or Natchez—as the site for the college. The full board rejected the report and accepted a generous offer by James and John Foster and Randall Gibson of a parcel of land near the town of Washington, the territorial capital. The trustees accepted the gift, then petitioned the legislature on July 25, 1803, to accept it and to name the Foster-Gibson site as the permanent home of Jefferson College. The legislature accepted the proposal, and on November 11, 1803, the site officially became the home of the college.[18] Unfortunately, the result, though reasonable, was unacceptable to Democratic-Republicans and Federalists alike. The dishonors were equal, and the college was launched amid grumbling and anger, not cheers and best wishes. That made financing the institution nearly impossible, since complaining folks are not often generous ones.

At the January 3, 1803, trustees' meeting in Washington, Governor Claiborne had been elected president of Jefferson College, William Dunbar vice president, Felix Hughes secretary, and Cato West treasurer. The trustees also appointed a committee to implement a lottery. The legislative act that created the college allowed a lottery but limited its earnings to a sum of $10,000 for the college, so the committee issued two thousand tickets at $5 each.[19] The cost of prizes offered deducted 15 percent from the total, giving the college $8,500 at the beginning of its fund-raising activities. With territorial ill will caused by the selection process, however, the lottery in support of Jefferson College failed miserably. In July 1803, it was reported that the lottery had been launched, but a communiqué dated January 28, 1804, reported, "The public has not responded to lottery." A report stated that the board had tried to float a loan from the legislature, but the response was negative. The final report concluded that "so far no money at all" had been collected for the college.[20]

Even with the failure of the lottery from both disinterest and ruffled feathers and the refusal of the legislature to fund the school even through a loan, the fate of Jefferson College really rested with Dunbar's petition to Congress seeking recognition of his ownership of the thirty acres on the cliffs of Natchez—an ownership patent he could prove beyond a reasonable doubt. Once again, however, partisan politics held center stage. The town of Natchez, stung by the placing of both the territorial capital and Jefferson College in nearby Washington, was determined to secure Congress's recognition of its ownership of the two town lots and the thirty acres on the cliffs. Lattimore found it difficult to urge legislators to vote against Natchez's wishes and still keep his nonvoting seat in the House of Representatives.[21] There was really too much power in Natchez for Lattimore to defy, so Dunbar's petition to Congress on the thirty acres and the resolution of town lot ownership dragged on year after year. Even though legislators were convinced Dunbar was right, congressional inaction worried the trustees, and when a decision was finally reached, they were not surprised at the contents of the report of the Public Lands Committee handed down on March 4, 1806—three long years after the congressional petition went forth.[22] The committee found for Natchez against William Dunbar, driving a knife through the heart of Jefferson College. At that point, the college was comfortably situated near Washington. Had the committee and Congress found in Dunbar's favor, and had he then given the land to Jefferson College to hold or sell, the institution would have had a fighting chance at survival. As it was, with lottery and loan failures, the institution faced tough times—even foreclosure.

It is difficult, however, to kill a college. When the board and other supporters started rallying citizens in support of the college in January 1803, they built their case on the platform of a public education institution for Mississippi's citizens. They knew it would be expensive to found a college and expensive to maintain it. Therefore, overall support was essential. A petition that made the case for the college concluded, "Such are our views, Fellow Citizens, of the importance of our present undertaking. We call on you then to lend your aid to an institution, which will be devoted to increase the common happiness. All are interested, let all contribute something to the common stock, let the rich give liberally and all others show their public spirit according to their abilities."[23]

During the politically charged site-selection process, many planters and business leaders made generous offers of financial support; those offers, however, were usually tied to the final location of the college. If it were located in Natchez, the college could count on the generosity of its leaders; the same was true for Greenville and its leaders.[24] As a site for the college, Washington had never been a major contender, so its selection may have been wise and nonpolitical, but it did not bring forth the generosity of partisan supporters. Dunbar was a contributor, but he based his generosity on the pending land gift and the hope that other leading planters and merchants in the territory would join in the noble effort by doing something similar.

By 1805, the college was all but dead, yet Dunbar, as vice president, offered curriculum recommendations at a June board meeting. If a student wished to follow a curriculum that included reading, writing, and basic arithmetic, the cost would be $20 per year. If the student preferred a more difficult curriculum, including Latin, Greek, French, and English grammar, the cost would be $30 a year. If the humanities, geometry, trigonometry, and other branches of mathematics were what the student wished to pursue, the cost would also be $30 a year. Board would be provided in various homes in Washington whose owners had agreed to be surrogate parents. As late as the summer of 1806, Governor Robert Williams, as president of the board, was seeking Dunbar's and President Jefferson's assistance in finding a president for the college—a person who would be willing also to teach half time for the yearly salary of $2,000.[25] The sad truth was that the governor had no college to sell. After the full board met on December 21, 1805, it did not meet again until April 1810.[26]

The partisanship of territorial governors had a great deal to do with the heat generated as the territory prepared itself for statehood after reaching the total of sixty thousand people required in the Northwest Ordinance of 1787. Who would be in charge? Where would the capital be located? Which groups would be favored? All of Mississippi's territorial governors had partisan goals that generated supporters and bitter enemies. Claiborne was one of them, so it is not difficult to visualize the problems he encountered from his enemies when he assumed the presidency of Mississippi's first college. The same was true of Robert Williams. Williams's successor, David Holmes, however, was a compromiser, always endeavoring to bring people together rather than split them further apart. Therefore, in 1810, during his governorship, tempers cooled, and for the most part partisan politics toward Jefferson College were abandoned. When Governor Holmes called a meeting of the board of trustees on April 28, 1810, Jefferson College was afforded an opportunity to survive. A proposal was offered that would allow the college to assume control of an academy that had recently been established in Washington by James Smylie.[27] Washington Academy had tried to sell lottery tickets with the same misfortune Jefferson College experienced eight years earlier. The two boards met, and Washington Academy's trustees voted to transfer their institution to the trustees of Jefferson College. The transfer was made on December 7, 1810; the academy's buildings were repaired or completed, and it was announced that "an academy under the superintendence of Dr. Edwin Reese, assisted by Mr. Sam Graham would open on the first of January."[28] Nine years after being chartered in 1802, Jefferson College was finally ready to begin making a positive educational mark on the territory and state it served.

Dunbar remained a trustee of Jefferson College until his death and even called a board meeting for April 12, 1810, shortly before he died. He did not live to see the union of the academy and college that allowed the continuation of his education dream. The entity that emerged in 1810 may not have been what Dunbar envisioned in 1802, but the new institution would serve long and well, if always precariously. Institution supporter J. Andrew Liddell wrote to John Liddell on July 3, 1848, that the institution "is getting to be a very disagreeable place indeed. Some of the boys are treating the professors so badly that they have had to resort to arms. . . . There is only fifteen or twenty students here now."[29] The buildings were again in disrepair. It is unfortunate that, as statehood beckoned and antebellum intellectual leadership and academic inquiry were desperately needed for a population far from the country's intellectual centers, a talented faculty and committed trustees and administrators were not afforded an opportunity to do much for educational pursuits in Mississippi.[30] Still, the college's founding demonstrated, as much as any other activity, the commitment to learning of William Dunbar, whose wealth guaranteed fine educational opportunities elsewhere for his own children. If he had cared only for self and family, he would not have contributed funds, ideas, and endless time to a college whose sole purpose was to elevate and diversify the learning options for those living around him in Mississippi. The effort may have failed; the idea did not.

16

Politics, Mississippi Style

William Dunbar constantly lamented the untidiness of politics; he told his family, friends, President Jefferson, and the world that he hated politics and was thankful that he was not a politician. Then again, he always maintained that he was not a businessman either, when in reality he was one of the shrewdest, most successful businessmen in Mississippi Territory. Dunbar's political instincts were among the keenest in an area that prided itself on politics as a game to be played and won. Though he never held high office, his political acumen underwrote his business success, enabling him to continue to succeed financially in the most turbulent of times as the very land he occupied was transferred from country to country, with attendant changes in leadership. Through it all, Dunbar seemed to know whom to befriend.

Dunbar thought and operated horizontally and not vertically. He saw business, science, exploration, education, and politics as ingredients of equal—or nearly equal—weight governing the way he lived his life. He grew up in a country in which his people ruled and needed not participate in politics to achieve success. Name, titles, land, influence, ample prestige to ensure a splendid education—all handed to them as a birthright. After primogeniture denied him Scottish lands and titles, Dunbar emerged in 1773 as a planter in England's West Florida colony, a place where mastering the art of politics would be necessary not only for success but for survival. Consider the 1778 environment in what is today Mississippi and Louisiana, with their fertile land, warm climate, ample rain, and access to America's most important river. It might appear that Dunbar could have selected no better place to seek his fortune than on the North American land between New Orleans and Natchez, but for one less politically astute, the instability of ownership and leadership of that area might well have led to failure.

Successful politics was key to economic success because of the history of that region. French explorers and colonists were the first whites to settle in the area, and they left behind a heritage rich and volatile. Next came the Spanish, who controlled East and West Florida for decades before losing it to the British in 1763, then regaining it from the British twenty years later. Then, in 1798, the Spanish lost Dunbar's Natchez region after Dunbar and Andrew Ellicott ran the thirty-first parallel line. Five years later, Spain lost the rest of Louisiana to France—a nation mired in a military quagmire in Europe, half a world away. France, then, less than a year after acquiring Louisiana, sold it all to the United States in the Louisiana Purchase. Napoleon was fighting on many European fronts, needed money, and had too few soldiers to occupy and defend the territory. Dunbar's task—huge by any measure—was to survive world politics, keep growing, and emerge economically successful. He had social plans and economic goals that depended upon astute political moves to succeed.

Indeed, few Americans living in the old Southwest during America's early decades ran the political gauntlet with more success than William Dunbar, and doing so forced him to improvise. He could not have foreseen multinational policies and Yazoo land frauds. He got his Manchac land grant from British authorities in 1773 and befriended English West Florida governors and other important West Florida officials who could help along the way. One might not consider his success with British officials as anything significant since he originated from the British Isles, was loyal to British authority, and was helping West Florida blossom. In 1783, after wartime setbacks at the hands of pesky colonists and angry Spaniards seeking revenge against the hated British, Spain received West Florida as a prize of war, rendering Dunbar subject to Spanish laws and whims. He made the transition with an ease that befuddled others. Dunbar became the confidante of all Spanish governors, with whom he moved with grace and sureness, serving as the French, English, and German language interpreter for each of them. Dunbar achieved high status in Spanish West Florida as an architect and surveyor while bestowing on officials agricultural gifts, accurate advice, and steadfast loyalty. It was no accident that in 1798 Governor Gayoso chose William Dunbar as the Spanish commissioner to determine the thirty-first parallel line. Realizing that he would soon be an American—his land holdings were situated slightly north of the thirty-first parallel—Dunbar could have tried to arrange with grateful Spanish officials a payment of land south of the border, on Spanish soil, for services rendered. Dunbar did accept land in payment for services, but it was land near Natchez in American, not Spanish, territory. He emerged from his days under British and Spanish rule—twenty-five years of political success—as far along in achieving his goal of economic success as any new American, with numerous British and Spanish land grants that translated into thousands of acres of fertile soil in the Natchez District and with a home unrivaled in the old Southwest.

By the time Mississippi Territory was created in 1798, Dunbar had become accomplished in practicing the art of politics, but he was by no means finished, for his political skills would be challenged for most of the rest of his life. It would have been far more promising for the Dunbar family in 1798 if Dunbar's West Florida holdings near Natchez had been south of the thirty-first parallel rather than north, except for the location of their plantation home. Both Dunbar and his friend Stephen Minor were tested immigrants who became favored non-Spaniards in West Florida. Before the Natchez cession by Spain to the United States, Minor was chosen to replace Gayoso as governor and thereafter lived in Natchez, representing Spanish interests in New Orleans until 1803.[1] Dunbar, conversely, chose to stay and construct a new political base within the boundaries of the United States; his relationship with Andrew Ellicott was significant in that rebuilding effort. Indeed, that proved to be the most fortunate friendship he ever formed, for Dunbar's intelligence, integrity, and knowledge so impressed Ellicott that he became Dunbar's eastern voice, thereby opening doors to scientific and philosophical circles hitherto closed to an unknown Dunbar. Even more significant, Ellicott opened the door to Dunbar's friendship with Thomas Jefferson.

To this point in the Dunbar biography, we have advanced a picture of the budding Jefferson-Dunbar friendship based upon scientific interests. That picture is accurate, but it is not complete; in truth, each needed the other—Jefferson the master national politician and Dunbar perhaps the best political operative his region had to offer. There evolved a marriage of political interests as well as a respect for each other's scientific talents. Why is that remarkable? There is no doubt that Dunbar was a Federalist in temperament and philosophy, for he had aristocratic ideals and pretensions, and he did not trust easily led masses. He believed gentlemen should rule—honorably of course—because they could rise above the pettiness on which common folks thrive. Spiritually and politically, Alexander Hamilton was Dunbar's hero and Federalist principles his hope, even though he preferred rural environments to cities. As a master player, however, Dunbar never preached those sentiments, preferring rather to live them. Still he had to be delighted that Mississippi Territory was going to be born under a Federalist president—perhaps the only truly Federalist president—John Adams. The territory appeared to be secure, dominated by conservatives on the national and local levels—the making of a Federalist heaven. It was a territory in which Dunbar had created for himself a place as an intellectual and economic force, soon to assist in making cotton of great importance in the South.[2]

If such was the picture in 1798, why was Dunbar on shaky political ground? First, Federalist Winthrop Sargent from Massachusetts, recent secretary of the Northwest Territory, was appointed to be Mississippi's first territorial governor. A worse choice could scarcely have been made. Though Sargent was a fine man who wanted to do a good job, he often said or did the wrong thing—doing what his heart, not his head, told him. Sargent had little political sense, and he knew nothing about Mississippi Territory. President Adams wanted harmony in a region recently ceded by Spain. Spanish officials left behind lawlessness and anarchy in the territory until an American government could take control, bringing along troops or police charged with enforcing a return to law and order. Colonel Anthony Hutchins and the entire Green clan—Democratic-Republicans to the core—were simply endeavoring to gain control of the territory before Sargent arrived. They were not trying to bring order out of chaos, as President Adams wanted; instead they were opportunists trying to achieve personal gain in an unsettled situation.[3]

During his years in America, Dunbar was never more vulnerable than in 1798; he was not an American, and he had been a Loyalist during the American Revolution. While he lived under the protection of Britain in West Florida, his plantation was sacked by patriots in 1778 and their Spanish allies a year later. After 1783, he lived under the protection of Spanish officials while the United States was coming into being. In the meantime, Americans such as Colonels Peter Brian Bruin and Thomas Green, Virginians with Revolutionary War records, as well as others such as Abijah Hunt, Thomas Rodney, and Cato West, migrated to the Natchez District from the East.[4] These men were economically successful for the most part, and they had high-level contacts among the powerful in the new nation that Dunbar— the new American—did not have. As we have seen, his position was precarious because land grants from other nations might not be honored by a new country seeking world acceptance and economic stability while moving from the Articles of Confederation in 1781 to the Constitution in 1787. Although the United States had promised to honor past land grants from France, England, Spain, and Georgia, it remained to be seen whether either government would do so. Ultimately, they would, because the America that entered the nineteenth century was an agrarian America, dependent upon the agricultural inventiveness and skills of Dunbar and others like him.

To make matters worse, in 1798 Natchez was a cesspool of lawlessness, with various families—more than just the Greens—and factions jockeying for position and power in a territory that could adopt a philosophy based on the whims of those in charge. How was Dunbar to protect his assets against others, many of whom envied his success and awaited the opportunity to undo his growing plantation empire? The key was in helping mold the philosophy of the first American territorial governor in Mississippi.

In evaluating the strengths and weaknesses of his situation, Dunbar rightly determined that he had two major advantages: first, his friendship with Andrew Ellicott and the publicity Ellicott might generate on Dunbar's behalf back East, and second, the Federalist philosophy espoused by both Adams and Sargent. It was not important that Sargent would be a disaster as governor, unable to bring harmony to a territory in need of leadership. That Sargent was as conservative as Dunbar made possible a friendship that could be beneficial to Dunbar as well as the territory.

When Sargent arrived in Mississippi Territory, William and Dinah Dunbar were the first to welcome him to his new home, and a friendship emerged nearly instantaneously.[5] Sargent already knew that cotton was becoming the staple of Mississippi Territory, and he asked Dunbar to provide him with a plan to ensure the quality of the cotton to be exported—a problem long on Dunbar's mind. Dunbar studied the issue, created a list of checks and balances that should go into a sound law, and on September 18, 1799, in a letter to Sargent, outlined his recommendations.[6] This assignment proved to be an important political victory for Dunbar in 1798, since it made him the major architect of a law that would regulate what he did for a living—raising, harvesting, ginning, and exporting cotton. Throughout the Sargent years, Dunbar advised on appointments and accepted assignments that would influence positively his agricultural activities. For example, Dunbar was offered the position of probate judge.[7] Sargent confessed to Dunbar that he did not know the limits of a probate judge's authority, so he recommended that Dunbar get a copy of a probate judge's duties as currently observed in the Northwest Territory and draft something based on that document for the governor to consider. Sargent concluded a November 4, 1798, letter to Dunbar by stating, "My Special Confidence in you . . . has induced me to select you for the Business, which perhaps is of more than Common Consequence, to the quiet and Contentment of our Country."[8] Within six months, Dunbar was the unofficial assistant governor, cleaning up Sargent's mistakes when he could and benefiting greatly from their friendship. Sargent's political favors to Dunbar were many and diverse.

The governor wanted to establish a customs house for a district south of the state of Tennessee that included all rivers and other waterways emptying into the Mississippi River from the territory. Dunbar recommended the waterways to be included, the locations of locks with lateral canals, the location of the customs house "in the neighborhood of Clarksdale," and the ideal customs collector. Dunbar wrote to Sargent on August 10, 1799, "I beg leave to say that I do not know any person whom I think better qualified by talents and integrity to occupy that charge, than James McIntosh Esquire." McIntosh was as conservative as Dunbar and was one of Dunbar's closest confidantes.[9]

One of the reasons Dunbar was able to be so influential in the Sargent years was that until a territory had five thousand free white males in its population, it was without a legislature; a governor and judges of his choosing ran the government, as required in the Northwest Ordinance of 1787. With a Federalist president and governor, this legal requirement allowed conservatives to be in charge of establishing a territorial government in Mississippi, even though a majority of its citizens were Democratic-Republicans— yeoman farmers who supported fellow southerner Thomas Jefferson. They hated Sargent, who made it easy for them to dislike him by being tactless and politically inept. Even Dunbar often worried over some needlessly foolish acts and statements of Sargent's. Dunbar wrote, "I am on as good terms as it is possible to be with a man of his phlegmatic and austere disposition. However good his intentions, it is impossible that a man so frigid and sour can give satisfaction to a free people."[10]

During the Sargent years (1798–1801), Dunbar served in several politically appointed positions. As conservator of the peace, he swore to "suppress all riots . . . and to take notice of all treasonable or seditious language and commit the authors . . . and to administer to all free male inhabitants who are considered permanent residents of the territory."[11] He served as probate judge, "to care for the estates of descendents according to his best judgment," as well as justice of the peace.[12] Dunbar wrote down his views on the organization of society, suggesting that there are three kinds of people: supporters of order, friends of government, and "disorganizers." Justices of the peace dealt with disorganizers. Dunbar also served as a legislator, elected when the first legislature was formed, as well as judge on the quarter session court, which heard everything from assault and battery to forgery to fraudulent deed cases.[13] Finally, Dunbar served as cotton gin inspector—a perfect post for a serious cotton planter. He took all of his assignments seriously, and he did a noteworthy job at each. As a cotton gin inspector, Dunbar wanted gins to undergo yearly inspections, cotton to be first rate and properly baled, records kept, and transactions notarized. In short, he wanted

Natchez cotton to be respected worldwide. Dunbar knew that if shoddy practices were allowed to go unpunished, the reputation of Natchez cotton would suffer—as would the reputation of good, honest cotton planters who provided a superior product. As a judge, Dunbar knew that a society could not progress with a foundation of lawless behavior that went unpunished. Regrettably, as he made and enforced law without the will of the people through legislative action, he made enemies who swore revenge.

Dunbar did not provide public service without an agenda. He made certain his British and Spanish land grants were approved. He won some of many antedated fights, but he lost some, too, notably his effort to give Jefferson College land on the Natchez bluffs. Certainly he looked out for his own interests, but he always associated those personal interests with the general good. He persuaded Governor Sargent to authorize the construction of a road that passed by the Forest, and when that action came before his court, he found it constitutional.[14] The road had long been planned and was needed, but Dunbar should have recused himself. Unfortunately, he intertwined public good with personal gain, and as a friend of an unpopular governor, he ensured that conservative Natchez laid the foundation for a territory outside Natchez—a Natchez determined to become more liberal.

One of the positive characteristics of William Dunbar was that he did not cast friends aside once their usefulness was exhausted. Winthrop Sargent was a friend of President John Adams, also from Massachusetts. One of the things an autocratic territorial governor could do in the initial stage of a territory was to create counties. Sargent promptly paid tribute to his Federalist brethren back East by creating both Adams and Pickering counties; Adams County included Natchez. In 1800 Sargent created Washington County, which included the area east of the Pearl River. Sargent was a poor choice to start a territory toward statehood, but he was not as bad as Democratic-Republican enemies made him out to be. He simply did not have a chance to succeed.[15] From the day he arrived, Democratic-Republicans who did not even know him thought of impeachment or, more realistically, a brief administration. Since Mississippi Territory already had the required number of free white males in 1798 for movement from first stage (governor and courts only) to second stage (an elected legislature, too), Democratic-Republicans immediately began petitioning Congress to move the territory quickly to the second stage—allowing the immediate election of a legislature to represent the people.[16] Sargent opposed that move and so did Dunbar. Dunbar maintained that the young territory simply was not ready for a legislature that would share governmental functions with an executive and courts. Like Dunbar, Sargent believed that the people were not yet ready to share in a free, democratic government.[17]

Despite the governor's disapproval, territorial liberal forces, led by Cato West, took their cause to Washington. Mississippi's first territorial representative to the U.S. House, Narsworthy Hunter, presented to the House a request to elevate Mississippi Territory to the second stage because it met Northwest Ordinance requirements for doing so. The petition was given to a congressional committee headed by Tennessean W. C. C. Claiborne, a Democratic-Republican supporter of Thomas Jefferson, who in early 1800 was preparing for his run for the presidency later that year. With Claiborne's support, the petition was approved in the summer of 1800,[18] thereby ending the autocratic rule of Winthrop Sargent.

Those who had chafed under Federalist rule for almost three years triumphed in November 1800 with the election of Thomas Jefferson as the third president of the United States, and Democratic-Republicans took over the reins of the federal government. The end of the Federalists and the rise of the Democratic-Republicans had great meaning in Mississippi Territory. One result predicted was the end of the political influence of William Dunbar, who, many thought, had swayed and duped English, Spanish, and American officials long enough. They predicted that the day of the Green family had arrived. To make matters worse for Dunbar, on May 25, 1801, Sargent was replaced by Claiborne, who created a legislature to do his bidding.[19] Winthrop Sargent did not return to Massachusetts, however; he remained in Natchez with his Mississippi wife, retained his friendship with Dunbar, and built Gloucester, one of the finest homes in the territory.

Once again the doubters were wrong; Dunbar's influence continued to grow, as he simply extended his circle of powerful friends. When he and Andrew Ellicott parted in 1798, they parted only in location, for a mutual respect had been forged that would never be broken. Beginning in 1799, Ellicott introduced Dunbar's credentials in scientific circles in the East, sang his praises to presidential candidate Thomas Jefferson, and with Jefferson as his partner, nominated and secured the election of William Dunbar to the American Philosophical Society. There began in 1800 a second friendship, a "friendship by correspondence," between Dunbar and Jefferson, as they discovered mutual scientific interests, exploration endeavors, and the relationship of education to progress. Though they would never shake hands with each other or converse over Madeira or tea, they became friends who shared ideas, trusted each other's judgment, and encouraged one another's curiosity. Now Jefferson—a Democratic-Republican hated and cursed by Federalists who believed him to be liberal enough to introduce mob rule into a new country that was not yet stable enough to keep the common folks in their rightful, subservient place—was the president of the United States.

To the consternation of local Democratic-Republicans, Dunbar's political influence increased under the three territorial governors who followed Sargent: Claiborne (1801–5), Robert Williams (1805–9), and David Holmes (1809–17). All four made contributions to the fabric that was to become Mississippi, but Williams was the weakest (he spent most of his time in North Carolina), and Holmes was the fairest and best. Holmes knew Dunbar the least because Dunbar died early in the Holmes years, but by 1809 the Dunbar legend was so solidly entrenched in Mississippi Territory that Holmes sought Dunbar's advice on several occasions, particularly concerning economic matters.

Not only did Dunbar become a close friend of Claiborne, but initially he retained all court and oversight posts granted him by Sargent. Ultimately, Dunbar relinquished some of Sargent's appointments, such as the probate court judgeship because of the negative comments he had to endure from neighbors and friends who lost through litigation in his court. Despite that Mississippi Democratic-Republicans denounced Dunbar as a Federalist masquerading as a Democratic-Republican, Dunbar's relationship with Jefferson and Ellicott prevailed, and Dunbar the Federalist became Dunbar the Democratic-Republican. He continued to hold at his pleasure a quarter session court judgeship, as well as the positions of justice of the peace and cotton gin inspector.[20] In addition, Dunbar did some surveying, helped organize a militia for the territory, arbitrated disputes, and offered counsel to Claiborne and Jefferson on such subjects as Spanish neighbors and the history of West Florida.[21] He also advised them as to the possibility of separating from Mississippi Territory the settlements far to the east on the Alabama and Tombigbee rivers, suggesting that the distance required the establishment of a new territory to the east.[22] Dunbar even gave blistering lectures to Claiborne and Jefferson on the uselessness of most lawyers in the territory and elsewhere.[23]

In 1801, Dunbar added two more powerful positions to his territorial résumé: he served in the first territorial legislature, and he worked with Claiborne to improve the quality of judges serving on the territorial supreme court. The court had three judges; one was trained in the law and was a sound judge, whereas the other two were simply friends of Sargent with "no legal background whatsoever."[24] Claiborne was wise enough to bide his time and not try to force either unqualified judge from office, but in 1802, when one of them abandoned his post and moved elsewhere, Claiborne appointed

David Ker, an attorney and the first presiding professor of the University of North Carolina.[25] Appointing skilled attorneys and judges to the supreme court resolved the quality issue, and it was Claiborne, advised by William Dunbar, who solved that problem.

Despite that Dunbar thought Mississippi Territory not ready for an elected legislature so soon after becoming a territory, he ran for a seat in the assembly and won. By 1803, he was serving as Speaker of the House, a position that allowed him to exert considerable influence in championing certain causes.[26] For example, as we have seen, Dunbar guided through important legislation that addressed smallpox in the territory. Anyone who knowingly brought smallpox into the territory would "be fined $2,000 and sentenced up to 12 mos. in jail." In addition, those who wanted a smallpox inoculation could get it free of charge, but no one would be forced to be inoculated. The governor was empowered to do all possible to "relieve the sufferers," and any costs involved would be paid by the territory. Finally, those who recovered from smallpox needed a certificate from a doctor noting full recovery.[27]

As a practical person, Dunbar played a leadership role in putting in place a tax structure. Sixteen items were to be taxed, including land, slaves (assessments depending upon age), houses, lots, billiard tables, pleasure carriages, pleasure horses, stallions, race horses, horned cattle, sales at auctions, warehouses, and retail shops. The act specifically noted that there would be no taxes on churches or schools.[28] Other laws Dunbar championed through to passage included An Act to Establish a Permanent Site of Justice for the District and County of Adams, An Act to Prevent the Evil Practice of Dueling, An Act Establishing the Fees of the Chief Justice and Registrar of the Several Orphans Courts in This Territory, An Act for the Relief of Creditors by Making Accommodation with Debtors, and An Act Making Further and More Official Provision for Establishing and Organizing the Militia of the Territory. Two acts that were special to Dunbar were An Act to Incorporate the Mississippi Society for the Acquirement and Dissemination of Useful Knowledge and An Act Empowering the Board of Trustees of Jefferson College to Elect New Trustees. His interests were many, including defense, suffering, education, taxes, and dueling—which he considered to be nothing less than sanctioned murder.

In the Mississippi Territory General Assembly, Dunbar could fight for laws he considered beneficial to cotton planters and people of wealth, and by serving on courts, he could enforce his definition of right and wrong and his own definition of justice. It would be inappropriate and unfair, however, to charge that Dunbar served as a justice of the peace, or even as a cotton gin inspector, out of self-interest alone. In a territory whose major staple was cotton, it was to almost everyone's benefit to produce, harvest, and export a product that was respected throughout the world. It was to the advantage of all for Dunbar to try to get creditors and debtors to solve money problems, to have a strong militia, and to keep in check all types of crime. By 1803, five years into the life of Mississippi Territory, only a few of Dunbar's land grants were still being challenged, and his name was uttered with respect in Philadelphia, in Liverpool, and at Monticello. By the end of 1803, his ability to secure the political friendship of Sargent and Claiborne, two quite dissimilar governors from different backgrounds and dispositions, had earned him not only success in most arenas but also the grudging respect of those who still claimed, albeit with softer voices, that he was an enemy in the Democratic-Republican camp.[29]

When the founding party would be out of office and out of favor after only two short years of governing, economic survival was not easy, but William Dunbar was able to survive, indeed thrive, during the years of inevitable political turmoil accompanying the birth of a territory and its government in a nation new and yet untested. When the Sargent years gave way to the Claiborne years, there were great changes in the territory, none of which Dunbar really opposed. Thomas Jefferson presented himself as a man of the people, whereas Alexander Hamilton, John Adams, and even George Washington were Federalists who believed that people were capable of great good if controlled and could generate great folly if not. They used the French Revolution and Jacobin excesses as proof of democracy gone mad. Jefferson, though he lived like a Renaissance prince at Monticello, believed in full involvement for all free white males in society, without pretensions. He wrote to James Monroe in March 1801 that "forms and ceremonies were to be set aside, and there were to be no privileges for one that another might not also enjoy."[30] In Mississippi Territory, the first general assembly was held on December 1, 1801; by the time it completed its labors, almost all laws were rewritten. Pickering County became Jefferson County, and in the following year mighty Adams County was split, the southern part becoming Wilkinson County (in honor of Democratic-Republican James Wilkinson). A new county north of Jefferson County was reorganized and named Claiborne County. The territory was, indeed, growing, and the Democratic-Republican stamp on it was never more evident than when Natchez was humbled—first in 1801, when Fort Dearborn was established in the small town of Washington, six miles from Natchez, and again in 1802, when the territorial capital was moved to Washington.[31] Dunbar approved all of these changes because new names and counties did not affect his life or lifestyle. After all, he lived in the country and had his own problems with haughty, self-satisfied Natchez.

By the time Claiborne left office and Robert Williams of North Carolina assumed the governorship in March 1805, Dunbar's interest in politics was waning. That Governor Williams stayed in North Carolina more than in Mississippi Territory did not bother Dunbar very much. As we know, he was busy experimenting with new cottonseeds, developing a press to bale cotton, tinkering with the cotton gin, exploring the Ouachita River and the hot springs, writing numerous articles for the *Transactions of the American Philosophical Society*, and trying to keep Mississippi's first college from dying. As Dunbar's areas of interest grew and his name became known across the region, he took little notice of occurrences affecting the territory: a band of cutthroats called the Kemper Gang was preying on travelers along the Natchez Trace; Aaron Burr was fomenting political chaos in the old Southwest; and legislators were expanding the suffrage.[32] In March 1809, David Holmes was appointed territorial governor, an event that theretofore would have elicited a great deal of attention from Dunbar, given his lifelong proclivity to befriend those in charge. If he had come to know Holmes better, perhaps they would have become friends. By almost any measure, David Holmes was the best governor Mississippi Territory had during its nineteen years of existence, and Dunbar admired him for his fairness and bipartisan leadership. The mild-mannered Holmes who guided the territory toward statehood was quite popular and well respected.

Except for the time he served as speaker of the legislature, 1803–5, William Dunbar was not a traditional politician, but his political skills were remarkable and critical to his success. His success might be termed a political wonder, especially since it was achieved by a man of science who claimed not to have any interest or expertise in either business or politics. His protestations have led some historians to accept his self-proclaimed dislike for politics and to dismiss his political record with little investigation of his disclaimer. Rowland wrote that Dunbar "never seemed to care for politics nor for political preferment, though all records show that he held the office as magistrate under Gov. Winthrop Sargent and rendered faithful public service in the beginning of the Commonwealth."[33] Even Andrew Ellicott wrote in 1798 that "Dunbar is never mentioned as a participant on either side" and in 1801 that "Mr. Dunbar writes to me that he has declined all publick business."[34] Yet Dunbar was a successful politician serving both territory and self. He arrived in America when colonists were deciding whether to support the crown or go with the resistance; he survived the tumultuous years of war and the period of changing government in the old Southwest, during which the leaders as well as the laws changed periodically. Few, if any, mastered more thoroughly the politics of survival and progress in that interesting yet complicated region during a period of constant changes than the scientist from Scotland, William Dunbar, and he did it in a way that appeared apolitical.

17

At Home

In many ways, Natchez, the town, and environs, including Second Creek, where the Dunbar family resided, mirrored William Dunbar the man. Natchez—and, indeed, early Mississippi—owed its persona to the territory's proximity to the Mississippi River and New Orleans, to its ability to handle ships coming and going on the river, and to its high-quality soil, warm weather, and relative isolation from Memphis, St. Louis, Louisville, and Pittsburgh to the north and east and New Orleans to the south. Natchez's location was tempered and flavored by French, English, and Spanish occupancy, Georgia foolishness, and the town's ability to remain above it all, aloof even from the Mississippi Territory it helped spawn. It was where folks came early, secured land, then welcomed others only if they could serve emerging plantations and cotton-related businesses. Natchez was not a place that shouted, "Y'all come." Perhaps the best chronicler of those times in Natchez was Thomas Rodney.

Rodney was a Mississippi failure who returned home to Delaware only to receive a generous political appointment from President Jefferson that afforded him an opportunity to return to Natchez and render successful service mediating land disputes. Rodney was a pleasant chap who enjoyed society and the good life, and in a remarkable journal he commented on all around him. He believed that a frontier outpost as well as an eastern metropolitan city could be measured by the "gentlemen" who lived there and more or less ran the town. He noted that in the early 1800s the Natchez area was ruled by thirty to forty gentlemen. The people (meaning the gentlemen and their families) were wonderful, the land was rich, and cotton had become the major crop in Mississippi Territory; corn and hogs were abundant, too, and would be more so if the price ever improved. He remarked that the town of Washington, the territorial capital, six miles from Natchez, was really a one-street town in the woods that was well located for pleasant living someday but was not a fit place for a capital.[1]

Rodney also remarked that by 1800 Natchez housed about two thousand families.[2] It was that population base that led Democratic-Republicans to believe that they need not put up with Winthrop Sargent's high-handed Federalist ways and to present a petition to Congress requesting second-level territorial status. Narsworthy Hunter, the territory's nonvoting representative to Congress, studied the petition before presenting it to Congress. Hunter was told that the governor had not authorized a formal census, but a conservative population estimate would suggest that by 1800 the territory had six thousand free male inhabitants, nine-tenths of whom were born in the United States. The problem Adams County had, suggested Cato West (the petition organizer), was that foreigners such as William Dunbar got to Natchez first with English land grants, which were reconfirmed by Spanish officials, who added Spanish land grants. That meant immigrants from other parts of the United States had to buy land from those already holding it, or they could go north and east in the territory onto rich lands grudgingly being ceded by the Choctaws, or, better still, they could go a few miles south into Spanish West Florida and take advantage of liberal Spanish land-granting policies. West and his Democratic-Republican friends who supported the petition pointed out that this was an interesting and unusual land circumstance: Americans had to go to Spanish West Florida, south of the thirty-first parallel, for land because American soil north of that line was held by foreign-born landholders, such as Dunbar and the Frenchman Peter Surget, along with the likes of Stephen Minor, an American long in sympathy with and in the employ of the Spanish. Unless a legislature was formed to represent the people in, among other things, challenging fraudulent Spanish land grants, there would be more out-migration than in-migration.[3] Though they accused Dunbar of currying favor with Spanish officials and thereby acquiring acres illegally, Dunbar's Democratic-Republican enemies could never make such charges stick, and nearly all challenges to grants he held were defeated. They could accuse; they could not convict.

By 1800, cotton had become a major crop in Mississippi, and one could expect to earn $1 per four pounds of clean cotton. Each active slave could yield from five hundred to eight hundred pounds at picking time, so slavery had expanded—there were now as many black as white inhabitants in the territory. By that year the territory was producing 3 million pounds of cotton each year, which brought in approximately $750,000 to planters and cotton-related businesses. A hungry market meant more production that, in turn, increased the number of slaves in the fields and dollars in the coffers.[4]

Observers of Natchez homes saw great similarities between West Indies and Natchez architecture, with balconies and piazzas that took advantage of both climate and view. They liked the small shops in Natchez run by free mulattos and French and Spanish creoles. They often mentioned "the great mixture of color of the people." They noted, too, that the streets were terrible, the high bluffs added a picturesque quality, and the activities in Natchez under the Hill were interesting. Often a diary would select one of the gentlemen as an example of life among the gentry in and around Natchez and would mention the size of his plantation tract, its gardens and orchards, and the quality of the homes: Oakland, Gloucester, the Forest.[5] Rodney stated that "every vegetable flourishes," that crime ran rampant after the Spanish left in 1798, and that for every gentleman there were many renegades.[6] He added with emphasis, though, that most citizens were good and were "animated by a firm active and energetic spirit of patriotism. . . . In fact this territory is the bulwark of the western country."[7]

People were as quick to point out bad qualities of the region as they were to note good ones. They spoke often of the yellow fever season, July to October—its relentless and contagious nature and the delirium and death it produced around the ninth day. Rodney believed that yellow fever came to the United States through New Orleans and swept up and down the Mississippi River.[8] After visiting Natchez, a British seaman complained about mosquitoes, alligators, and heat. He wrote, "Damn my precious eyes if I would not rather be at allowance of a moldy biscuit a day, in any part of Old England, or even New York, Pennsylvania, or Maryland than I would be obliged to live in such a country."[9] Most negative comments, however, were reserved for diseases and fevers encountered—and the abundance of liquor consumed everywhere.

As late as 1809, Washington was described as a small town of thirty scattered houses, one store, one drugstore, three taverns, and a jail, all on the same street.[10] Few liked Washington, and visitors were fairly split on Natchez—emphasizing, on the plus side, the diversity of its people, the view from the bluff, the presence of a hospital and a theater, and the quality of the land, and on the negative side, the heat, mosquitoes, and the fear of fevers that were frequently fatal.[11] A number of comments related to churches. Until 1798, during Spanish days, no Protestant churches were allowed in the area. Most of the Americans who migrated to Natchez were Protestants from the East, and some related lawlessness to the absence of churches. Many, including the Dunbars, supported a movement to build Protestant churches and "establish a settled Ministry."[12] Governor Claiborne did try to inculcate a respect for law, but until Dunbar helped to pass a law creating a militia, and until that militia was in place at Fort Dearborn in Washington, judges like Dunbar tried criminals and put them in flimsy jails, only to see the absence of funds to maintain or improve those jails lead authorities to impose fines and then grant pardons to prisoners.[13] One might contend that there was no more lawless spot in America in the first decade of the nineteenth century than the Natchez region, with thugs called the Mason Gang pillaging and killing along the Natchez Trace and criminals in town getting away with crimes ranging from theft to murder. At the same time, visitors and residents alike spoke of the beauty of the area and the opportunities the Mississippi River afforded for wealth, communication, and personal and business transportation.[14]

The Dunbar family thrived and lived comfortably among all their neighbors—Federalists, Democratic-Republicans, and those who supported neither party. Dunbar was much admired, even revered, as the turmoil of 1798 gave way to a decade in which his business interests improved yearly, as did his reputation as a scientist, educator, and explorer. The Dunbar family lived as well as any in the territory, and Dunbar bought only the best scientific instruments, carriages, linens, and liquor. He was one of a group of wealthy area planters who, in September 1804, ordered from France "1720 casks of Claret, 2400 bottles of St. Estephe Medoc, 15 pipes of brandy, sweet oil and bottles, Cambricks, 756 ells, Linen for sheets, 520 ells, Britapies, 1200 ells, 70 doz. men's white silk stockings, 18 gross white playing cards, 312 doz. kid gloves of assorted finishes, lengths, and colours, 96 reams of 'faint blue' common uncut paper, Wall paper of various kinds, including; 9 muses dark grounded, 209 boxes of soap (9544 pieces), and 44 Damas Jeans containing 902 soft shelled almonds." The total cost of these goods was 144,238.38 francs.[15] Records of goods ordered from stores in Natchez, New Orleans, Philadelphia, and overseas reveal that only the best goods were ordered for the Dunbar family. From Abijah Hunt's store in Natchez, Dunbar bought fifty-one yards of fine linen, one piece of coarse linen, a wool hat, and some fine tea. The total bill was 107.75 francs.[16]

Dunbar wanted the best, but he was well aware of cost and was always searching for a financial advantage. From John Vaughn in Philadelphia, he ordered a fine "coach for a family, for 4 grown persons & drawn by 2 horses." Dunbar wanted the coach to be handsome, well finished "with plated mounting but nothing gaudy or superfluous." He told Vaughn that his friend Stephen Minor wanted the same thing, hoping that ordering two coaches would lower the cost of each to $500–$600. He showed both his frugality and his patrician turn of mind when he added, "Maybe you can find one almost new and paint it up for me, as I presume it is not very fashionable among you republicans to have your coats of arms painted upon your carriages."[17] Dunbar repeated the remark, hoping that Vaughn would take the hint and paint the Dunbar Scottish coat of arms on the carriage, but not outright asking him to do so lest he offend Republican-Democratic principles. He did enjoy distinctiveness.

A fairly typical Dunbar negotiation story—and there are many—took place in 1806 when he wrote to Green and Wainwright in London telling them, at length, that he was considering seriously allowing their firm to sell that year's Dunbar cotton crop, despite that many other agents were offering tempting terms in the hope of winning the honor. Dunbar's reputation for honesty and high-quality cotton was such that the opportunity to sell his cotton was a privilege sought by many agents. After giving Green and Wainwright hope, he ordered a gold watch "to be made in its most perfect state" at a good price, as well as other articles, from a lady's breast pin to many pairs of cork-sole shoes for both men and women.[18] The relationship between winning the cotton contract and filling his order at a "good" and "fair" price was not lost on Green and Wainwright, and the firm got the cotton shipment that year. Throughout his life, Dunbar wanted value for money. He fought inflated invoices and dismissed forever businesses that tried to deceive him.

In 1806, Dunbar suffered a tragic business loss. In December, while attending a territorial supreme court session as a juror, he lost his cotton gin, millhouse, carriage, and all outbuildings to a fire. The loss included 300,000 pounds of cotton. Rodney estimated the loss at $16,000 to $20,000 and noted that such a loss would put many other planters out of business, but Dunbar, he wrote, "is very wealthy."[19] Indeed, Dunbar hardly mentioned the loss (he discussed the fire in only one letter), for he considered such as a part of life endured by planters living in a frontier society.

Despite illnesses—fever, loss of energy, and headaches—that seemed to recur frequently; extensive business and scientific activities; political, legal, and legislative activities of many kinds; Jefferson College duties as an administrator and trustee; and an expedition that lasted 103 days and required endless future work on journals, William Dunbar no longer neglected his wife and children. Love of family and constant hospitality are the hallmarks of many nationalities, but Scots are well known for their family ties, generosity of spirit, and eagerness to engage others, and William Dunbar was no exception.[20] His parents were recognized for their hospitality at both Duffus and Thunderton houses. Dunbar was well schooled in the art of entertaining and turning various occasions into opportunities to make new friends and discuss contemporary issues. It took a long time for a letter from Natchez to make its way to Philadelphia, to say nothing of London or his home-town, Elgin. When he left in 1771, Dunbar left behind a mother, brother, and sister he would never see or talk to again, except in letters that might not get there. He traveled a good deal in America between 1771 and 1792, the year he and his family finally occupied the Forest, but it was in a limited area up and down the Mississippi River. Dunbar's treks from Philadelphia to Pittsburgh, from there to Manchac, to Jamaica, to Pensacola, and back to Manchac were long. How many times did he travel from Manchac to New Orleans and back again, befriending merchants and Spanish officials, and how much time was spent traveling that route recovering from the sacking of his home in both 1778 and 1779? Once he inhabited the Forest, however, he seemed determined not to travel great distances again. It seems strange that he did not travel east to visit Andrew Ellicott and George Hunter, to meet the president of the United States whose correspondence he saved and treasured and who regarded him above most others. Would one not expect him to visit the American Philosophical Society—in whose journal he pub-lished a number of articles between 1803 and 1810—or to see his daughter in Philadelphia and his son at Germantown Academy? He did not undertake one single trip to enhance his name or enlarge his importance as a scientist or explorer. He stayed first in West Florida and then in Mississippi Territory, and never, as far as his correspondence indicates, contemplated an eastern or European trip. For one who supposedly craved recognition—a Dunbar logo on the family carriage and a red jacket in his official portrait—Dunbar labored at home, enjoyed his family, and with Dinah played the role of gra-cious and busy host in Mississippi Territory.

We would know little about Dunbar's family life had it not been for social butterflies such as Thomas Rodney, who seemed always to be here and there among high-society folks, officiating at marriages, delivering framed marriage certificates, and discussing who was in love with whom.[21] He opened the world of the Forest to those seeking glimpses of an impos-ing plantation home that later burned to the ground, never to be rebuilt. Rodney called the Forest "a perfect paradise," with rooms filled most of the year with flowers from colorful gardens. He commented that the Dunbar girls were beautiful, and they were splendid hostesses in a home that seemed to be perpetually used for entertainment on some level, whether honoring a visiting dignitary or hosting a wedding reception, a young people's gather-ing, or a pleasant evening of dinner and conversation with friends.[22] Rodney never tired of telling others that Dunbar was one of the wealthiest and most respected men in the territory. "He is hospitable and lives like a nabob," Rodney wrote.[23]

Many young men were said to be in love with the Dunbars' daughter Peggy, and Rodney acted as advisor to one would-be suitor (though he ultimately married her to another man). Rodney instructed the young man not to be so shy around Peggy. Alas, the young man never did make contact with Peggy and was never able to put Rodney's courting instructions to use. In 1802, young attorney James Dunlop came to Mississippi Territory. He met Peggy in 1803, courted her for two years, and married her at the Forest on September 14, 1806, with Thomas Rodney officiating. She was considered "the most eligible maiden in the territory,"[24] and the grand wedding and reception were fondly remembered for years to come by many in attendance. There were many weddings at the Forest during the first decade of the nineteenth century, and Dunbar and Dinah made each one special and memorable. On February 18, 1808, their son James married Elizabeth Bisland at the Forest, again with Rodney officiating, and again the local newspaper proclaimed the occasion as grand.[25] The only controversial marriage of a Dunbar offspring took place four months after Dunbar's death. The Surgets were a prominent Natchez area family. Peter Surget, a native of Rochelle, France, migrated to the Natchez District from New York in 1785, seven years before Dunbar took up residence there. Surget became eminently successful, but his son, Francis, a bit of a rake, was accused of raping Mary Ellis. Whether he was guilty was never determined by Natchez's slowly emerging court system, and the incident was hushed up. On March 9, 1811, Francis married the Dunbars' daughter Eliza—as the newspaper declared, "a woman of rich inheritance." Claiborne praised Peter Surget as the "most extensive and successful planter"; still, tongues wagged over this marriage.[26]

There is no way of knowing what Dunbar might have thought of this union. Over the years, he wrote little about his children, but he seemed to be as considerate as any father of that day. Perhaps the greatest tribute the Dunbar children bestowed on their father was the music they played, the quotes they passed along, and the tales they told for decades. Apparently, all Dunbar and Dinah required of their children was that they work hard, do their best at all endeavors, enjoy each other, and of course be frugal with their money.[27]

William Dunbar was not a self-deprecating man, but he was not self-aggrandizing either. He could have visited the White House and studied the architecture of that building, which was first occupied by Jefferson; he could have studied the evolving community architectural plan that would turn swampland into the nation's capital. Most likely he would have enjoyed the experience, and he might even have added an idea or two for consideration.

No one would have viewed his doing so as an effort to show others he knew leaders in high places. Yet Dunbar chose not to do so, not even to consider the possibility. He gained his visibility through published articles and success as a planter, plus other activities that naturally put his name in print, such as leading an expedition into southern Louisiana Purchase lands. At no time in his life did Dunbar add "Sir" to his name, even though he would not have minded having the Dunbar crest affixed to his family carriage.[28] In the latter case, he was showing pride in family history in Scotland; in the former case, he would have perpetuated an untruth that would dishonor his name and heritage. He was William Dunbar, son of Alexander and Anne Dunbar—period. He may have been a nabob in Rodney's eyes, and he did live at the top of the social chain, but he was republican enough to consider affectations unnecessary in a country that afforded all white males a chance at success.

What he did relish were his laboratory, gardens, orchards, views, inventions, family, and life at the center of the universe—Second Creek and the Forest. People visited and enjoyed themselves not only on special occasions now and again; the Dunbars entertained several times a week. Adults chatted, sipped, and dined; children played, romped about, visited with adults, and dined separately.

Christmas was a special time in the Dunbar home. While in New Orleans on business in late 1799, Dunbar wrote Dinah asking what special needs she had for the Christmas celebration that year. He would buy what she requested while in New Orleans and bring it up the river with him when he returned home. He wrote with his usual commentary on attention to frugality but mingled it with a joy of season and family: "Don't spare little things, all we have to do is avoid extravagance. So that anything to make your daughters fine, your table fine, are always approved, provided it does not produce vanity, but leaves us as it found us."[29]

Throughout his life, Dunbar kept commitments to rules and regulations for his slaves, for himself, and for his family. One episode with a humorous twist concerns a preacher's encounter with one of Dunbar's inventions. It cannot be verified by the Dunbar original source material I studied, but it is part of family lore and one that fits his personality. Supposedly, Dunbar invented the famous southern rotating fan for porch and house. Records show that he tinkered with such a fan, but there is no proof that he was the actual inventor. As legend has it, Dunbar installed a fan through the ceiling above the edge of their dining room table. A slave on the floor above slowly turned the fan and could move it up and down as well. Dunbar and Dinah often had a preacher to Sunday dinner, typically the minister who served the Forest church. By all accounts, Dunbar instructed ministers to keep the blessing to one minute. One Sunday a minister stood to offer the blessing just below the fan. When he kept praying after a minute had passed, upon a signal from Dunbar, the operator above dropped the level of the fan while still turning it, allowing a blade to knock the preacher in the head, rendering him unconscious. If this story is true, it is reflective of Dunbar's attention to instructions and shows that he could be a bit of a prankster, too.

Visitors to the Forest often commented on the gardens. One foreign visitor wrote that "the South is emphatically the land of flowers." He remarked that the southern United States was filled with trees of every odor and shape, and flowers—one kind or another—lasted most of the year. He continued that he had "visited a garden on a plantation which is the first in Mississippi and to which all others are more or less approximate. I would describe it could my pen do adequate justice." The guest wrote about casia, a creeping plant with a pink flower, boxwoods by the hundreds, and lofty shrubs bordered by diminutive hedges. He described a terraced walkway that ended at an artificial pond surrounded by flowers and shrubs. Around the pond were a number of diamond-shaped beds of violets "from which rose a cloud of fragrance." As he toured, he wrote about forests beyond the property, primeval in nature and feeling.[30]

A typical Sunday noon at the Forest might find three or four local officials dining with the Dunbars. By 1804, folks were calling Dunbar "old Mr. Dunbar" because William Jr. was growing into a fine young man and soon would be off to Philadelphia and prep school. After lunch, visitors might say that Dinah and William Dunbar "entertained superbly." Many guests did not leave at dinner's end but "stayed there all night"; it seemed all were "greatly pleased with [Dunbar] and his family." An observer stated that he received ten invitations to the Forest for every one he could accept. "Great friendliness & hospitality" were words used repeatedly.[31]

Again, we have Thomas Rodney to thank for insights into daily life at the Forest. Whenever he went—and that was frequently—he usually stayed at least two days and often more. Rodney wrote about daily life, which included much study time with the governess for all the children. In 1804, Rodney noted that although Dunbar was fifty-four years of age, his family was young. His children were seven or eight in number (he could never remember the exact number—it was nine), and their birth dates ranged from the time Dinah and Dunbar married twenty years earlier.[32] Though Dunbar was a formal person, the atmosphere at the Forest was informal after studies were completed. By 1804, the eldest daughter, Anne, was away at school in New Orleans, and the second daughter, Peggy, was fast becoming the belle of the territory.[33] Rodney remarked often about the friendliness of everyone in the family. By 1810, two young Dunbars had gone east to study in boarding schools and universities in Pennsylvania and New Jersey; they would miss their father's funeral. Dunbar would not have wanted them to neglect their studies just to attend his funeral; travel was such that they would have lost a whole semester in doing so. Rodney's parting comments as Dunbar was buried were how remarkable his family was, and how someone could "become wealthy in this country."[34] Both comments were offered as a way of praising a friend who was special and who shared himself with others.

While researching this work, I happened upon a series of Dunbar stories printed in an unpublished family journal called the "Forester," dated June 1844. The stories were based on Dunbar's custom of keeping "a sort of running account of what was going on at The Forest." They spoke of the continuing family tradition of entertaining often and with many different groups, discussing everything from ghost stories to rattlesnakes getting into the house, to church services at the Forest church, to the distinguished careers of the Dunbar sons (who pursued educational options as father instructed), and "the laughter and singing along the way." One short notation indicated clearly that fun and hospitality did not die when Dunbar did. The "Forester" noted a continuous parade of guests who came to the Forest. "They seemed to come from everywhere, the Dunbars have acquaintances & they come for many reasons and stay for a long time. Seems like an open house or an inn. This seems to be the normal for the Forest."[35] Indeed it was for sixty years, from 1792, when the Forest became the Dunbars' home, until fire destroyed property but not memories.

From the time Dunbar landed in Philadelphia in 1771, his correspondence, plantation and expedition journals, and notes contained references to illnesses that were never really identified. He wrote about fevers, colds, aches, and pains. Such infirmities usually put him to bed for a few days— the length was rarely stipulated in records—and there is nothing more about that illness until another notation indicates that he was working but with a fever or pain. There are no detailed notations on what was ailing him. The references were no worse when his feet were wet during much of the painful trip to and from the hot springs—approximately one thousand miles in all—than they were on the Manchac plantation, running the thirty-first parallel line, or home at the Forest. The references were constant and abbreviated, and Dunbar never seemed to describe life-threatening diseases, such as yellow fever or malaria. Rodney often included comments on Dunbar's health in his diary. One 1804 comment concerned killing a rattlesnake and taking it to Dunbar, who was studying snakes at the time. Rodney wrote that "Mr. Dunbar had not got well. Tho his fever had left him . . . he was still in bed awaiting Dr. Hunter" so they could get started on the Ouachita expedition adventure.[36] This was a typical situation for Dunbar—ill, in bed, a fever.

It became obvious that Dunbar was really ill when the *Mississippi Messenger* reported in 1808 that he had failed to pick up his mail at the Natchez post office, when for years he had been faithful in doing so. On January 18, there had been in his post office box twenty-four letters, and no one had been to the box since January 1. The article suggested that Dunbar might be gone, or busy, or sick.[37] He normally picked up his mail, or had someone check on his mail, daily, for he was too structured to do otherwise. Dunbar would never have gone nearly three weeks without checking his mailbox. He was not away, and he was always busy. This suggests, instead, that he was quite ill that month.

Dunbar recovered once again, but on July 2, 1808, he wrote to William Jr., at school in Philadelphia, that the family had lost their son and his brother, Tommy, who died on June 27 of an "ulcerous putrid sore throat." He continued by telling young Dunbar of the sorrow that had swept the whole family. "Your mama & sisters are greatly affected by this severe stroke of providence," he wrote, "and we know you will greatly lament the loss of so good and so promising a boy." He shared with the young man his fear that the infection was contagious and might spread to other members of the family, although thus far it had not. He closed the sad letter by advising his son to "take great care of your own health & run no risk by violent play or exercise in hot or wet weather to get yourself overheated."[38]

There is little doubt that the first decade of the nineteenth century was the most rewarding one in the life of William Dunbar. It is equally obvious, however, that the pace of his life since arriving in West Florida in 1773 was taking its toll on his health. Vacations were unheard of in his schedule. He had goals for his life; he lived according to those dreams and succeeded probably beyond his expectations. In setting a pace that would wear down the best of us, and by ever diversifying his interests and activities, he very likely shortened his life by several years. He died at age sixty in 1810. It is true that age sixty was old for the place and time in which Dunbar lived, but his friend Thomas Jefferson was born seven years before him and died sixteen years after him. Jefferson's desire to learn something new each day never waned. Dunbar's did not either.

18

The End of a Life

William Dunbar died on October 16, 1810, "the victim of a most af-
flicting malady."[1] In that time and place, the cause of death was seldom spelled out in medical terms unless it was smallpox, malaria, cancer,
yellow fever, or some other obvious illness. Dunbar died, I think, of inquisitiveness. He devoted each day of his majority to re-creating what he
would have had in Scotland had he been the firstborn son and, more important, satisfying his personal scientific curiosity about nearly everything. As a
youth, he tested dust in Morayshire and water in the Firth of Moray. As an
adult, he embraced North America and understood well its natural wealth
and potential for greatness. Dunbar never looked back; he never doubted
his goals; he allowed inquisitiveness to deny him rest, safety, holidays, and
periods of relaxation. The failure to pause physically and mentally took its
toll: it killed William Dunbar before his time. He may have had wet feet
every day of his historic 103-day journey to hot waters that baffled him
until death, but figuratively he had wet feet all of his life. He could not stop
studying, pondering, inventing, inquiring, and learning.

His son-in-law and close friend Samuel Postlewaite and wife, Dinah,
were his selected joint executors of his will.[2] They, especially Postlewaite, labored for six years settling the debts of a very orderly, organized man. Postlewaite had to settle accounts with at least eleven firms that served Dunbar's
business needs in, among other places, New Orleans, Philadelphia, New
York, London, and Liverpool. They purchased goods on behalf of the Dunbar family; handled legal matters; shipped cotton and other commodities
to the East, the Indies, and Europe; and advised on financial options. Correspondence for decades with agents such as Green and Wainwright, Chew
and Relf, and John Vaughn fill Dunbar's letters and journals, in addition to
saved bills and receipts.[3] These records tell a story of a man who imported

and exported constantly at a time when doing so was expensive, agonizingly time consuming, and extremely confusing. Often what was ordered in January would not be received until the next January, or later.

Dunbar's business practices were more complicated because he used many different agents for various services. He shipped bale upon bale of cotton to Liverpool through New Orleans and Philadelphia, sold it at a pre-arranged price, and seldom took cash alone for the transaction. Along with every shipment, Dunbar sent a list of goods he wanted in return—always at a good price—and he left with his agents a sum of money to be used to fill future orders when cotton was not shipped while the remaining cash was shipped to him or, more likely, to John Vaughn in Philadelphia or Chew and Relf in New Orleans. Seldom did cash or money drafts go from Manchester or Liverpool, through several hands on different boats, all the way to St. Catherine's landing and the Forest. Money was moved about like so many chess pieces, and it took a financial acumen such as Dunbar's to keep up with what was where. Now the unraveling of all those records fell into the lap of Samuel Postlewaite.

Postlewaite was not only the husband of the eldest Dunbar daughter, Anne, but also a successful businessman-planter and friend of Dunbar and Dinah. By the end of October 1810, he was writing to all agents and other known creditors informing them of Dunbar's death, thanking them for past service, and unscrambling business transactions while asking for bills due and the status of current accounts. He told them also that "Mrs. Dunbar is joining me in the desire to extinguish every just claim against the estate."[4] The task was almost a full-time job—one that Postlewaite undertook willingly because of the love he felt for his in-laws. Shortly after Dunbar's death, he wrote Dinah, "My heart has already been melted so often."[5]

Serving as the executor of the Dunbar will was time consuming for Postlewaite because of problems not with longtime and trusted agents but with others to whom debts were owed and, more especially, those who contacted Postlewaite with bills he knew nothing about and could not confirm. Postlewaite was a fine business and agriculture student of Dunbar, and he handled the payment of debts only after careful scrutiny of provable data. When contacting known debtors, Postlewaite wrote the person or firm, informing them that the estate wanted to settle known debts and requesting a bill with a list of payments already made by Dunbar and the exact amount still due. He promised to study the bill carefully to verify Dunbar's purchase and the amount necessary to close the account. Then, and only then, did the executors pay the bill. Postlewaite stated, "I will endeavour to satisfy myself from an examination of the deceased's papers," and he did just that.[6]

Postlewaite was no pushover trying to bring about a quick settlement of the estate. If he asked for a bill and one was not forthcoming in a reasonable time, he wrote interesting reminders. One stated, "I am bound by my respect for the deceased's memory and in justice to his estate, to bring again to your notice" the amount due or the need for a bill. If he thought someone was testing his attention to detail or was seeking more than was due, he might write, "Your mode of calculating interest is a ruinous one to the unfortunate debtor";[7] then he would refigure the interest and send the amended amount, noting that the debt was now paid in full.

William Simmons of the War Department requested an accounting of government supplies still stored at St. Catherine's landing from the 1804–5 expedition and the one scheduled for a year later. Postlewaite dutifully gave a listing, noting what should be reclaimed by the military and what should be discarded.[8] When Dinah Dunbar ordered goods, Postlewaite handled those matters through agents he was hoping to discharge as quickly as possible.[9] He even took the occasion to serve as surrogate father to the young Dunbar children, advising them on the need to be frugal in life. While William Jr. was away at school in Philadelphia, Postlewaite wrote, "I will not my dear Dunbar preach about economy," and then offered a written lecture on economy. He wrote also, "Check your ardor and industry in pursuit of your studies."[10] Regardless of their ages, Samuel kept all of the Dunbar children, and Dinah, up to date on his efforts to settle William Dunbar's estate.

An additional executor's chore handled by Samuel Postlewaite had to do with the estate of Dunbar's best friend, Alexander Ross. As mentioned earlier, Alexander died four years earlier than Dunbar, on July 18, 1806, and Dunbar was appointed executor of Alexander's estate. Upon Dunbar's death in 1810, Postlewaite assumed the completion of the work. As the executor of Ross's estate, Dunbar was to settle all of his accounts, sell all of his property, and see that the proceeds were forwarded to Ross's kin in Elgin, Scotland. The Ross family was not known to Dunbar in Scotland, but the family's admirable work habits had impressed Dunbar's father. On November 7, 1810, Postlewaite wrote to Sir Archibald Dunbar, Dunbar's nephew in Elgin who now owned the Dunbar estates, that he would be sending to him 5,000 pounds sterling to be given to James Ross for distribution among Ross family members as James saw fit.[11]

What further complicated matters for Postlewaite was that cotton shipped in 1808 and 1809 was, in some cases, still in transit, and the 1810 crop had only cleared or was clearing New Orleans on its way to Philadelphia and Liverpool when Dunbar died. Postlewaite wrote to Chew and Relf on November 5, 1810, that he had just sent down the Mississippi River to

New Orleans by flatboat 105 bales of cotton to be added to the 350 bales already in New Orleans awaiting shipment. Chew and Relf were instructed to insure all in the usual way and then send the bales on Liverpool.[12] Cotton agents could not be discharged, however, while cotton was still being raised on the Dunbar plantations and shipped to Liverpool. What Postlewaite wanted was to settle Dunbar's accounts through 1810[13] and secure the right for William Jr., as the eldest son, to decide whether to retain all or some of the agents. In his will, Dunbar gave two of his plantations to his four sons, but they could not assume control until the will had been fully executed. Therefore, there was a great deal of correspondence between Postlewaite and all agents in 1811–16 as he tried to complete his duties as executor. Most debts were handled within two years; cotton lingered on. The payment of all just debts was formally completed and accepted by the probate court of Adams County on August 28, 1816, when the court authorized the formal listing of the remaining assets for distribution. The court concluded, "We do grant, and commit unto Samuel Postlewaite and Dinah Dunbar the administration of all . . . in the will." They were charged to "file in the Registrar's office of this Court a true and perfect inventory thereof within three months from this date and render a just account of their Executorship when thereto legally required."[14]

In many ways, paying debts took less time than inventorying and determining the worth of all property, including land, plantation homes and other buildings, town lots, slaves, and scientific equipment. Dinah and Dunbar were married in 1784, when he was thirty-four and she was fifteen. They had nine children, four girls and five boys: Anne, born in 1786; Margaret (Peggy), born in 1788; Eliza, born in 1791; Helen, born in 1796; William, born in 1793; Archibald, born in 1796; Thomas, born in 1801; Robert, born in 1803; and Alexander, born in 1806. Eight of the children were alive when Dunbar passed on in 1810.[15]

Dunbar's will stipulated that the two plantations, along with their slaves, were to be equally divided among the four boys. Margaret and her family lived on one half of another plantation, River Place, and she was to be allowed to keep that half; Eliza, when she married, could live on the other half of that plantation. When Helen married, she would be given a plantation of 450 acres at Bayou Pierre. Dunbar willed to Dinah the right to live in the major house at the Grange plantation if she married a second time. If not, she could remain at the Forest throughout the remainder of her life. On the days of their marriages, both Eliza and Helen were to be given ten slaves each—eight to work in the fields, one to do domestic labor, and one (around fourteen years of age) to be taught to be a waiter. William Jr. was to get all of the chemical, astronomical, and philosophical apparatus (hoping he would make good use of it, Dunbar noted); Dinah was to get all of his electrical machines, microscope, and other instruments to be "dispensed of as she shall think fit." Dunbar reiterated that the dispensation decisions of Dinah and "my very dear friend" Samuel Postlewaite were final.[16]

For a man as exact and precise as Dunbar, the will was quite general. The children would have to get together to determine who got what, and they did so without rancor. Maybe the amiability with which the eight children went about splitting assets had to do with the fact that they were still young. The oldest was Anne at twenty-four, and only one other, Margaret, was beyond the teen years. The four boys who inherited plantations with slaves were four, seven, twelve, and seventeen. Yet age may not have had a great deal to do with the feeling they had for each other, for Dinah and Dunbar had raised a family that looked out for one another. The classes with tutors; the field trips with a scientist father pointing out grasses, trees, and water; the free run of their home, even with guests about; and the care and love of parents who truly belonged together really made a difference. Each child began life by entering a loving and caring family, and the affection one had for the others continued throughout their years, even after they bought land in Kentucky,[17] Louisiana, Arkansas, and other parts of Mississippi. The thread tying the family together never broke as distances expanded.

By January 1825, the family had made some determinations. First, Dunbar owned four plantations—the Forest, the Grange, Hedges, and River Place. Add to that all of the slaves, stock, farming utensils, books, and various other items. All would be divided equally among the four sons. Second, the balance of the real property—lots and land—would be divided equally among all heirs. Third, the four male heirs must set aside a stipulated fifty-four acres of wooded land and then hire two appraisers to determine the value of all the land and slaves, but not stock, on the four plantations. Fourth, an heir who got real property with debt attached could sell or exchange that property with another heir or sell it to other possible purchasers. Fifth, once an heir accepted a portion of the estate, he or she was responsible for it thereafter.[18] The Dunbar children decided on this division of assets on January 17, 1825, and their wishes were accepted in court two days later. They sought agreement and court ratification quickly for two reasons: "For the purpose of avoiding any interference of strangers, and to prevent the costs & expenses of legal proceedings."[19]

The appraisers were hard at work legally defining what belonged to William Dunbar and then evaluating each portion of each piece one at a time. For example, they valued various kinds of land at different per-acre amounts: they looked separately at the acres for cultivation, the acres around the house and quarters, cleared land versus wooded land, and upper land versus low land that tended to flood.[20] Finally, in the March 1828 term of Adams County probate court, the court accepted the final accounting of the Dunbar estate. It accepted that there was a total of $85,701.69 in debts, all of which had been paid in full. It verified that Samuel and Anne Postlewaite (she replaced her husband as executor upon his death) were paid $119,137.83 for executor duties performed since 1810 and that the appraisers and accountants were paid a total of $187,394.16 for services rendered.[21] It had taken eighteen years to reach this final settlement; if the heirs had been contentious and unwilling to share equally, the settlement on holdings so diversified, purchased from or granted by English West Florida, Spanish West Florida, and the United States, could have remained in court decades longer.

It is hard to imagine what William Dunbar's story might have been without his wife, Dinah. From the year of their marriage until they relocated from Manchac to Natchez District, Dunbar was gone as many as ten months a year, leaving Dinah behind to resurrect a looted plantation, manage slaves, diversify crops, complete experiments, and raise a family. Their daughter Anne (named for Dunbar's mother) was born a year after their marriage, and Margaret (named for Dunbar's sister) two years later. In all, three girls were born to Dinah and William Dunbar during those difficult years, to a woman herself only sixteen to twenty-two years of age. Dunbar hardly saw the girls and mentioned them only in closing letters to Dinah filled with instructions and additional chores. When the family moved to the Forest, Anne was five years old, Margaret three, and Eliza only months old. During the three years they lived in the carriage house at the Forest, Dinah planned and oversaw the construction of a kitchen while Dunbar supervised the building of his laboratory and library. In short, following the customs of that day, Dinah tended to family matters, supported greatly by domestic servants she respected and appreciated. During those carriage house years, William Jr. was born, giving Dinah additional responsibilities while her husband went back and forth to New Orleans, absenting himself from home as he chased a dream constructed nearly forty years past.

After William Dunbar's death, Dinah, at age forty-one, retired into herself for more than a year, a length of time that worried the children. Still, she was too active to mourn forever, and she had a large family to raise. During his lifetime, Dunbar was always puttering and constantly improving the Forest. Though the plantation home was large enough for his family, Dunbar was forever trying out new things, and he dreamed of adding dormer windows just under the roof line on all four sides of the home, as well as building a captain's walk with a seating area on the roof so that he and Dinah could sit, sip their Madeira, and view their holdings, their fields, and their next possible acquisition. Dunbar made plans for the dormer windows and the positioning of the walk and seating area, but little construction was done. When Dunbar died, work on the project slowed considerably because workers were not sure of Dinah's intentions. Finally, Dinah decided that she would fulfill Dunbar's dream for the home he loved, and she directed and worked the men as hard as Dunbar ever did. In went dormer windows and as fine a captain's walk as anyone had ever seen. Dinah was a sight to see, sitting on a comfortable bench on that walk atop her home with columns on all four sides, looking out on property that surrounded the house as far as the eyes could see. As historian Harnett Kane wrote, "Here the widow knew good years, watching her estate prosper, the children marry well."[22]

Dinah Dunbar died at the Forest on November 15, 1821, at the age of fifty-two. She was the one who had nurtured the children and guided them into adulthood, while helping turn the Forest into a plantation home that frequently welcomed guests who admired and respected her. She deserves a biography of her own, for she gave lie to the image of well-manicured, upper-class southern women who waved hankies and looked beautiful behind fans while doing little else and leaving all of the work to domestic help. Indeed, Dinah scrubbed floors, and so did the children; she helped make meals and put flowers in all rooms. The family appears little in this biography because of the youth of the children and the fact that none were rascals to be scolded or bailed out of jail. Apparently, they learned from Dunbar and Dinah, talented tutors, and hardworking slaves who taught them to appreciate learning and work before they were sent to prep schools or colleges. All later returned home to marry and make lives in the South.

I remember well, long years ago, searching for the right dirt road in Second Creek that would take me to the remains of the Forest. What I saw in 1960 when first I ventured to the site were abandoned orchards and gardens, a vine-covered family grave, and still-sturdy massive columns reaching toward the sky. I could envision the orchards, pond, and gardens. My mind's eye could see the forests, and I could almost see children running about, slaves bringing beauty from the earth, and adults living a life that few others were living at that time.

I recall the delight of meeting Marian Patty, a descendant who lived in the carriage house. I remember too our decision to clean up the long-neglected Dunbar family graveyard. I probably did not swing at those vines, weeds, and cane nearly as long as I remember doing, but I got to see work-men bring to life a patch of ground holding the remains of William Dunbar, Dinah, and several of their children, grandchildren, and great-grandchildren as well. The graveyard faced what had been the Forest and its gardens, and I could not help but think that it was somehow unbefitting for one of Mis-sissippi Territory's first families to be cited in textbooks yet nearly forgotten by a state that knows and cherishes history. I sat in that cemetery and copied the words on each of the tombstones, and I reread them again from time to time. I cherish the simple words on Dinah's tombstone: "In Memory of Dinah Dunbar, Consort of the late Wm. Dunbar." It includes dates of birth and death. I like the word "consort." Though it has several meanings, consort meant then what it means today: partner. She was, indeed, William Dunbar's partner, and she deserves that recognition.

While following the trail of Dunbar's last will and testament from the initial reading to its execution eighteen years later, one cannot help but note, even in passing, the growth of children and grandchildren into contribut-ing adults. I sat on the stone border of that small cemetery with twenty-five graves, including those of four Dunbar children—Thomas, Alexander, Margaret, and William Jr.—and I tried to determine if they, too, had a plan for life, a personal mission. One of Dunbar's Scottish professors advised him in 1769 about living and dying. He wrote, "The prospect of Death . . . is a gloomy prospect at best, but to have it always in view would of course embitter all the sweets of life."[23] That advice reflects Dunbar's creed—know that death awaits you but give life your all for so long as breath is in you. He had a plan; he adhered to that plan; and he crafted a life even he could not have predicted as he sailed westward to America.

America has a way of giving us one great man or woman per family, not often followed by succeeding generations also securing the elusive good fortune. There was one George Washington, Thomas Jefferson, Abraham Lincoln, and Franklin and Eleanor Roosevelt, but no others from each line. Yes, there was a stream of successful members of the Adams family, but such a tradition is not often duplicated in this land of opportunity, individual-ity, and diversity. William Dunbar was unique. Generational greatness was not the hallmark of the Dunbars in Scotland, nor was it to be in the land Dunbar claimed and loved during tumultuous but exciting years. William Jr. became a doctor, but he did not have the scientific inquisitiveness of his father. Dunbar left him most of his astronomical equipment in the hope that it would awaken a dormant scientific inquisitiveness in his eldest son.[24] Apparently, it did not. A grandson, Field Dunbar, attended Princeton and was described by family as "a good math student like his father & grandfather," but he ended his college career thirty-third in a class of forty-nine.[25] That would not have pleased Dunbar.

The Dunbar children were good people who strayed only short distances—to Arkansas, Louisiana, and Pennsylvania—but they were mainly planters without a scientific interest, honest businessmen who simply wanted to accumulate, citizens who were respected but not emulated. They seemed not to wonder what was over that far hill or around that always-elusive corner. One son, Robert, was a self-proclaimed humanitarian and a founder of the American Colonization Society.[26] The society, founded in 1819, was dedicated to ending slavery in this country. Its stated goal, however, was to send slaves to Liberia, a country from which none of them came. The slaves of the second decade of the nineteenth century were the descendants of those whose enslavement had begun centuries earlier. None of the slaves in the fields of 1820 came from Liberia or had any holdings there to start life anew, and few were clamoring to go to a continent they had never known. Yes, they wanted freedom, but here in America, not in a new country on some faraway continent that was no longer home. The ending of slavery was a noble goal, but sweeping slavery under the rug by returning blacks to Africa as if they had simply been borrowed since the sixteenth century was a ridiculous notion that would have heaped hardship upon hardship already too heavy to bear.

In his will, Robert left his entire library to Jefferson College and all of his property, including slaves, to his wife, Elizabeth, to do with as she would. If he survived Elizabeth, he would leave his property to Robert Dunbar Jr., who, at his own death, would turn all slaves over to the American Colonization Society "for the purpose of transporting said slaves to the colony in Liberia in Africa."[27] If Robert had freed his slaves during his lifetime, one could call him a humanitarian. His will does not lead one to that conclusion.

Decades later, Virginia Dunbar McQueen would write in her valuable journal of her grandfather William Dunbar, "He died in Natchez at the forest in 1810, aged sixty-one years. Buried in the Dunbar graveyard, his resting place was marked by shafted marble bearing this inscription: 'Sacred to the memory of William Dunbar of the Forest. A native of Scotland, son of Sir Archibald Dunbar of Thunderton Hall, Elgin. His wife laments a tender husband, his children an affectionate parent, his friends a valuable acquaintance, science a distinguished notary.'"[28]

19

The Legacy

Was William Dunbar a great American? If diversity of interests and inquisitiveness are the yardstick, he certainly was extraordinary. If recognition beyond his lifetime is the yardstick, he was not. But Dunbar certainly deserves recognition for the quality of his astronomical calculations at the thirty-first parallel in 1798, for his achievements as a scientific explorer, for his part in founding a college, for his significant scholarly contributions to the American Philosophical Society, for his improvements in the taking of longitude, and for his remarkable political skills.

And then there was cotton. There can be no question about the leadership role Dunbar played in making cotton a significant product in the old Southwest and elsewhere. In that effort, he determined the staple for Mississippi for decades to come. The seed, the weather, the soil, and the Mississippi River, plus the demand for high-quality cotton in Britain, made the Natchez region a perfect place for cotton planting, harvesting, and exportation on a grand scale, and from the beginning Dunbar recognized that opportunity.

The growth of cotton as a crop in Mississippi Territory can be viewed both positively and negatively. As demand increased for cotton, the price went up, and more and more cotton was planted. To make planting and exporting of cotton work economic wonders for the planter, there needed to be a plentiful supply of cheap labor. For that reason, the institution of slavery that had plagued America—particularly the South—since the seventeenth century was enhanced by the emergence of cotton as the staple. After the success of the colonies in the American Revolution, slavery had appeared to be waning. The words "life, liberty, and the pursuit of happiness" were taken seriously as southern Americans reconsidered the economic value of slavery. Leaders such as Washington, Franklin, Paine, Jefferson, Adams, and Hamilton saw slavery as a failed and shameful system soon to vanish in an America founded on the principle of freedom. Historians have argued for generations over the contention that slavery might soon have disappeared—one can argue convincingly either way—but there is no doubt that the emergence of cotton as the staple of the lower South, where warm weather came early and stayed late, reversed any movement toward ending this shameful practice.

As one who has studied Dunbar's life and admired his ethical principles, I am surprised at his failure ever to criticize the institution of slavery and his willingness to punish slaves severely. He seldom wrote kindly about a slave—even those tending his wife and children—and he never freed one for meritorious service. By the standards of the time, Dunbar did not mistreat slaves, nor did he impose upon them cruel rules to obey. He just did not treat them as fellow human beings.

Throughout decades of research on this remarkable man, I have tried to understand his unqualified acceptance of an institution other educated southern men questioned during the period of his rise to economic power. Clues allow the door to understanding to open a bit, but only a bit. Dunbar's personality was fashioned very much by his mother rather than his father. Dunbar was born to Scottish aristocracy. The family was recognized and respected throughout the land, especially in the northeastern part of the country; their lineage goes back to medieval times. Dunbar's three elder half-brothers acted like normal gentry youngsters who needed not work for a living. They played, caroused, and simply awaited majority and family responsibilities, with the eldest succeeding to their father's titles and lands upon his death. Dunbar's experience was different. From the day he was born, his mother preached studies and scholarship—that which family name made possible. Quite unlike his half-brothers, Dunbar was a loner, and he shunned carousing in favor of research, contemplation, and scholarship.

What he did with his youth was as admirable as it was unusual, but one reviewing the life of William Dunbar should not confuse any of his habits with democracy or a love for people. As much as, if not more than, his brother and half-brothers, Dunbar was an aristocrat of the gentry class. He and his mother knew that he had the opportunity to stretch and test his mind because he did not have to plant seeds in overworked soil or live in a hovel. Dunbar lived in two beautiful homes in and around Elgin, and he liked doing so; he was an aristocrat who knew that he probably would lose everything when his father died. I do not believe that he studied as hard as he did, and led his class at King's College, simply to prepare himself for an effort to recoup losses after primogeniture deprived him of home. Records do not show that he harbored such notions growing up. Neither did Dunbar study so that his learning would help others. He appears to have felt no empathy for the peasants who labored in Dunbar fields; he never even mentioned them. As far as I could determine, Dunbar never gave a thought to the less fortunate. He wore his standing in society as a badge that rightly belonged to him. Dunbar was the firstborn son of a mother from the lower English gentry class who was fortunate enough to marry an aristocrat, and she knew very well the opportunities that marriage brought to herself and her children.

There is no doubt that Dunbar came to America to become a member of the gentry class in agricultural colonies owned and controlled by Britain. It was a land of opportunity seen clearly by his mother—a land that welcomed an immigrant who was willing to work hard for the economic progress that was possible on abundant land not worn out by years of constant cultivation. It was upon that land that Dunbar would build what ancestors before him had built in Scotland. His goal was not just success; it was gentry-class status—the top of the mark back home and in America. Hence the Forest: the ultimate American symbol of standing. Dunbar did not believe that anyone was going to hand him success simply because he was the product of the gentry class in a European country. Instead he worked hard over a long time for the success he craved, never altering his goal despite hardships and major setbacks. He was driven; he was committed.

What made possible Dunbar's dream of entering a new American aristocracy in the South shaped by the Britain he knew and loved was the institution of slavery—cheap labor to work rich and plentiful land. Dunbar never openly questioned his sense of entitlement, which rested upon the backs of peasants and slave labor. For nearly four exciting decades, which saw the birth of a new nation, Dunbar apparently remained oblivious. In his correspondence and journal about life in English and Spanish West Florida between 1773 and 1791, he never questioned in any way the institution of slavery, the allocation of land based on the number of slaves available to work that land, or the morality of one individual's enslaving another. I suppose I should not have been surprised by the absence of any defense for or criticism of slavery by Dunbar, for it was not his style to debate issues based upon nonscientific arguments. He was interested in finding answers to questions using natural law and scientific evidence. Is there a better way to measure longitude? What seeds will yield the best cotton crop in the old Southwest? How can we better bale cotton? What grows best along this river? What subjects should be included in a broadly based college curriculum? Is there something over that hill or around the bend that will answer a question that has stumped me for years? William Dunbar was the consummate mathematician-scientist who believed that the answers to hard, black-and-white scientific questions would both satisfy his curiosity and benefit society in some undefined way.

As an inquiring scientist, Dunbar sought answers to questions that both interested and puzzled him. The moral or ethical side of a question, if there was one, was of minor interest to him. Often, however, his inquiries did benefit society. For example, his journal notes regarding sick slaves and his postmortem study of them led to a better understanding of stomach blockage problems and, probably, efforts to save sufferers. Dunbar's efforts to help settle honorably the thirteen-year thirty-first parallel line disagreement between Spain and the United States relieved future local squabbles between settlers, thereby saving lives. Dunbar should also be credited with the lives he helped save by paying to inoculate all in the Mississippi Territory who would allow it during the 1802 smallpox epidemic. His improvements in cotton baling saved the lives of many slaves doomed to die by previous inhumane baling practices. Dunbar's inquiries helped move society forward; his discoveries benefited a young, expanding nation, as did his generous acts. Yet these advances—and there were many—were the positive results of other aspirations, economic fulfillment, unquestioned social status, and an uninterrupted outlet for an inquiring mind. Seldom in life does one achieve all of one's dreams; Dunbar came close. Seldom does one, in a single generation, create a legacy that endures for most of a century; Dunbar did. Seldom does a new immigrant capture much of a nation's intellectual attention; Dunbar lived to walk intellectually with a president and other leading scientists in the early years of a fast-growing new country, and he came to earn and enjoy respect for his many contributions.

Was America better off for William Dunbar's having come its way? Absolutely. He was a scientific pioneer in a nation boasting few others. He accepted American citizenship in 1798 and never dishonored that allegiance or yearned again for British or Spanish rule. Dunbar became an American in every way one wants to define that word, and he worked hard for the improvement of a region of the new nation as its boundary moved slowly westward.

Still, after uncovering the details of Dunbar's life and attempting to assess his standing among others who lived during that age, I admit to being unable to draw a conclusion as to his historical significance. Dunbar is not easy to assess because he was not one dimensional. He led the old Southwest and Mississippi Territory in fields as varied as surveying, architecture, gardening and horticulture, exploring, inventing, planting, scientific inquiry, politics, education, and public service, and he was considered the most valuable regional contributor in all those fields by friends and foes, a president, and members of the American Philosophical Society. By any evaluation criteria, William Dunbar emerges as the most important contributor who labored and prospered in British and Spanish West Florida and Mississippi Territory.

Dunbar lived in a region with few people—a section little known by most Americans—where it was easier to be the best, the most admired. Still, living far away from the great centers of scholarship offered challenges not faced by East Coast scientific colleagues with libraries and laboratories close at hand. To allow location to be the yardstick is not only unfair, it is also foolhardy. New regions, particularly ones as rich as Mississippi Territory, attract the adventurous and talented, not the unmotivated. Warm climate, fine soil, a staple in demand, and cheap labor completed a magnet that attracted those to whom opportunity meant real possibilities and possibilities meant potential success. The Adams County of the first decade of the nineteenth century was no place for one without vision; it was made for risk taking. It was made for William and Dinah Dunbar.

Mississippi, as is true of all fifty states, has produced many significant Americans in myriad fields. It is tempting to compare one with another, and to suggest that a successful forerunner like Dunbar is among the top five, the top ten, or the top fifty contributors Mississippi has produced. I choose not to play that game, mainly because it is impossible to compare a writer with a political leader or an opera singer, or a Choctaw leader with a scientist, or someone living and contributing in 1803 with another in 1961. It is possible, however, to evaluate success among those living, let us say, during Mississippi Territory years, and when one does, William Dunbar emerges as a genuine American success story in many fields of interest. The Mississippi that gained statehood in 1817 was built upon a foundation forged during territorial days, and it is important to evaluate those who led during those exciting and important years. That historical examination shows clearly that William Dunbar stands tall among peers who also contributed much to forming that foundation.

As I evaluate the many dimensions of Dunbar's successful life, I am convinced that his most significant accomplishment was his journey to the hot springs, despite that it was an afterthought when the major Red-Arkansas rivers venture was scrapped. At age fifty-four, Dunbar did not have to accept Jefferson's challenge to lead that expedition into the unknown, with dangers lurking, to study the mystery of the hot springs of Arkansas. He had to put his fragile health and life on the line to make that trip. He could not do otherwise. He had to explore the unknown; he had to evaluate that which had not yet been discovered. Moreover, he was willing to do the same thing the next year, and the year after that, thereby separating himself from all other satisfied and successful planters enjoying the bounty that was theirs. The acceptance of that opportunity to explore made all the difference in Dunbar's life. It served also as advice, both to contemporaries and to future generations: do not allow economic success to dampen the curiosity and imagination that make success possible. "Live with curiosity all your days" would appear to be Dunbar's legacy, for to him nothing was as special as an inquiring mind. The cost of inquiry may be death, as it has been for many through the ages. The need to know and the willingness to suffer in pursuit of knowledge elevate William Dunbar to the first rank of late-eighteenth- and early-nineteenth-century American contributors. It is not possible to appreciate fully the evolution of Mississippi Territory without understanding the role played by William Dunbar.

Postscript

A Note on the History of the Forest Plantation in Natchez

It would be difficult, if not impossible, to overstate the significance of William Dunbar's home, the Forest, to the story of his life; indeed, throughout this book, I, along with various other historians, Dunbar's descendants, Dunbar himself, guests of the Dunbars, and an assortment of authors writing during Dunbar's lifetime, have made reference to the Forest as reflective of Dunbar's values, mission, and place in society. In every case, it was assumed that there was only one mansion built on the plantation.

Early in my research for this work, I journeyed to Second Creek, Mississippi, and met Dunbar descendant Marian Patty, who lived in the carriage house on the grounds of the Forest. Patty showed me around the remains of the fabled plantation and confirmed my understanding that the dwelling had burned to the ground in 1852.

After this work had gone to press, however, historian Elbert Hilliard, director emeritus of the Mississippi Department of Archives and History, recalled something about there having been two houses built on the Dunbar plantation. Consultation with Mimi Miller of the Historic Natchez Foundation, as well as Miller's subsequent review of the work of the late Alma Carpenter, substantiated the claim that there were, indeed, two houses built on the plantation, the second built by Dinah Dunbar after William Dunbar's death. I am most appreciative to Hilliard and Miller for calling this to my attention and to the University Press of Kentucky for allowing me to append this brief note to the manuscript.

The following records support the premise that there were two houses built on the Forest plantation. Perhaps the earliest account is found in an 1817 letter from William and Dinah's son Archibald to his mother: "So I shall never see the old mansion again! I certainly have a great attachment to the house I was born in and the back room I have had so many frolics in. But as I suppose it necessary for a new one to be built I shall not repine."

Two grandsons-in-law also left written records indicating that Dinah Dunbar built the fabled mansion at the Forest. Dr. John C. Jenkins, grandson-in-law of Dinah Dunbar, recorded in his diary on January 13, 1852, that the house had burned and that another had been "erected by my wife's grandmother."

It would appear, then, that the references to the Forest written before Dunbar's death in 1810 were describing the original plantation house, designed by William Dunbar himself. The first house, built in the early 1790s, was described by the ornithologist Alexander Wilson as "a big square white plantation house deep in the oak woods. . . . The plantation was not elaborate, but it was spacious. . . . The veranda of the plantation house . . . stood one floor above the ground." Wilson's description indicates that the 1790 house was frame and painted white, with a veranda (full-width porch). The reference to the veranda standing "one floor above the ground" indicates that the frame house rested on a raised brick basement story.

We might suggest, then, that the Dunbars' first house, as described by Wilson, would have been no more impressive than many early plantation houses in the lower Mississippi Valley. Still, the earlier house must also have been quite spacious, since records suggest that the Dunbars entertained often and in an elegant fashion. A newspaper cited herein termed the Forest a "princely estate . . . a mansion," and we know from Dunbar's papers that he landscaped the formal gardens. One guest of the Dunbars' wrote that he had "visited a garden on a plantation which is the first in Mississippi and to which all others are more or less approximate."

To some extent the legend of the Forest was built upon Dinah and William Dunbar's hospitality rather than the size or opulence of their plantation home. Describing one of their parties, William Dunbar Jr. estimated that more than one hundred people attended the lavish affair and drank champagne into the night. Frequent guest Thomas Rodney called the Forest "a perfect paradise" and wrote that Dunbar "is hospitable and lives like a nabob."

As late as June 1844, a series of stories printed in the "Forester" discusses the continuing family tradition of entertaining "a continuous parade of guests" who "come from everywhere" with "laughter and singing along the way." The "Forester" also notes that the descendants carried on William Dunbar's passion for music by having guests sing Dunbar's original compositions.

While it is generally accepted that Dinah carried out William Dunbar's plans for the addition of dormer windows and a widow's walk to the original Forest, it comes as a surprise that she built an entirely new mansion. Then again, the widow Dunbar might simply have been carrying out her husband's legacy. In 1793, shortly after they moved into the first home, Dunbar wrote to his wife, urging her to invite three English ladies who were visiting Natchez to dine with her and spend the night. He then declared that the Dunbars would be hospitable to all people regardless of their station in life, and there is no record of either of them going back on that.

Notes

Introduction: Rediscovery

1. John K. Bettersworth, *Mississippi: A History* (Austin, TX: Steck, 1959), 159; Dunbar Rowland, *History of Mississippi, the Heart of the South* (Chicago and Jackson, MS: Clarke, 1925), 1:27.

2. J. F. H. Claiborne, *Mississippi as a Province, Territory, and State* (Jackson, MS: Power and Barksdale, 1880), 1:101.

3. *The Journal of Andrew Ellicott* (Chicago: Quadrangle Books, 1962), 88.

4. Virginia Dunbar McQueen, "Remembrances of My Grandfather, Sir William Dunbar," in the possession of Douglas McQueen.

5. Trey Berry, Pam Beasley, and Jeanne Clements, eds., *The Forgotten Expedition, 1804–1805: The Louisiana Purchase Journals of Dunbar and Hunter* (Baton Rouge: Louisiana State University Press, 2006).

1. The Dunbar Family of Elgin, Scotland

1. McQueen, "Remembrances of My Grandfather."

2. "Plantation Plundered," 1779, in *Life, Letters and Papers of William Dunbar of Elgin, Morayshire, Scotland, and Natchez, Mississippi*, ed. Eron Rowland (Jackson: Press of the Mississippi Historical Society, 1930), 69–70.

3. Cecil Johnson, "The Distribution of Land in British West Florida," *Louisiana Historical Quarterly* 16 (1833): 544–45.

4. Quoted in John Sinclair, ed., *The Statistical Account of Scotland, Drawn Up from the Communications of the Ministers of the Different Parishes* (Edinburgh: Creech, 1794), 5:5–19, 8:384–400, 10:623–37, 11:508–13.

5. Ibid., 5:11–12, 8:390–92.

6. D. Matheson, *The Place Names of Elginshire* (Stirling, Scotland: MacKay, 1905), 139; Charles Rampini, *A History of Moray and Nairn* (Edinburgh: Blackwood, 1897), 267.

7. Quoted in Rampini, *History of Moray*, 268.

8. Ibid., 142–45. The Gaelic name Dunbar came from the family's lands and possessions; "dun" means hill and fortress. C. L'Estrange Ewen, *A History of Surnames of the British Isles: A Concise Account of Their Origin, Evolution, Etymology, and Legal Status* (London: Paul, Trench, Trubner, 1931), 380.

9. Ewen, *History of Surnames*, 144–45; *Black Agnes, or the Defense of Dunbar*

by Agnes, Countess of March, in the Year 1338 (London: Renington, 1804); Robert Young, *Annals of the Parish and Burgh of Elgin, from the Twelfth Century to the Year 1876, with Some Historical and Other Notices Illustrative of the Subject* (Elgin, Scotland: *Moray Weekly News* Office, 1879), 648.

10. Duncan Forbes, ed., *Ane Account of the Familie of Innes* (Aberdeen, Scotland: Spaulding Club, 1864), 189–90; Alexander Erskine to Archibald Dunbar, April 27, 1716, in *Social Life in Former Days Chiefly in the Province of Moray, Illustrated by Letters and Family Papers*, ed. E. Dunbar (Edinburgh: Edmonston and Douglas, 1865), 1:66.

11. Young, *Annals of the Parish*, 649.

12. Alexander Erskine to Archibald Dunbar, April 2, 1716, in Dunbar, *Social Life in Former Days*, 1:66.

13. Robert Douglas, *The Land Provosts of Elgin: Historical and Biographical Sketches* (Elgin, Scotland: Walker, 1926), 56–57.

14. Young, *Annals of the Parish*, 649.

15. William Cramond, ed., *The Records of Elgin, 1234–1800* (Aberdeen, Scotland: Milne and Hutchison, 1903), 1:453.

16. Young, *Annals of the Parish*, 649.

17. Ibid., 648–50.

18. William Dunbar to Archibald Dunbar, August 6, 1742, in Dunbar, *Social Life in Former Days*, 1:321–22.

19. Young, *Annals of the Parish*, 650.

20. Dunbar, *Documents Relating to Moray*, 58.

21. Archibald Dunbar to unknown addressee, August 1702, in Dunbar, *Social Life in Former Days*, 1:22.

22. Lieutenant R. Hay to Archibald Dunbar, March 2, 1757, in Dunbar, *Social Life in Former Days*, 1:63.

23. William Sutherland to Archibald Dunbar, December 1710, in Dunbar, *Social Life in Former Days*, 1:64.

24. Dunbar, *Social Life in Former Days*, 2:14.

25. Ibid., 2:146–47.

26. Archibald Dunbar to Earl of Moray, April 14, 1758, in Dunbar, *Social Life in Former Days*, 1:221.

27. Earl of Moray to Archibald Dunbar, April 3, May 10, 1758, in Dunbar, *Social Life in Former Days*, 161–62; Archibald Dunbar to Earl of Moray, April 14, 1758, in Dunbar, *Social Life in Former Days*, 145–46.

28. Archibald Dunbar to William Dunbar, August 6, 1742, in Dunbar, *Social Life in Former Days*, 1:321–22.

29. Certificate, n.d., in Dunbar, *Social Life in Former Days*, 1:99–100.

30. J. W. Watson, *Morayshire Described: Being a Guide to Visitors Containing a Notice of Ecclesiastical and Military Antiquities, Topographical Description and the Principal County Residencies, Towns and Villages, and Genealogical Notes of the Leading Families in the County with Map and Illustrations* (Elgin, Scotland: Russell and Watson, 1868), 74–75.

31. Ibid., 149.

32. Lachlan Shaw, *The History of the Province of Moray* (Glasgow: Morison, 1882), 2:15–16.

33. Ibid., 2:16; Watson, *Morayshire Described*, 150; William Rhind, *Sketches of the Past and Present State of Moray* (Edinburgh: Shortrede, 1839), 55–56.

34. Shaw, *History of the Province*, 2:15.

35. Watson, *Morayshire Described*, 149–50.

36. "Inventory of Thunderton House," May 25, 1708, in Dunbar, *Social Life in Former Days*, 1:205–19.

37. Peter Townend, ed., *Burke's Genealogical and Heraldic History of the Peerage, Baronetage, and Knightage* (London: Burke's Peerage, 1963), 780.

2. The Youthful Years

1. Sinclair, *Statistical Account of Scotland*, 5:14–15.

2. "An Outline of the Antiquities and History of Elgin with an Account of the Number, Extent, and Grandeur of the Religious Establishments in and around the City," n.d., Elgin Public Library, Elgin, Scotland.

3. William Dunbar Papers, Mississippi Department of Archives and History, Jackson (hereafter cited as WDP-MDAH).

4. Archibald Dunbar to William Dunbar, August 3, 1776, March 14, 1777, December 9, 1777, August 14, 1779, William Dunbar Papers, in the possession of Marian Patty; Townsend, *Burke's Genealogical*, 780.

5. All of the letters between Dunbar and his mother were filled with love and concern one for the other. To my knowledge, however, he never corresponded with his elder half-brother Alexander. WDP-MDAH.

6. Many childhood pictures, collections, and essays written by William Dunbar show the diversity of his interests. Dunbar Family Papers, in the possession of Sir Edward Dunbar.

7. John Jeans to William Dunbar, March 1766, in *Life, Letters and Papers of William Dunbar*, 16–18.

8. P. Hume Brown, "Scotland in the Eighteenth Century," *Scottish Historical Review* 6 (1909): 355.

9. Quoted in Henry W. Meikle, "The Learning of the Scots in the Eighteenth Century," *Scottish Historical Review* 7 (1910): 291.

10. D. B. Horn, "Some Scottish Writers of History in the Eighteenth Century," *Scottish Historical Review* 40 (1961): 1.

11. Cosmo Innes, ed., *Selections from the Records of the University and King's College of Aberdeen, 1796–1854* (Aberdeen, Scotland: Spaulding Club, 1854), vii.

12. Cramond, *Records of Elgin*, 1:445.

13. "Outline of the Antiquities."

14. William Falconer to Archibald Dunbar, April 23, 1754, in Dunbar, *Social Life in Former Days*, 1:11.

15. Archibald Dunbar to John Brulet, October 20, 1755, in ibid., 1:12.

16. *Life, Letters and Papers of William Dunbar*, 9.

17. Peter John Anderson, ed., *Roll of Alumni in Arts of the University and King's*

College of Aberdeen, 1596–1860 (Aberdeen, Scotland: University of Aberdeen, 1900), 84.

18. Even his father was becoming aware of Dunbar's scholarly curiosity and began writing people about his brilliance. Archibald Dunbar to Earl of Moray, February 22, 1761, Dunbar Family Papers.

19. W. Innes Addison, ed., *The Matriculation Albums of the University of Glasgow from 1728 to 1858* (Glasgow: MacLehose, 1913); W. Innes Addison, ed., *A Roll of the University of Glasgow from 31st December 1727 to 31st December 1897, with Short Biographical Notes* (Glasgow: MacLehose, 1898).

20. Rev. Lachlan Shaw to Archibald Dunbar, September 17, 1763, in Dunbar, *Social Life in Former Days*, 1:9–10.

21. Thomas Reid to Archibald Dunbar, September 4, 1755, in Dunbar, *Social Life in Former Days*, 1:7.

22. Innes, *Selections from the Records*, 65.

23. Anderson, *Roll of Alumni in Arts*, 77–79, 226.

24. Reid to Dunbar, September 4, 1755, 1:5–7.

25. Ibid., 1:5.

26. Peter John Anderson, ed., *Lists of Officers of the University and King's College of Aberdeen, 1495–1860* (Aberdeen, Scotland: University of Aberdeen, 1893), 76.

27. Ibid., 3, 5, 14, 15, 27, 34, 36, 42, 49, 63, 71, 74, 76, 88, 92.

28. Anderson, *Roll of Alumni in Arts*, 84; Peter John Anderson, ed., *Officers and Graduates of the University and King's College of Aberdeen* (Aberdeen, Scotland: Melne and Hutchison, 1893), 246.

29. John Leslie to Archibald Dunbar, February 9, 1764, Dunbar Family Papers.

30. Lord Provost to Archibald Dunbar, March 26, 1736, in Dunbar, *Social Life in Former Times*, 1:243–45.

31. Lord Lovot to Archibald Dunbar, April 9, 1737, in ibid., 1:246; W. D. Brodie to Archibald Dunbar, May 20, 1737, in ibid., 1:249.

32. "Extracts from Presbyterian Minutes during the Ministry of Joseph Sanderson, 1703–27," in *The Church of Alves*, ed. William Cramond (Elgin, Scotland: Courant and Courier Office, 1900), 65.

33. Stephen Ree, *Parish Ministers of the Presbytery of Elgin, 1560–1912* (Elgin, Scotland: Walker, 1912), 20.

34. J. B. Craven, *History of the Episcopal Church in the Diocese of Moray* (Kirkwall, Scotland: Pierce, 1889), 174, 83, 192.

35. Young, *Annals of the Parish*, 650.

36. Brown, "Scotland in the Eighteenth Century," 347–52; Ramsay quoted in ibid., 351; Gregory quoted in ibid., 349; ibid., 350.

37. John Jeans to William Dunbar, March 1766, in *Life, Letters and Papers of William Dunbar*, 16–17.

38. John Jeans to William Dunbar, March 26, 1769, in ibid., 21.

39. John Jeans to William Dunbar, March 1766, in ibid., 16–18.

40. Ibid., 19.

41. Jeans to Dunbar, March 26, 1769, in ibid., 22.

42. Jeans to Dunbar, March 1766, March 26, 1769, in ibid., 10–20, 22.

43. Margaret I. Adam, "The Highland Emigration of 1770," *Scottish Historical Review* 16 (1919): 283; Margaret I. Adam, "Eighteenth Century Highlands and the Poverty Problem," *Scottish Historical Review* 19 (1921): 4; Sinclair, *Statistical Account of Scotland,* 5:20; John M. Dickie, "The Economic Position of Scotland in 1760," *Scottish Historical Review* 18 (1920): 26–29; Brown, "Scotland in the Eighteenth Century," 23–45; Sinclair, *Statistical Account of Scotland,* 5:2.

44. Quoted in Adam, "Highland Emigration of 1770," 289.

45. *Life, Letters and Papers of William Dunbar,* 9.

46. Sinclair, *Statistical Account of Scotland,* 5:20; Grant quoted in Broughton and Cally Papers, Scottish Record Office, Register House, Edinburgh.

47. Archibald Dunbar, will recorded July 7, 1769, Scottish Record Office.

48. Passenger ticket and invoice of goods, *Pennsylvania* packet, March 1771, WDP-MDAH.

3. From Pennsylvania to Louisiana

1. J. Hector St. John de Crèvecoeur quoted in *American Colonial Documents to 1776,* ed. Merrill Jensen, vol. 9 of *English Historical Documents,* ed. David C. Douglas (New York: Oxford University Press, 1955), 476.

2. J. Hector St. John de Crèvecoeur, *Letters from an American Farmer* (Garden City, NY: Doubleday), 67.

3. *Life, Letters and Papers of William Dunbar,* 9.

4. Evarts Boutell Greene, *The Revolutionary Generation, 1763–1790* (New York: Macmillan, 1945), 49.

5. Solon J. Buck and Elizabeth Hawthorn Buck, *The Planting of Civilization in Western Pennsylvania* (Pittsburgh: University of Pittsburgh Press, 1939), 130–31, 136; Croghan quoted in ibid., 136.

6. Harnett T. Kane, *Natchez on the Mississippi* (New York: Morrow, 1947), 44.

7. Thomas Lynch Montgomery, ed., *Forfeited Estates, Inventories and Sales,* Pennsylvania Archives, 6th series (Harrisburg, PA: Harrisburg Publishing, 1907), 7–9, 24–26.

8. Johnson, "Distribution of Land," 544–45.

9. Ibid., 541–42.

10. John W. Monette, *History of the Discovery and Settlement of the Valley of the Mississippi by the Three Great European Powers, Spain, France and Great Britain, and the Subsequent Occupation, Settlement, and Extension of Civil Government by the United States until the Year 1846* (New York: Harper, 1846), 1:405–6, 360, 405.

11. Montgomery, *Forfeited Estates,* 8–9.

12. Kane, *Natchez on the Mississippi,* 44–45.

13. *Life, Letters and Papers of William Dunbar,* 9–10.

14. Johnson, "Distribution of Land," 545–46.

15. Cecil Johnson, "Expansion in West Florida, 1770–1779," *Mississippi Valley Historical Review* 20 (1934): 495.

16. Johnson, "Distribution of Land," 546–47.

17. Johnson, "Expansion in West Florida," 487–88.

18. Quoted in C. N. Howard, "Some Economic Aspects of British West Florida, 1763–1768," *Journal of Southern History* 6 (1940): 220, 219; James A. James, "Spanish Influence in the West during the American Revolution," *Mississippi Valley Historical Review* 6 (1917): 194; Clarence E. Carter, "Some Aspects of British Administration in West Florida," *Mississippi Valley Historical Review* 1 (1914): 370–74.

19. Lewis Cecil Gray, *History of Agriculture in the Southern United States to 1860* (Gloucester, MA: Smith, 1958), 1:77, 73–74.

20. Ibid., 1:74–75, 69–71; Lawrence Kinnaird, ed., *Spain in the Mississippi Valley, 1765–1794* (Washington, DC: GPO, 1949), 237–38.

21. Gray, *History of Agriculture*, 6–67; planter quoted in ibid., 66–67.

22. Ibid., 66, 68–69.

23. Rodney C. Loehr, "The Influence of English Agriculture on American Agriculture, 1775–1825," *Agricultural History* 11 (1937): 3–4.

24. Rowland, *History of Mississippi*, 1:296; *Life, Letters and Papers of William Dunbar*, 10; Philip Pittman, *The Present State of the European Settlements on the Mississippi with a Geographical Description of That River Illustrated by Plans and Draughts* (London: Nourse, 1770), 23–24.

25. *Montgomery (AL) Advertiser*, December 14, 1941.

26. Anne Dunbar to William Dunbar, July 24, 1776, WDP-MDAH.

27. William Dunbar, plantation diary entries, *Life, Letters and Papers of William Dunbar*, 34, 51, 44, 39, 42.

28. John Swift to William Dunbar, September 5, 1775, WDP-MDAH.

29. Dunbar, plantation diary entries, 28–32, 54–55, 26.

30. The diary, from beginning to end, includes a discussion of the manufacture of barrel staves and why such an enterprise is an appropriate activity for a plantation and its slaves. Ibid., 41.

31. Ibid., 43.

32. Ibid., 23, 24, 35, 36, 40–42, 48–50, 52, 43.

33. Ibid., 24, 25, 29–34, 45, 39, 40, 47, 48.

34. Ibid., 29–30, 39, 40, 47, 48, 24, 56.

35. Ibid., 55.

36. Ibid., 51.

37. Ibid., 72.

38. Ibid., 27–30.

39. Ibid., 45–47.

40. Ibid., 47.

4. The American Revolution in Manchac

1. James, "Spanish Influence in the West," 204–5.

2. Kathryn T. Abbey, "Peter Chester's Defense of the Mississippi after the Willing Raid," *Mississippi Valley Historical Review* 22 (1935): 31, 21; Dunbar, plantation diary entry, 61; Abbey, "Peter Chester's Defense," 21–22.

3. Dunbar, plantation diary entries, 60–63; John Caughey, "Willing's Expedition down the Mississippi, 1778," *Louisiana Historical Quarterly* 15 (1932): 11; Kane, *Natchez on the Mississippi*, 45; Abbey, "Peter Chester's Defense," 21–22.

4. Dunbar, plantation diary entry, 60.

5. Ibid., 60–61.

6. Ibid., 61–62, 63.

7. Caughey, "Willing's Expedition," 8. The following are some of the goods Willing and his party confiscated from plantations and stores coming down the Mississippi: 615 deer skins, 41 bundles of worsted and thread stockings, 2 kegs of gunpowder, 3 scale beams, 1 box of soap, 200 pounds of indigo, 21 cotton counterpanes, 6 carpets, 2 bundles of women's clothes, 2 baskets of silver buckles, 1 pair brass and 1 pair wooden scales, 1 empty case, 5 ink stands, 1 pewter cup, 1 desk, 1 trunk, 1 watch, 22 pairs of silk ferreting, 6 leather pocketbooks, medicines, 50 shirts and trousers, and assorted other items. Kinnaird, *Spain in the Mississippi Valley*, 2:282–84.

8. Monette, *History of the Discovery*, 1:433–38; Gálvez quoted in Kinnaird, *Spain in the Mississippi Valley*, 2:272.

9. Caughey, "Willing Expedition," 26–27, 36; Wilbur H. Siebert, "The Loyalists in West Florida and the Natchez District," *Proceedings of the Mississippi Valley Historical Association* 8 (1914–15): 110–11.

10. Siebert, "Loyalists in West Florida," 111.

11. Willing quoted in Kinnaird, *Spain in the Mississippi Valley*, 2:278–79.

12. Dunbar, plantation diary entries, 64–65.

13. Ibid., 66.

14. McQueen, "Remembrances of My Grandfather."

15. Dunbar, plantation diary entries, 65–66.

16. Ibid., 66, 68, 69.

17. Henry P. Dart, ed., "West Florida: The Capture of Baton Rouge by Galvez, September 21st, 1779," *Louisiana Historical Quarterly* 12 (1929): 258–62.

18. Dunbar, plantation diary entries, 69–70.

19. Isaac Joslin Cox, "The Louisiana-Texas Frontier," pt. 1, *Quarterly of the Texas State Historical Association* 10 (1906): 39; George L. Rives, "Spain and the United States in 1795," *American Historical Review* 4 (1898): 64–65.

20. Rives, "Spain and the United States," 64–65.

21. Kinnaird, *Spain in the Mississippi Valley*, 2:345–46, 355–56; Dart, "West Florida," 258–62.

22. Dart, "West Florida," 258–62.

23. Kinnaird, *Spain in the Mississippi Valley*, 2:358.

5. From Darkness to Light

1. Dunbar, plantation diary, 71.

2. Ibid., 70–71.

3. McQueen, "Remembrances of My Grandfather."

4. Dunbar, plantation diary, 71–74.

5. Ibid., 74.

6. Kinnaird, *Spain in the Mississippi Valley*, 2:425; John Caughey, "The Natchez Rebellion of 1781 and Its Aftermath," *Louisiana Historical Quarterly* 16 (1933): 51–63.

7. James E. Winston, "Notes on the Economic History of New Orleans, 1803–1836," *Mississippi Valley Historical Review* 11 (1924): 200–201.

8. Kinnaird, *Spain in the Mississippi Valley*, 3:1–5; Arthur Preston Whitaker, ed., *Documents Relating to the Commercial Policy of Spain in the Floridas with Incidental Reference to Louisiana* (Deland: Florida State Historical Society, 1931), 33–37.

9. McQueen, "Remembrances of My Grandfather."

10. Gray, *History of Agriculture*, 2:602–5, 589–90.

11. Jack D. L. Holmes, *Gayoso: The Life of a Spanish Governor in the Mississippi Valley, 1789–1799* (Baton Rouge: Louisiana State University Press, 1965), 91–94, 95.

12. William Dunbar to Diana Dunbar, April 4, May 8, 1790, in the possession of Sarah Ayres (hereafter cited as SA).

13. Kane, *Natchez on the Mississippi*, 47–48; William Baskerville Hamilton, *Anglo-American Law on the Frontier: Thomas Rodney and His Territorial Cases* (Durham, NC: Duke University Press, 1953), 86.

14. *Life, Letters and Papers of William Dunbar*, 12–13; Kane, *Natchez on the Mississippi*, 48.

15. Diana Dunbar to William Dunbar, October 25, 1789, April 6, 9, 1790, WDP-MDAH.

16. Kane, *Natchez on the Mississippi*, 47–48.

17. Diana Dunbar to William Dunbar, August 11, 1789, SA.

18. Diana Dunbar to William Dunbar, October 25, 1789, April 6, 9, 1790, SA; William Dunbar to Diana Dunbar, April 4, 17, 22, May 3, 1790, SA; William Dunbar to Diana Dunbar, April 5, 1791, WDP-MDAH.

19. Diana Dunbar to William Dunbar, October 25, 1789, SA.

20. Diana Dunbar to William Dunbar, April 6, 1790, SA.

21. William Dunbar to Diana Dunbar, April 4, 1790, SA.

22. William Dunbar to Diana Dunbar, October 25, 1789, SA.

23. Sarah Ayres's and Marian Patty's collections of Dunbar papers and McQueen's "Remembrances of My Grandfather" contain numerous references to Dunbar's and Diana's activities during this period of time.

24. William Dunbar to Diana Dunbar, April 5, 1791, WDP-MDAH.

25. Arthur H. DeRosier Jr., "Carpenter's Estimate on the Building of 'The Forest,'" *Journal of Mississippi History* 27 (1965): 259–64.

26. Ibid.

27. Ibid.

28. *Montgomery (AL) Advertiser*, December 14, 1941.

6. A Dream Realized

1. John Davis, *Travels in Louisiana and the Floridas in the Year 1802, Giving a Correct Picture of Those Countries* (New York: Riley, 1806), 136.

2. Marcus L. Hansen, "The Population of the American Outlying Regions in 1790," *Annual Report of the American Historical Association* 1 (1931): 405.

3. Quoted in Kinnaird, *Spain in the Mississippi Valley*, 3:137.

4. Ellicott quoted in Francis Baily, *Journal of a Tour in Unsettled Parts of North America in 1796 and 1797* (London: Baily Bros., 1856), 278–80.

5. Ellicott quoted in ibid., 283–85.

6. Ellicott quoted in ibid., 285.

7. Ellicott quoted in ibid., 351–52; *Journal of Andrew Ellicott*, 135.

8. Pittman, *Present State of the European Settlements*, 37–39.

9. *Journal of Andrew Ellicott*, 192.

10. Arthur Herman, *How the Scots Invented the Modern World: The True Story of How Western Europe's Poorest Nation Created Our World and Everything in It* (New York: Crown, 2001), viii; Scott quoted in ibid.

11. Haydn cited in Elizabeth Dunbar Murray, *Early Romances of Historic Natchez* (Natchez, MS: Natchez Printing and Stationery, 1938), 15.

12. G. P. Whittington, ed., "The Journal of Dr. John Sibley July–October, 1802," *Louisiana Historical Quarterly* 10 (1927): 490.

13. Holmes, *Gayoso*, 115.

14. William Dunbar to Diana Dunbar, October 16, 1791, SA.

15. William Dunbar to Diana Dunbar, May 5, 1794, SA.

16. Holmes, *Gayoso*, 131–32; William Dunbar to Diana Dunbar, June 4, 1792, SA.

17. William Dunbar to Diana Dunbar, February 28, 1794, WDP-MDAH.

18. William O. Scroggs, "Early Trade and Travel in the Lower Mississippi Valley," *Proceedings of the Mississippi Valley Historical Association* 2 (1909): 235.

19. William Dunbar to Diana Dunbar, June 9, 1792, SA.

20. William Dunbar to Diana Dunbar, April 12, 1793, SA.

21. William Dunbar to Diana Dunbar, April 27, 1792, SA.

22. William Dunbar to Diana Dunbar, May 5, 1794, SA.

23. William Dunbar to Diana Dunbar, May 19, 1794, SA.

24. Holmes, *Gayoso*, 131–32; Kane, *Natchez on the Misissippi*, 46–47; Holmes, *Gayoso*, 126, 60, 48–49.

25. Irving A. Leonard, "A Frontier Library, 1799," *Hispanic American Historical Review* 23 (1943): 26–27.

26. *Natchez (MS) Democrat*, pilgrimage ed., 1965.

27. William Dunbar to Diana Dunbar, March 12, 1793, SA.

28. Rev. H. Beach to William Dunbar, December 31, 1803, WDP-MDAH.

29. William Dunbar Jr. to George T. Olmsted (brother-in-law), June 20, 1839 (typed copy), WDP-MDAH.

30. *Montgomery (AL) Advertiser*, December 14, 1941.

31. Ibid.; Theodora Britton Marshall and Gladys Crail Evans, *They Found It in Natchez* (New Orleans: Pelican, 1940), 53–54.

32. William Dunbar to Diana Dunbar, June 18, 1792, SA.

33. Leonard, "Frontier Library," 22–23.

34. Kinnaird, *Spain in the Mississippi Valley*, 19–20.

35. Kane, *Natchez on the Mississippi*, 47.

36. William Dunbar to Diana Dunbar, March 12, April 1, 1794, SA.

37. William Dunbar to Diana Dunbar, April 27, 1794, SA.

7. Emergence on the National Scene

1. Rives, "Spain and the United States," 76.

2. Holmes, *Gayoso*, 177.

3. Catharine Van Cortlandt Mathews, *Andrew Ellicott: His Life and Letters* (New York: Grafton Press, 1908), 148, 155.

4. *Journal of Andrew Ellicott*, 68, 70.

5. Ibid., 67–68, 90.

6. Ibid., 19; Mathews, *Andrew Ellicott*, 4.

7. *Journal of Andrew Ellicott*, 177–78; Monette, *History of the Discovery*, 1:532.

8. *Life, Letters and Papers of William Dunbar*, 76–77.

9. Ibid., 76; William Dunbar to Mr. Hutchins, June 25, 1797, SA. An arpent is a French unit of land measurement, commonly used in Canada and the southern United States, equal to about 0.85 acre.

10. Holmes, *Gayoso*, 198–99; Peter J. Hamilton, "Running Mississippi's South Line," *Publications of the Mississippi Historical Society* 2 (1899): 160–61.

11. *Journal of Andrew Ellicott*, 179–80.

12. "Running the Line," May 31–June 7, 1798, in *Life, Letters and Papers of William Dunbar*, 79.

13. Holmes, *Gayoso*, 232–35.

14. "Running the Line," June–early July 1798, 79–80; *Journal of Andrew Ellicott*, 180.

15. William Dunbar to Dinah Dunbar, August 18, 1798, SA.

16. Rowland, *History of Mississippi*, 1:324–25.

17. Ibid.; "Running the Line," August 1–18, 1798, 80–81.

18. William Dunbar to Dinah Dunbar, June 6, 1798, SA.

19. William Dunbar to Dinah Dunbar, June 23, 1798, SA.

20. William Dunbar to Dinah Dunbar, June 6, 1798, SA.

21. Ibid.

22. William Dunbar to Dinah Dunbar, August 21, 1798, SA.

23. Mathews, *Andrew Ellicott*, 159–60, 158–59.

24. William Dunbar to Dinah Dunbar, June 23, August 18, 1798, SA.

25. William Dunbar to Dinah Dunbar, June 23, 1798, SA.

26. William Dunbar to Dinah Dunbar, August 18, 1798, SA.

27. William Dunbar to Dinah Dunbar, August 21, 1798, SA; "Running the Line," August 20–31, 1798, 81–82.

28. *Journal of Andrew Ellicott*, 182.

29. Ibid., 183–84.

30. David Bradford to David Redick, November 8, 1798, David Bradford Letters, Department of Archives and Manuscripts, Louisiana State University, Baton Rouge.

31. Mathews, *Andrew Ellicott*, 160.

32. *Journal of Andrew Ellicott*, 183, 187.

33. Ibid., 193–94.

34. Mathews, *Andrew Ellicott*, 23; Holmes, *Gayoso*, 259–60.

35. Holmes, *Gayoso*, 60.

36. Dunbar Rowland, ed., *The Mississippi Territorial Archives*, vol. 1, *1798–1804, Executive Journals of Governor Winthrop Sargent and Governor William Charles Cole Claiborne*, (Nashville, TN: Brandon), 162–63.

37. Clarence Edwin Carter, ed., *The Territorial Papers of the United States* (Washington, DC: GPO, 1937), 5:158–59.

38. *Journal of Andrew Ellicott*, 48.

39. Andrew Ellicott to William Dunbar, April 18, 1800, in *Life, Letters and Papers of William Dunbar*, 105–6.

40. *Journal of Andrew Ellicott*, 43.

8. Scientist

1. One unknown writer, an engineer, wrote to Dunbar's grandson, "I am doing just the kind of work now that was done by your grandfather when he established the 31° of north latitude & you can imagine of what interest his manuscript would be to me. As a scientific document I would even have it published in the transactions of the American Society of Engineers." Unknown writer to Field Dunbar, [late 1840s?], William Dunbar Papers, in the possession of Marian Patty.

2. Wilson quoted in Milford F. Allen, "Thomas Jefferson and the Louisiana-Arkansas Frontier," *Arkansas Historical Quarterly* 20 (1961): 45.

3. It was on one evening in 1798, while encamped on a bluff overlooking the Mississippi River, that Dunbar wrote about the trees and plants growing in Mississippi Territory and adjoining Spanish territory. He noted the following: "Sugar Cane; Indigo, 2 species; Cotton, 2 varieties, distd by seed only; Tobacco; Indian Corn, 8 or 10 varieties; Rice; Okra; Squash; Sweet Potato; Irish Potato; Every species of root & leguminous plant, which are the productions of the Gardens of Europe or the U.S.; Apricots, not common. It is expected they will do well; Figs, 3 or 4 species, produce abundantly and in great perfection. There are three crops in the year of which the middle one yields plenty; Pomegranate large & fine; Much flowering, with a great variety of flowers, ornamental shrubs and medicinal herbs; Guinea Corn; Brown Corn; Millet; Pumpkins; Musk and Water Melons; Tomatoes; Egg plant; Ground nuts; Quinces, very fine & very large; Almonds succeed well; Spanish Walnut, very rare, but the climate is doubtless congenial to it; Cherries do not succeed well; Plums, plenty and good, but the first European plums bear not plentifully and often miss entirely; Peaches, excellent and in great abundance; Apples thrive but indifferently; Pears rare; Nectarines, subject to rot upon the trees." *Life, Letters and Papers of William Dunbar*, 98–99.

4. Ibid., 94.

5. Ibid., 96–97, 95–97, 95, 85–88, 94, 95, 87–88, 82–83.

6. Ibid., 92–93.

7. Simon Gratz, ed., "Thomas Rodney," pt. 2, *Pennsylvania Magazine of History and Biography* 44 (1920): 59, 62.

8. "Notes on Encampment," August 1798, in *Life, Letters and Papers of William Dunbar*, 90; Kane, *Natchez on the Mississippi*, 49.

9. "Notes on Encampment," August 1798, 90.

10. A. Williamson to William Dunbar, June 24, 1800, in *Life, Letters and Papers of William Dunbar*, 205–6.

11. Joseph Dunbar Shields, *Natchez: Its Early History* (Louisville, KY: Morton, 1930), 233.

12. *Life, Letters and Papers of William Dunbar*, 117–18, 121–22.

13. Hamilton, *Anglo-American Law*, 86–87.

14. William Dunbar to Edward Troughton, October 20, 1805, in *Life, Letters and Papers of William Dunbar*, 325–27; William Dunbar to [indecipherable addressee], October 20, 1805, in *Life, Letters and Papers of William Dunbar*, 328; William Dunbar to John Swift, June 20, 1806, in *Life, Letters and Papers of William Dunbar*, 361.

15. Dunbar to Troughton, October 20, 1805, 325–27.

16. William Dunbar, letter book, October 20, 1805, 322–25, Mississippi Department of Archives and History.

17. Charles S. Sydnor, *A Gentleman of the Old Natchez Region, Benjamin L. C. Wailes* (Durham, NC: Duke University Press, 1938), 121–22.

18. William Dunbar to John Vaughn, February 1806, in *Life, Letters and Papers of William Dunbar*, 328–29.

19. Ibid.; *Life, Letters and Papers of William Dunbar*, 11–12.

20. Hamilton, *Anglo-American Law*, 87.

21. William Dunbar, journal entry, April 10, 1806, WDP-MDAH.

22. William C. C. Claiborne to William Dunbar, April 16, 1802, in *Official Letter Books of W. C. C. Claiborne, 1801–1816*, ed. Dunbar Rowland (Jackson, MS: State Department of Archives and History), 1:83–84; ibid., 1:193–201; Joseph T. Hatfield, "The Public Career of William C. C. Claiborne" (PhD diss., Emory University, 1962), 154–55; Rowland, *History of Mississippi*, 1:384–85.

23. *Official Letter Books of W. C. C. Claiborne*, 1:85; Lattimore quoted in ibid.

24. *Life, Letters and Papers of William Dunbar*, 214–15.

25. William Dunbar, meteorological observation notes, June 30, 1803, WDP-MDAH; William Dunbar, "Monthly and Annual Results of Meteorological Observations," *Transactions of the American Philosophical Society* 6 (1804): 188–89.

26. "Concerning Philip Nolan," *Quarterly of the Texas State Historical Association* 7 (1904): 314–15.

27. Ibid., 315–16; Thomas Jefferson to William Dunbar, August 1800, in *Life, Letters and Papers of William Dunbar*, 111–12; Thomas Jefferson to American Philosophical Society, January 16, 1801, in William Dunbar, "Meteorological Observations for One Entire Year," *Transactions of the American Philosophical Society* 6 (1804): 9–23: *The Writings of Thomas Jefferson*, memorial ed., ed. Andrew A.

Lipscomb and Albert Ellery Bergh (Washington, DC: Thomas Jefferson Memorial Association of the United States, 1903), 10:191–92.

28. "Concerning Philip Nolan," 315–17.

29. Dunbar, meteorological observation notes, June 30, 1803, WDP-MDAH.

30. William Baskerville Hamilton, *Thomas Rodney, Revolutionary and Builder of the West* (Durham, NC: Duke University Press, 1953), 86–87; "Notes on Encampment," August 1798, in *Life, Letters and Papers of William Dunbar*, 88–90.

31. Gratz, "Thomas Rodney," pt. 2, 52–53.

32. *Life, Letters and Papers of William Dunbar*, 104–5.

33. Dunbar, "Meteorological Observations for One Entire Year," 9–23.

34. *Writings of Thomas Jefferson*, ed. Lipscomb and Bergh, 191–92.

35. *Life, Letters and Papers of William Dunbar*, 209–14.

36. Ibid.

9. Land Policies

1. Francis P. Burns, "The Spanish Land Laws of Louisiana," *Louisiana Historical Quarterly* 11 (1928): 559–60.

2. Ibid., 561.

3. Johnson, "Distribution of Land," 551.

4. Ibid., 548–49.

5. Charles A. Bacarisse, "Baron de Bastrop," *Southeastern Historical Quarterly* 58 (1955): 323–25.

6. Beatrice M. Stokes, "John Bisland, Mississippi Planter, 1776–1821" (master's thesis, Louisiana State University, 1941), 96.

7. Holmes, *Gayoso*, 34–35.

8. William Dunbar to Don Manuel Gayoso de Lemos, April 11, 1797, in *Life, Letters and Papers of William Dunbar*, 76; Governor Gayoso to William Dunbar, April 19, 1797, in *Life, Letters and Papers of William Dunbar*, 77–78.

9. *Life, Letters and Papers of William Dunbar*, 76–77.

10. Burns, "Spanish Land Laws," 503–4, 576–79.

11. William Dunbar to Gen. George Mathews, December 9, 1797, Mathews Family Papers, Department of Archives and Manuscripts, Louisiana State University.

12. *The Natchez Court Records: Abstracts of Early Records, 1767–1805* (Greenwood, MS: N.p., 1953), 2:97, 205, 216, 239, 304, 456, 459, 557, 564, 591; *Mississippi Messenger*, March 18, 1806; proclamations, October 1, 1803, February 6, 1804, WDP-MDAH; land grants, May 2, 1795, December 8, 1796, WDP-MDAH.

13. Land grants, December 31, 1791, November 1793, March 3, 1804, December 15, 1794, WDP-MDAH.

14. *Journal of Andrew Ellicott*, 154; *Journals of the General Assembly of the Mississippi Territory: Journal of the Legislative Council, Second General Assembly, Second Session, October 3–November 19, 1803*, ed. William D. McCain (Hattiesburg, MS: Book Farm), 21–22, 26; Hatfield, "Public Career of William C. C. Claiborne," 133–34.

15. *Journal of Andrew Ellicott*, 154–55.

16. *Journals of the General Assembly*, 21–22, 26.

17. Carter, *Territorial Papers*, 5:142–45; Hatfield, "Public Career of William C. C. Claiborne," 134.

18. Carter, *Territorial Papers*, 5:156–58; Hatfield, "Public Career of William C. C. Claiborne," 135.

19. Hatfield, "Public Career of William C. C. Claiborne," 135–36.

20. *American State Papers: Public Lands* 1:123–25.

21. Arthur H. DeRosier Jr., *The Removal of the Choctaw Indians* (Knoxville: University of Tennessee Press, 1970), 28–29.

22. *American State Papers: Public Lands* 1:123–25; Hatfield, "Public Career of William C. C. Claiborne," 136.

23. Carter, *Territorial Papers*, 5:192–205; Hatfield, "Public Career of William C. C. Claiborne," 137–38.

24. Carter, *Territorial Papers*, 5:272–75; Hatfield, "Public Career of William C. C. Claiborne," 138–39.

25. Rowland, *Mississippi Territorial Archives*, 1:340; Hatfield, "Public Career of William C. C. Claiborne," 139.

26. Hamilton, *Thomas Rodney*, 66–67.

27. R. S. Cotterill, "The National Land System in the South: 1803–1812," *Mississippi Valley Historical Review* 16 (1930): 495–96, 498–99.

28. Ibid., 499.

29. Hamilton, *Thomas Rodney*, vii–viii; other historians quoted in ibid.

30. Ibid., viii.

31. Hamilton, *Anglo-American Law*, 186–87.

32. Certificate signed July 9, 1805, WDP-MDAH.

10. Cotton and Slavery

1. William B. Hamilton, "Early Cotton Regulation in the Lower Mississippi Valley," *Agricultural History* 15 (1941): 20–21.

2. Kinnaird, *Spain in the Mississippi Valley*, 3:307.

3. William Dunbar to Winthrop Sargent, February 2, 1801, Winthrop Sargent Papers, Massachusetts Historical Society, Boston (hereafter cited as WSP-MHS).

4. Minter Wood, "Life in New Orleans in the Spanish Period," *Louisiana Historical Quarterly* 22 (1939): 666–67.

5. Ibid., 667–68.

6. Gray, *History of Agriculture*, 2:633.

7. Baily, *Journal of a Tour*, 286, 345–46.

8. M. B. Hammond, *The Cotton Industry: An Essay in American Economic History* (New York: Macmillan, 1897), 45, 76, 77.

9. McQueen, "Remembrances of My Grandfather"; Bienville quoted in ibid.

10. Ibid.; Gray, *History of Agriculture*, 2:678, 695.

11. Whitaker, *Documents Relating to the Commercial Policy*, 201, 203.

12. McQueen, "Remembrances of My Grandfather."

13. Stanley Dumbell, "Early Liverpool Cotton Imports and the Organization of the Cotton Market in the Eighteenth Century," *Economic Journal* 33 (1923): 362–64.

14. Ibid., 371–72, 367.

15. Ibid., 370.

16. It is understandable but ironic that southern migrants from coastal communities moved westward to the Mississippi River seeking agricultural opportunities. There they found a staple crop—cotton—in demand at home and in Europe, that created a rural, agricultural environment as well as cities to handle and transport crops produced for export, thereby following both the Jeffersonian and Hamiltonian visions for a growing industry.

17. Thomas Ellison, *The Cotton Trade of Great Britain* (London: Wilson, 1886), 85–86.

18. Dumbell, "Early Liverpool Cotton Imports," 362.

19. *Liverpool Daily Post Supplement,* "The Ambassador of Commerce," June 3, 1927.

20. Dumbell, "Early Liverpool Cotton Imports," 367–69.

21. Gray, *History of Agriculture,* 2:681–82.

22. William Dunbar to Chew and Relf, October 5, 1810, in *Life, Letters and Papers of William Dunbar,* 377–80.

23. William Dunbar to Samuel Breek Jr., Esq., January 12, 1802, in *Life, Letters and Papers of William Dunbar,* 114.

24. William Dunbar to Bird and Co., July 5, 1802, in *Life, Letters and Papers of William Dunbar,* 115–16.

25. William Dunbar to Bird and Co., August 23, 1802, in *Life, Letters and Papers of William Dunbar,* 117.

26. William Dunbar to Pearce and Crawford, November 11, 1802, in *Life, Letters and Papers of William Dunbar,* 118–19.

27. William Dunbar to Bird and Co., January 17, 1803, in *Life, Letters and Papers of William Dunbar,* 120–21.

28. In addition to the letters cited above, see William Dunbar to Daniel W. Cope, October 4, 1809, in *Life, Letters and Papers of William Dunbar,* 264; William Dunbar to James and Thomas H. Perkins, November 22, 1809, in *Life, Letters and Papers of William Dunbar,* 281; and Gray, *History of Agriculture,* 2:708–9.

29. Rowland, *History of Mississippi,* 1:296.

30. Gray, *History of Agriculture,* 1:336.

31. L. C. Gray, "Economic Efficiency and Competitive Advantages of Slavery under the Plantation System," *Agricultural History* 4 (1930): 35–36; Frederick Law Olmsted, *A Journey in the Seaboard Slave States, with Remarks on Their Economy* (New York: Dix and Edwards, 1856), 114–16.

32. Gray, "Economic Efficiency," 37–38.

33. Edgar T. Thomson, "The Climatic Theory of the Plantation," *Agricultural History* 15 (1941): 60.

34. Ulrich B. Phillips, "The Economic Cost of Slaveholding in the Cotton Belt," *Political Science Quarterly* 20 (1905): 266.

35. Ibid., 259.

36. Gray, "Economic Efficiency," 35; Robert Worthington Smith, "Was Slavery Unprofitable in the Ante-Bellum South?" *Agricultural History* 20 (1946): 62–63.

37. Smith, "Was Slavery Unprofitable," 63–64.

38. Gray, *History of Agriculture*, 2:687–88.

39. Crèvecoeur, *Letters from an American Farmer*, 167–68.

40. Washington quoted in Paul S. Taylor, "Plantation Laborer before the Civil War," *Agricultural History* 28 (1954): 2.

41. Jefferson quoted in ibid.

42. Ibid., 1–2.

43. William Dunbar to John Ellis, May 4, 1802, in *Life, Letters and Papers of William Dunbar*, 113; William Dunbar to Winthrop Sargent, March 16, 1807, WSP-MHS.

44. Ibid.

45. William Dunbar to Colonel Morehouse, March 22, 1806, in *Life, Letters and Papers of William Dunbar*, 333–34.

46. William Dunbar to Mr. Girod, March 22, 1806, in *Life, Letters and Papers of William Dunbar*, 335–36.

47. *Mississippi Messenger*, June 17, 1806; Adams County Board of Supervisors, *Transcription of County Archives of Mississippi, No. 2, Adams County (Natchez): Minutes of the County Court, 1802–1804* (Jackson, MS: N.p., 1942), 2:15.

48. William Dunbar to Thomas Turno and Hohn Price, February 1, 1807, in *Life, Letters and Papers of William Dunbar*, 351–52.

11. Agricultural Experimenter

1. Taylor, "Plantation Laborer," 3.

2. Gray, *History of Agriculture*, 2:703, 700–701.

3. Charles S. Sydnor, "Historical Activities in Mississippi in the Nineteenth Century," *Journal of Southern History* 3 (1937): 141–42.

4. Avery O. Craven, "The Agricultural Reformers of the Ante-bellum South," *American Historical Review* 33 (1928): 305, 307–9, 312–13.

5. John Hebron Moore, "Cotton Breeding in the Old South," *Agricultural History* 30 (1956): 95, 96; C. A. Browne, "Some Historical Relations of Agriculture in the West Indies to That of the United States," *Agricultural History* 1 (1927): 30.

6. Moore, "Cotton Breeding," 96–98; John Hebron Moore, *Agriculture in Ante-bellum Mississippi* (New York: Bookman Associates, 1958), 32–33; William Dunbar to Green and Wainwright, October 2, 1807, WDP-MDAH.

7. Moore, "Cotton Breeding," 97.

8. Moore, *Agriculture in Ante-bellum Mississippi*, 44–45, 49.

9. Hammond, *Cotton Industry*, 78; Gray, *History of Agriculture*, 2:701–2.

10. Gray, *History of Agriculture*, 2:793–94.

11. Holmes, *Gayoso*, 100–101.

12. Gratz, "Thomas Rodney," pt. 1, 348.

13. William Dunbar to Winthrop Sargent, February 14, 1802, WSP-MHS.

14. William Dunbar to Winthrop Sargent, November 21, 1799, WSP-MHS.

15. Cleo Hearon, "Mississippi and the Compromise of 1850," *Publications of the Mississippi Historical Society* 14 (1914): 86.

16. Holmes, *Gayoso*, 99, 20–21, 100; Moore, *Agriculture in Ante-bellum Mississippi*, 22.

17. Dunbar quoted in Moore, *Agriculture in Ante-bellum Mississippi*, 25.

18. William Dunbar to Matthew Pearce and James Crawford, 1802, in *Life, Letters and Papers of William Dunbar*, 119–20.

19. William Dunbar to Green and Wainwright, February 25, 1806, in *Life, Letters and Papers of William Dunbar*, 328.

20. Holmes, *Gayoso*, 100–101.

21. McQueen, "Remembrances of My Grandfather."

22. Gray, *History of Agriculture*, 2:705.

23. Moore, *Agriculture in Ante-bellum Mississippi*, 51–52.

24. *Life, Letters and Papers of William Dunbar*, 10.

25. Moore, *Agriculture in Ante-bellum Mississippi*, 52.

26. Gray, *History of Agriculture*, 2:705.

27. Sydnor, *Gentleman of the Old Natchez Region*, 122.

28. Gray, *History of Agriculture*, 2:710.

29. W. D. Shue, "The Cotton Oil Industry," *Publications of the Mississippi Historical Society* 8 (1904): 267.

30. Bettersworth, *Mississippi*, 111–12.

31. McQueen, "Remembrances of My Grandfather."

32. Hammond, *Cotton Industry*, 79–80.

33. Riley quoted in Shue, "Cotton Oil Industry," 267.

34. Bettersworth, *Mississippi*, 350–51.

35. Shue, "Cotton Oil Industry," 269.

36. Gray, *History of Agriculture*, 2:710.

37. Shue, "Cotton Oil Industry," 266.

38. James Mean [Mease] to William Dunbar, March 9, 1808, in *Life, Letters and Papers of William Dunbar*, 198.

12. An Invitation to Serve

1. Jefferson quoted in Isaac Joslin Cox, "The Exploration of the Louisiana Frontier, 1803–1806," *Annual Report of the American Historical Association*, 1904, 153–54.

2. Thomas P. Abernethy, *The South in the New Nation, 1789–1819* (Baton Rouge: Louisiana State University Press, 1961), 252.

3. William Dunbar to Bird and Co., July 25, 1802, in *Life, Letters and Papers of William Dunbar*, 116.

4. William Dunbar to John Vaughn, September 1, 1803, in *Life, Letters and Papers of William Dunbar*, 123; Isaac Joslin Cox, "The Louisiana-Texas Frontier," pt. 2, *Quarterly of the Texas State Historical Association* 17 (1913): 7–8.

5. Dunbar to Vaughn, September 1, 1803, 123.

6. *The Western Journals of Dr. George Hunter, 1796–1805*, ed. John Francis McDermott (Philadelphia: American Philosophical Society, 1963), 8–9.

7. William O. Scroggs, "Rural Life in the Lower Mississippi Valley about 1803," *Proceedings of the Mississippi Valley Historical Association* 8 (1914–15): 275–76.

8. Isaac Joslin Cox, "The New Invasion of the Goths and Vandals," *Proceedings of the Mississippi Valley Historical Association* 8 (1914–15): 192–93.

9. Cox, "Louisiana-Texas Frontier," pt. 2, 144–45; Charles Gayarré, *History of Louisiana*, vol. 4, *The American Domination* (New York: Widdleton, 1856), 82–83.

10. *Le Telegraphe* (New Orleans), February 8, 1804.

11. *Writings of Thomas Jefferson*, ed. Lipscomb and Bergh, 11:23; *Journals of Dr. George Hunter*, 8–9.

12. *Writings of Thomas Jefferson*, ed. Lipscomb and Bergh, 11:23.

13. *Journals of Dr. George Hunter*, 9.

14. John Francis McDermott, "Sketch of Dr. George Hunter," in ibid., 5–6; *Journals of Dr. George Hunter*, 8–9.

15. Cox, "Louisiana-Texas Frontier," pt. 2, 143–44, 141–43.

16. *Journals of Dr. George Hunter*, 8–10.

17. William Dunbar to Henry Dearborn, May 13, 1804, in *Life, Letters and Papers of William Dunbar*, 128–29.

18. William Dunbar to Thomas Jefferson, May 13, 1804, in *Life, Letters and Papers of William Dunbar*, 130–31.

19. Ibid., 130–33.

20. Cox, "Exploration of the Louisiana Frontier," 154–55; *Journals of Dr. George Hunter*, 10.

21. *Journals of Dr. George Hunter*, 10.

22. William Dunbar to Peter Walker, June 10, 1804, in *Life, Letters and Papers of William Dunbar*, 135–37.

23. Dunbar to Freeman, June 14, 1804, 138.

24. Dunbar to Dearborn, June 15, 1804, 139.

25. *Journals of Dr. George Hunter*, 11.

26. Ibid.

27. William Dunbar to Thomas Jefferson, June 9, 1804, in *Life, Letters and Papers of William Dunbar*, 133–35; William Dunbar to Lt. Col. Thomas Freeman, June 14, 1804, in *Life, Letters and Papers of William Dunbar*, 137–38.

28. Dunbar to Jefferson, June 9, 1804, 133–35; William Dunbar to Henry Dearborn, June 15, 1804, in *Life, Letters and Papers of William Dunbar*, 138–39.

29. *Journal of Dr. George Hunter*, 11; Thomas Jefferson to William Dunbar, July 17, 1804, WDP-MDAH.

30. Allen, "Jefferson and the Louisiana-Arkansas Frontier," 47; Gratz, "Thomas Rodney," pt. 2, 54–55; Dunbar to Jefferson, June 9, 1804, 135–36.

31. *Journals of Dr. George Hunter*, 11; Jefferson to Dunbar, July 17, 1804, WDP-MDAH.

32. *Journals of Dr. George Hunter*, 10.

33. Ibid., 11; William Dunbar to Thomas Jefferson, August 18, 1804, in *Life,*

Letters and Papers of William Dunbar, 122–23, 139–40; Cox, "Exploration of the Louisiana Frontier," 155–56.

34. Dunbar to Jefferson, August 18, 1804, 139–40.

35. Bill of sale, August 30, 1804, WDP-MDAH.

36. William Dunbar to Thomas Jefferson, October 14, 1804, in *Life, Letters and Papers of William Dunbar*, 140–41; William Dunbar to Thomas Jefferson, October 15, 1804, in *Life, Letters and Papers of William Dunbar*, 160–62.

37. Dunbar to Jefferson, October 14, 1804, 144.

38. Dunbar to Jefferson, October 15, 1804, 161.

39. Dunbar to Jefferson, October 14, 1804, 140–41.

13. One Hundred Three Days

1. William Dunbar, "Journal of a Voyage Commencing at St. Catherine's Landing, on the East Bank of the Mississippi, Proceeding Downwards to the Mouth of the Red River, and from Thence Ascending That River, the Black River and the Washita River, as High as the Hot-Springs in the Proximity of the Last Mentioned River," October 16, 1804–January 26, 1805, day 1, October 16, 1804, in *Life, Letters and Papers of William Dunbar*, 216.

2. *Journals of Dr. George Hunter*, 13.

3. Dunbar, "Journal of a Voyage," day 2, October 17, 1804, 216–17.

4. Ibid., day 3, October 18, 1804, 217.

5. Ibid., day 4, October 19, 1804, 217.

6. Ibid., day 5, October 20, 1804, 218–19.

7. Ibid., day 6, October 21, 1804, 219–20.

8. Ibid., day 8, October 23, 1804, 221–23.

9. Ibid., day 10, October 25, 1804, 224–26; ibid., day 11, October 26, 1804, 227.

10. Ibid., day 12, October 27, 1804, 227–28.

11. Ibid., day 16, October 31, 1804, 230–31; ibid., day 18, November 2, 1804, 232; ibid., day 17, November 1, 1804, 231–32.

12. Ibid., day 18, November 2, 1804, 232.

13. Ibid., day 22, November 6, 1804, 235–36.

14. Ibid., day 27, November 11, 1804, 238–39; Jennie O'Kelly Mitchell and Robert Dabney Calhoun, "The Marquis de Maison Rouge, The Baron de Bastrop, and Colonel Abraham Morehouse, Three Ouachita Valley Soldiers of Fortune," *Louisiana Historical Quarterly* 20 (1937): 393.

15. Dunbar, "Journal of a Voyage," days 23–26, November 7–10, 1804, 236–38.

16. *Journals of Dr. George Hunter*, 13.

17. Dunbar, "Journal of a Voyage," day 28, November 12, 1804, 239.

18. Ibid., day 29, November 13, 1804, 239–40.

19. Ibid., day 30, November 14, 1804, 240–41.

20. Ibid., day 31, November 15, 1804, 241–42; *Journals of Dr. George Hunter*, 13.

21. *Journals of Dr. George Hunter*, 13–14; Dunbar quoted in ibid.

22. Dunbar, "Journal of a Voyage," day 31, November 15, 1804, 241–42.

23. Ibid., day 32, November 16, 1804, 242–43.

24. Ibid., day 33, November 17, 1804, 243–44.

25. Ibid., day 39, November 23, 1804, 249–50.

26. Ibid., day 42, November 26, 1804, 252–53.

27. Ibid., day 43, November 27, 1904, 253–54.

28. Ibid., days 44, 45, November 28, 29, 1804, 255–57.

29. Ibid., day 48, December 2, 1804, 259–60.

30. Ibid., day 49, December 3, 1804, 260–62. The chutes are located near present-day Rockport, Arkansas.

31. Ibid., day 50, December 4, 1804, 263–64.

32. Ibid., day 51, December 5, 1804, 264–66.

33. Ibid., day 52, December 6, 1804, 266–67.

34. Ibid., days 53, 55, December 7, 9, 1804, 267–72.

35. Ibid., day 53, December 7, 1804, 267–68.

36. Ibid., day 55, December 9, 1804, 269–72.

37. Ibid., day 54, December 8, 1804, 268–69.

38. Ibid., day 57, December 11, 1804, 274–75.

39. Ibid., day 56, December 10, 1804, 272–74.

40. Ibid., day 58, December 12, 1804, 275–76.

41. Ibid., day 59, December 13, 1804, 276–79.

42. Ibid., day 70, December 24, 1804, 289–92. Dunbar's fascination with the springs is also evident in observations from December 15 (day 61) to December 23 (day 69), 279–289, when, weather permitting, he returned time and again to the hot springs for further study and additional samples to take back to his laboratory at the Forest for study.

43. Ibid., day 70, December 24, 1804, 289–92.

44. Ibid., day 71, December 25, 1804, 292.

45. Ibid., days 73, 74, December 27, 28, 1804, 294–95.

46. Ibid., day 73, December 27, 1804, 294.

47. Ibid., day 74, December 28, 1804, 296–97.

48. Ibid., day 76, December 30, 1804, 299–300.

49. Ibid., day 81, January 4, 1805, 302.

50. Ibid., day 85, January 8, 1805, 304–5.

51. Ibid., day 86, January 9, 1805, 305.

52. Ibid., day 87, January 10, 1805, 306–9.

53. Ibid., day 92, January 15, 1805, 312–14.

54. Ibid., days 93, 95, 96, January 16, 18, 19, 1805, 314.

55. Ibid., days 95, 96, January 18, 19, 1805, 314.

56. Ibid., day 97, January 20, 1805, 314–16.

57. Ibid., days 98, 99, 102, January 21, 22, 25, 1805, 317–20.

58. Ibid., day 103, January 26, 1805, 320.

14. Moments of Success and Disappointment

1. William Dunbar to Thomas Jefferson, February 12, 1805, in *Life, Letters and Papers of William Dunbar*, 142–43.

2. Jack D. L. Holmes, ed., *Documentos ineditos para la historia de la Luisiana, 1798–1810* (Madrid: Ediciones Jose Pormu Turanzas, 1963), 361.

3. Cox, "Exploration of the Louisiana Frontier," 158–59.

4. Jefferson quoted in Allen, "Jefferson and the Louisiana-Arkansas Frontier," 53–54.

5. William Dunbar to Thomas Jefferson, February 13, 1805, in *Life, Letters and Papers of William Dunbar*, 144.

6. Dunbar to Jefferson, February 12, 1805, 142–43.

7. Dunbar quoted in *Journals of Dr. George Hunter*, 14–15.

8. Allen, "Jefferson and the Louisiana-Arkansas Frontier," 54–55.

9. William Dunbar, *Journal of a Geometrical Survey Commencing at St. Catherine's Landing, on the East Shore of the Mississippi Descending to the Mouth of the Red River, and from Thence Ascending That River, the Black River and River of the Washita as High as the Hot Springs in the Proximity of the Last Mentioned River* (Boston and New York: Houghton Mifflin, 1904), 64.

10. Dunbar to Jefferson, February 13, 1805, 144.

11. Ibid., 13–15.

12. *Journals of Dr. George Hunter*, 15.

13. William Dunbar to Thomas Jefferson, February 15, 1805, in *The Writings of Thomas Jefferson: Being His Autobiography, Correspondence, Reports, Messages, Addresses, and Other Writings, Official and Private*, ed. H. A. Washington (Washington, DC: Taylor and Maury, 1854), 4:15.

14. Allen, "Jefferson and the Louisiana-Arkansas Frontier," 54–55.

15. William Dunbar to Thomas Jefferson, March 9, 1805, in *Life, Letters and Papers of William Dunbar*, 144.

16. Thomas Jefferson to William Dunbar, March 14, 1805, in *Life, Letters and Papers of William Dunbar*, 152.

17. Henry Dearborn to William Dunbar, March 25, 1805, in *Life, Letters and Papers of William Dunbar*, 150–52.

18. John Sibley to William Dunbar, April 2, 1805, in *Life, Letters and Papers of William Dunbar*, 162–77.

19. William Dunbar to Henry Dearborn, May 4, 1805, in *Life, Letters and Papers of William Dunbar*, 148–50.

20. Henry Dearborn to William Dunbar, May 24, 1805, in *Life, Letters and Papers of William Dunbar*, 152–53.

21. *Writings of Thomas Jefferson*, ed. Washington, 4:577, 578–90.

22. *Official Letter Books of William C. C. Claiborne*, 3:119.

23. *Writings of Thomas Jefferson*, ed. Washington, 4:577, 579–80; *Journals of George Hunter*, 15.

24. Carter, *Territorial Papers*, 5:554.

25. *Official Letter Books of William C. C. Claiborne*, 3:119–20, 128–29.

26. William Dunbar to Thomas Jefferson, July 6, 1805, in *Life, Letters and Papers of William Dunbar*, 154–56.

27. William Dunbar to Thomas Jefferson, July 9, 1805, in *Writings of Thomas Jefferson*, ed. Washington, 5:19.

28. William Dunbar to Thomas Jefferson, November 10, 1805, in *Life, Letters and Papers of William Dunbar*, 184.

29. Henry Dearborn to William Dunbar, July 10, 1805, in *Life, Letters and Papers of William Dunbar*, 156–57.

30. William Dunbar to Henry Dearborn, July 21, 1805, in *Life, Letters and Papers of William Dunbar*, 158–59.

31. *Official Letter Books of William C. C. Claiborne*, 3:141–42.

32. William Dunbar to Thomas Jefferson, October 8, 1805, in *Life, Letters and Papers of William Dunbar*, 182–84.

33. William Dunbar to Thomas Jefferson, December 17, 1805, in *Life, Letters and Papers of William Dunbar*, 187–88.

34. *Official Letter Books of William C. C. Claiborne*, 3:206–7.

35. Dan L. Flores, ed., *Jefferson and Southwestern Exploration: The Freeman and Custis Accounts of the Red River Expedition of 1806* (Norman: University of Oklahoma Press, 1984), 81, 86; Henry Dearborn to Peter Custis, January 14, 1806, in *Life, Letters and Papers of William Dunbar*, 193–94; Peter Custis to Henry Dearborn, September 24, 1806, in *Life, Letters and Papers of William Dunbar*, 214–15.

36. Allen, "Jefferson and the Louisiana-Arkansas Frontier," 56–57.

37. Thomas Jefferson to the U.S. Congress, February 19, 1806, in *A Compilation of the Messages and Papers of the Presidents*, ed. James D. Richardson (Washington, DC: GPO, 1897), 1:386–87. Jefferson enclosed a copy of Dunbar's journal of the trip.

38. *Discoveries Made in Exploring the Missouri, Red River, and Washita, by Captains Lewis and Clark, Doctor Sibley, and William Dunbar, Esq. with a Statistical Account of the Countries Adjacent* (Natchez, MS: Marschalk, 1806), 113–64; Henry Dearborn to William Dunbar, August 14, 1805, in *Life, Letters and Papers of William Dunbar*, 177; *Mississippi Herald and Natchez Gazette*, May 27, 1806; *Mississippi Messenger*, June 10, 1806.

39. William Dunbar to Thomas Jefferson, December 17, 1805, in *Life, Letters and Papers of William Dunbar*, 187–88.

40. *Official Letter Books of William C. C. Claiborne*, 3:261–64.

41. Ibid., 3:265, 267; W. C. C. Claiborne to William Dunbar, February 12, 1806, in *Life, Letters and Papers of William Dunbar*, 190.

42. William Dunbar to Henry Dearborn, February 25, 1806, in *Life, Letters and Papers of William Dunbar*, 329–30.

43. William Dunbar to Thomas Jefferson, February 25, 1806, in *Life, Letters and Papers of William Dunbar*, 330–31.

44. Thomas Jefferson to William Dunbar, March 28, 1806, in *Life, Letters and Papers of William Dunbar*, 192–93.

45. William Dunbar to Henry Dearborn, March 18, April 1, May 6, 1806, in *Life, Letters and Papers of William Dunbar*, 194–95, 331–33, 336–37; William Dunbar to Thomas Jefferson, May 6, 1806, in *Life, Letters and Papers of William Dunbar*, 342.

46. William Dunbar to Henry Dearborn, June 24, September 6, 1806, in *Life, Letters and Papers of William Dunbar*, 347–48; Cox, "Exploration of the Louisiana Frontier," 159–60, 168, 173; G. P. Whittington, ed., "Letters of Dr. John Sibley

of Louisiana to His Son Samuel Hopkins Sibley, 1803–1821," *Louisiana Historical Quarterly* 10 (1927): 500–501.

47. William Dunbar to Thomas Jefferson, March 16, 1806, in *Life, Letters and Papers of William Dunbar*, 147–48; William Dunbar to Chew and Relf, April 4, 1807, in *Life, Letters and Papers of William Dunbar*, 153; Allen, "Jefferson and the Louisiana-Arkansas Frontier," 55–56.

48. Henry Dearborn to William Dunbar, March 30, 1807, in *Life, Letters and Papers of William Dunbar*, 197–98.

49. Dearborn quoted in William Dunbar to Lt. Col. Kingsberry, June 6, 1807, in *Life, Letters and Papers of William Dunbar*, 354–55.

50. William Dunbar to William Simmons, August 9, 1809, in *Life, Letters and Papers of William Dunbar*, 366–70; Secretary of War to William Dunbar, November 2, 1809, WDP-MDAH.

51. *Journals of Dr. George Hunter*, 5; Cox, "Exploration of the Louisiana Frontier," 151.

52. Mary D. Hudgins, "William Dunbar, History Maker," *Arkansas Historical Quarterly* 1 (1942): 331.

15. The Importance of Education

1. William Dunbar to John Vaughn, May 2, 1808, in *Life, Letters and Papers of William Dunbar*, 361–62.

2. Ibid.

3. Ibid., 363.

4. William Dunbar to William Dunbar Jr., July 28, 1808, WDP-MDAH.

5. Ibid.

6. Ibid.

7. William B. Hamilton, "The Southwestern Frontier, 1795–1817, an Essay in Social History," *Journal of Southern History* 10 (1944): 396–97.

8. An Act to Incorporate the Mississippi Society for the Acquirement and Dissemination of Useful Knowledge, *Acts Passed by the Second General Assembly of the Mississippi Territory, during Their First Session* (Jackson, MS: Marschalk, 1804), 16–17; Hamilton, *Thomas Rodney*, 87; Sydnor, *Gentleman of the Old Natchez Region*, 124–25.

9. Act to Incorporate the Mississippi Society, 17.

10. William B. Fowler, "The History of Jefferson College of Washington, Mississippi, Prior to the War for Southern Independence" (master's thesis, Louisiana State University, 1937), 22–24.

11. Hatfield, "Public Career of W. C. C. Claiborne," 127–28.

12. Ibid., 128; Fowler, "History of Jefferson College," 28–29; Dunbar Rowland, "The Mississippi Valley in American History," *Proceedings of the Mississippi Valley Historical Association* 9 (1915–16): 65.

13. An Act to Establish a College in the Mississippi Territory, *Acts Passed at the Third Session of the First General Assembly of the Mississippi Territory* (Natchez, MS: Marschalk, 1804), 7–8; An Act Empowering the Board of Trustees of Jefferson College to Elect New Trustees, *Acts Passed by the Second General Assembly of the*

Mississippi Territory, during Their First Session, 17–18; Fowler, "History of Jefferson College," 35–36.

14. William B. Hamilton, "Jefferson College and Education in Mississippi, 1798–1817," *Journal of Mississippi History* 3 (1941): 262–64, 269; Hatfield, "Public Career of W. C. C. Claiborne," 130–32.

15. Natchez common council, minutes book, August 16, 1803, March 3, 1804, May 20, 1805, May 8, 1806, microfilm roll 481, Mississippi Department of Archives and History; Carter, *Territorial Papers,* 5:346–49.

16. Natchez common council minutes book, August 16, 1803, March 3, 1804, Mississippi Department of Archives and History; Carter, *Territorial Papers,* 5:347–49; Hamilton, "Jefferson College," 265–66.

17. Fowler, "History of Jefferson College," 29.

18. Hamilton, "Jefferson College," 266–68; Monette, *History of the Discovery,* 2:350–51; *Journals of the General Assembly of the Mississippi Territory,* 1.

19. Rowland, *History of Mississippi,* 1:385–86; Andrew Marschalk Papers, Mississippi Department of Archives and History.

20. J. K. Morrison, "Early History of Jefferson College," *Publications of the Mississippi Historical Society* 2 (1899): 183.

21. Natchez common council, minutes book, August 18, 1803, November 22, 1804, March 19, 1805, Mississippi Department of Archives and History; Thomas Rodney to Dunbar Lattimore, January 22, 1806, Thomas Rodney Papers, Mississippi Department of Archives and History; House Committee on Public Lands, *Report of the Committee on Public Lands, March 4, 1806,* 9th Cong., 1st sess., 1806 (Washington, DC: Way, 1806), 8–11; William Dunbar to Thomas Jefferson, January 18, 1804, in *Life, Letters and Papers of William Dunbar,* 126–27; *Mississippi Messenger,* April 15, 1806; Fowler, "History of Jefferson College," 33, 37.

22. House Committee, *Report of the Committee on Public Lands,* 3–8; *Mississippi Messenger,* April 15, 1806.

23. Morrison, "Early History of Jefferson College," 182–83.

24. Hatfield, "Public Career of W. C. C. Claiborne," 128–30.

25. Hamilton, "Jefferson College," 271–72; Act to Establish a College, 7–8.

26. Hamilton, "Jefferson College," 271–72; *Natchez (MS) Weekly Chronicle,* December 2, 1809; Morrison, "Early History of Jefferson College," 184.

27. Morrison, "Early History of Jefferson College," 184; *Natchez (MS) Weekly Chronicle,* April 2, 1810.

28. Morrison, "Early History of Jefferson College," 184.

29. J. Andrew Liddell to John Liddell, July 3, 1848, Liddell Family Papers, Department of Archives and Manuscripts, Louisiana State University.

30. John Bisland to William Steele, August 30, 1817, letter copy book, Bisland Family Papers, Department of Archives and Manuscripts, Louisiana State University.

16. Politics, Mississippi Style

1. Whittington, "Letters of Dr. John Sibley," 487; Kane, *Natchez on the Mississippi,* 81–82.

2. William Dunbar's political activities were such that if he were living today he would most likely be a Republican. Though he agreed with Washington, Jefferson, and others that the nation would be better served without political parties, he believed that if parties were to exist, they should serve the needs of those supporting national goals. In his view, parties existed to serve citizens, not the other way around. That belief allowed him to serve Federalist as well as Democratic-Republican leaders without changing his political convictions.

3. Holmes, *Gayoso*, 256–57.

4. William B. McGroarty, ed., "Diary of Captain Philip Buckner," *William and Mary College Quarterly Historical Magazine* 6 (1926): 201, 190, 203–4, 202.

5. William Dunbar to Winthrop Sargent, November 8, 1798, September 18, 1799, WSP-MHS.

6. Dunbar to Sargent, September 18, 1799, WSP-MHS.

7. Dunbar to Sargent, November 8, 1798, WSP-MHS; Rowland, *Mississippi Territorial Archives*, 1:78–79.

8. Rowland, *Mississippi Territorial Archives*, 1:78–79.

9. William Dunbar to Winthrop Sargent, August 10, 1799, in *Life, Letters and Papers of William Dunbar*, 102–3; William Dunbar to Winthrop Sargent, August 31, 1800, WSP-MHS.

10. Dunbar quoted in Kane, *Natchez on the Mississippi*, 116.

11. Rowland, *History of Mississippi*, 1:354–55; Dunbar to Sargent, November 8, 1798, WSP-MHS.

12. William Dunbar to Winthrop Sargent, November 8, 1798, October 29, 1800, March 16, 1801, WSP-MHS; Winthrop Sargent, proclamation, April 5, 1799, WDP-MDAH; Winthrop Sargent to William Dunbar, April 3, June 7, 1799, in *Life, Letters and Papers of William Dunbar*, 99–100; Winthrop Sargent to John Marshall, August 25, 1800, in Rowland, *Mississippi Territorial Archives*, 1:274–75; Dunbar Rowland, *Courts, Judges, and Lawyers of Mississippi, 1799–1935* (Jackson, MS: Hederman, 1935), 1; Rowland, *History of Mississippi*, 1:363; Winthrop Sargent, proclamation, April 6, 1799, WDP-MDAH; justice of the peace commission, December 31, 1799, WDP-MDAH; justice of the peace commission, July 2, 1800, in Rowland, *Mississippi Territorial Archives*, 1:257; Winthrop Sargent to William Dunbar, October 20, 1800, in Rowland, *Mississippi Territorial Archives*, 1:298–99; Winthrop Sargent to William Dunbar, April 6, 1799, in *Life, Letters and Papers of William Dunbar*, 101; Rowland, *Courts, Judges and Lawyers*, 4; *Official Letter Books of W. C. C. Claiborne*, 1:64.

13. Carter, *Territorial Papers*, 5:133–34; Adams County Board of Supervisors, *Transcriptions of County Archives of Mississippi, No. 2, Adams County (Natchez): Minutes of the Court of General Quarter Sessions of the Peace, 1799–1801* (Jackson, MS: N.p., 1942), 1:1, 4, 56, 66, 148; Adams County Board of Supervisors, *Minutes of the County Court*, 2:82; Natchez mayor's court, letter book, 1803–5, microfilm, roll 481, Mississippi Department of Archives and History; charge delivered to grand jury by Quarter Sessions Court Judge William Dunbar, June 4, 1800, in *Life, Letters and Papers of William Dunbar*, 10–11, 106–8; Mississippi Territory General Assembly, A Law to Provide for the Inspection of Cotton Gins, Cotton Presses and Cot-

ton, Intended for Exportation from the Mississippi Territory, *Laws of the Mississippi Territory, September 21–October 5, 1799* (Jackson, MS: N.p., n.d.), 14–16; Adams County Board of Supervisors, *Minutes of the Court of General Quarter Sessions*, 1:36; Hamilton, "Early Cotton Regulation," 21–23.

14. Adams County Board of Supervisors, *Minutes of the Court of General Quarter Sessions*, 1:56; Adams County Board of Supervisors, *Minutes of the County Court*, 2:82.

15. Carter, *Territorial Papers*, 5:122–23; *Natchez (MS) Green's Impartial Observer*, March 7, 1801; William L. Jenks, "Territorial Legislation by Governor and Judges," *Mississippi Valley Historical Review* 5 (1918): 36, 44; Robert V. Haynes, "The Revolution of 1800 in Mississippi," *Journal of Mississippi History* 19 (1957): 246–47.

16. Jenks, "Territorial Legislation," 36, 44; Haynes, "Revolution of 1800," 246–47; Mississippi Territory House of Representatives, *Report, in Part, of the Committee to Whom Were Referred on the 13th Ultimo, a Petition of Cato West, and Others, in Behalf of Themselves and the Other Inhabitants of the Mississippi Territory*, February 18, 1800 (Jackson: Mississippi Territory House of Representatives, 1806), 3–9.

17. Mississippi Territory House, *Report, in Part, of the Committee*, 3–9; Adams County Board of Supervisors, *Minutes of the Court of General Quarter Sessions*, 1:106.

18. Carter, *Territorial Papers*, 5:110–15.

19. Bettersworth, *Mississippi*, 124.

20. Adams County Board of Supervisors, *Minutes of the Court of General Quarter Sessions*, 1:177; An Act Supplementary to an Act Entitled "An Act Providing for the Inspection of Cotton" Passed the 10th day of March, 1803, *Acts Passed by the Second General Assembly of the Mississippi Territory, during Their First Session*, 2–3; Hamilton, "Early Cotton Regulation," 20–25.

21. Carter, *Territorial Papers*, 5:152, 637; Haynes, "Revolution of 1800," 240–42; Douglas C. McMurtrie, ed., *The Mississippi Militia Law of 1799: A Note on This Natchez Imprint of February, 1799, Accompanied by a Complete Facsimile of the Apparently Unique Copy of the Law Preserved in the Archivo General de Indias at Seville, Spain* (Chicago: John Calhoun Club, 1933), 2–11; Carter, *Territorial Papers*, 5:483–84, 488–89; Hamilton, *Anglo-American Law*, 138; Thomas Jefferson to William Dunbar, March 3, 1803, [other date blurred], in *Life, Letters and Papers of William Dunbar*, 158–59, 204–5.

22. Carter, *Territorial Papers*, 5:297–98.

23. Hamilton, *Anglo-American Law*, 138.

24. Hatfield, "Public Career of W. C. C. Claiborne," 121–22; Adams County Board of Supervisors, *Minutes of the Court of General Quarter Sessions*, 1:169; McGroarty, "Diary of Captain Philip Buckner," 189.

25. Hatfield, "Public Career of W. C. C. Claiborne," 122–23.

26. Ibid., 120–21; Rowland, *History of Mississippi*, 1:370, 373, 476.

27. An Act to Prevent the Importation and Spreading of the Small-pox within This Territory, *Acts Passed by the Third Session of the First General Assembly of the Mississippi Territory* (Jackson, MS: Marschalk, 1804), 10–11; A Law Concerning

Aliens and Contagious Diseases, *Laws of the Mississippi Territory, 1799* (Natchez, MS: Marschalk, 1799), 106–7.

28. An Act Supplementary to the Acts of the General Assembly Providing for the Raising of a Revenue Passed the 30th of January 1802 and the 12th of March 1803, *Acts Passed by the Second General Assembly of the Mississippi Territory, during Their First Session*, 6.

29. Carter, *Territorial Papers*, 5:267, 274–75.

30. Jefferson quoted in Gaillard Hunt, "Office-Seeking during Jefferson's Administration," *American Historical Review* 3 (1898): 270–71.

31. Bettersworth, *Mississippi*, 125.

32. George Granger to Robert Williams, November 20, 1806, Robert Williams Papers, Mississippi Department of Archives and History; Thomas P. Abernethy, "Aaron Burr in Mississippi," *Journal of Southern History* 11 (1949): 19–21.

33. Rowland quoted in *Life, Letters and Papers of William Dunbar*, 12.

34. Ellicott, *Journal of Andrew Ellicott*; Ellicott quoted in Carter, *Territorial Papers*, 5:132.

17. At Home

1. Gratz, "Thomas Rodney," pt. 1, 209–11.

2. Ibid., 211.

3. Mississippi Territory House, *Report, in Part, of the Committee*, 10–11.

4. Ibid.

5. Allen, "Jefferson and the Louisiana-Arkansas Frontier," 201–2.

6. Rodney quoted in Davis, *Travels in Louisiana and the Floridas*, 105.

7. Gratz, "Thomas Rodney," pt. 2, 181–82.

8. Davis, *Travels in Louisiana and the Floridas*, 105.

9. Fortescue Cuming, *Sketches of a Tour to the Western Country, through the States of Ohio and Kentucky: A Voyage down the Ohio and Mississippi Rivers, and a Trip through the Mississippi Territory, and Part of West Florida, Commenced at Philadelphia in the Winter of 1807 and Concluded in 1809* (Cleveland, OH: Clark, 1904), 310.

10. Ibid., 319.

11. Ibid., 315–16, 319–23; McGroarty, "Diary of Captain Philip Buckner," 187.

12. Stokes, "John Bisland," 30–31.

13. Hatfield, "Public Career of W. C. C. Claiborne," 146–48.

14. McGroarty, "Diary of Captain Philip Buckner," 187.

15. Mack Swearingen, ed., "Luxury at Natchez in 1801: A Ship's Manifest from the McDonogh Papers," *Journal of Southern History* 2 (1937): 189.

16. Abijah Hunt, record book, June 1, 1797–May 10, 1799, Mississippi Department of Archives and History.

17. William Dunbar to John Vaughn, 1806, in *Life, Letters and Papers of William Dunbar*, 337–38.

18. William Dunbar to Green and Wainwright, 1806, in *Life, Letters and Papers of William Dunbar*, 343–45.

19. Gratz, "Thomas Rodney," pt. 2, 298.

20. Ibid., 186–87; ibid., pt. 1, 359.

21. Ibid., pt. 2, 86–87; Thomas Rodney, diary entry, 1804, Mississippi Department of Archives and History.

22. Gratz, "Thomas Rodney," pt. 2, 187.

23. Ibid., pt. 1, 359.

24. Hamilton, *Anglo-American Law*, 150; *Mississippi Messenger*, September 16, 1806.

25. *Mississippi Messenger*, February 25, 1808.

26. Hamilton, *Anglo-American Law*, 422–23.

27. Gratz, "Thomas Rodney," pt. 1, 334, 353.

28. Kane, *Natchez on the Mississippi*, 50–51.

29. McQueen, "Remembrances of My Grandfather."

30. *Montgomery (AL) Advertiser*, December 14, 1941.

31. Cuming, *Sketches of a Tour*, 323–26, 360–61; Gratz, "Thomas Rodney," pt. 1, 360–61; Gratz, "Thomas Rodney," pt. 2, 189.

32. Gratz, "Thomas Rodney," pt. 1, 360–61.

33. Ibid., 189; ibid., pt. 2, 360–61.

34. Ibid., pt. 1, 189.

35. "Forester," June 5, 1844, WDP-MDAH.

36. Rodney, diary entry, 1804, Mississippi Department of Archives and History.

37. *Mississippi Messenger*, January 21, 1808.

38. William Dunbar to William Dunbar Jr., July 2, 1808, WDP-MDAH.

18. The End of a Life

1. Samuel Postlewaite to Green and Wainwright, November 22, 1810, in *Life, Letters and Papers of William Dunbar*, 389.

2. Samuel Postlewaite to John Vaughn, November 27, 1810, in *Life, Letters and Papers of William Dunbar*, 399; Samuel Postlewaite to Chew and Relf, March 15, 1811, in *Life, Letters and Papers of William Dunbar*, 399; William Dunbar, will proven January 8, 1816, records of wills, no. 1, Adams County, Mississippi.

3. Samuel Postlewaite to Chew and Relf, November 5, 1810, in *Life, Letters and Papers of William Dunbar*, 380–82; Samuel Postlewaite to Green and Wainwright, November 22, 1810, May 5, June 14, 1811, in *Life, Letters and Papers of William Dunbar*, 389–90, 400–401; Samuel Postlewaite to John Vaughn, June 25, 1811, in *Life, Letters and Papers of William Dunbar*, 401–2; accountant's balance, February 27, 1812, WDP-MDAH.

4. Postlewaite to Chew and Relf, November 5, 1810, March 15, 1811, 380–82, 399; Postlewaite to Green and Wainwright, November 22, 1810, 389–90.

5. Samuel Postlewaite to Dinah Dunbar, October 26, 1810, WDP-MDAH.

6. Samuel Postlewaite to Chew and Relf, November 5, 15, 1810, in *Life, Letters and Papers of William Dunbar*, 380–82; Samuel Postlewaite to Matthew Pearce, November 15, 1810, in *Life, Letters and Papers of William Dunbar*, 382.

7. Samuel Postlewaite to Matthew Pearce, February 11, 1811, in *Life, Letters and Papers of William Dunbar*, 395–96.

8. Samuel Postlewaite to William Simmons, February 4, 1811, in *Life, Letters and Papers of William Dunbar*, 394–95.

9. Samuel Postlewaite to Chew and Relf, November 16, 1810, in *Life, Letters and Papers of William Dunbar*, 383.

10. Samuel Postlewaite to William Dunbar Jr., January 29, 1811, William Dunbar, letter book, Mississippi Department of Archives and History.

11. Samuel Postlewaite to Archibald Dunbar, November 17, 1810, in *Life, Letters and Papers of William Dunbar,* 383–85; Samuel Postlewaite to James Ross, November 17, 1810, in *Life, Letters and Papers of William Dunbar*, 386–87.

12. Postlewaite to Chew and Relf, November 5, 1810, 380–82.

13. Samuel Postlewaite to Chew and Relf, November 21, 1810, in *Life, Letters and Papers of William Dunbar*, 387–88.

14. Abstract no. 701, Covering the South 160 Acres of the Marian Davis Ogden 510 Acre Tract out of "The Forest Plantation," August 28, 1816, Adams County, MS, Mississippi Department of Archives and History.

15. Birth, marriage, and death of Dunbar children, WDP-MDAH.

16. William Dunbar, will recorded October 13, 1810, WDP-MDAH.

17. A. B. Wooley to Field Dunbar, February 4, 1848, WDP-MDAH.

18. Abstract no. 701, Mississippi Department of Archives and History.

19. Dividing Dunbar Estate, January 17, 1825, Adams County, MS, WDP-MDAH.

20. Stephen Duncan to George Banks, January 23, 1825, WDP-MDAH.

21. Final Account of Dunbar's Estate, March 1828, Adams County, MS, WDP-MDAH.

22. Kane, *Natchez on the Mississippi*, 51–52.

23. John Jones to William Dunbar, March 13, 1769, in *Life, Letters and Papers of William Dunbar*, 19–20.

24. Dunbar, will proven January 8, 1816.

25. Circular, May 18, 1846, in the possession of Douglas McQueen.

26. Robert T. Dunbar, will recorded December 4, 1837, WDP-MDAH.

27. Ibid.

28. McQueen, "Remembrances of My Grandfather."

Selected Bibliography

Unpublished Manuscript Collections

Scottish Record Office, Register House, Edinburgh
Broughton and Cally Papers

Elgin Public Library, Elgin, Scotland
"An Outline of the Antiquities and History of Elgin with an Account of the Number, Extent, and Grandeur of the Religious Establishments in and around the City"

Mississippi Department of Archives and History, Jackson
William Dunbar, letter book, 1805–12
William Dunbar Papers
Abijah Hunt, record book, June 1, 1797–May 10, 1799
Andrew Marschalk Papers
Natchez common council, minutes book, 1803–14, microfilm roll 481
Natchez mayor's court, minutes book, 1803–5, microfilm roll 481
Thomas Rodney, diary, 1804
Thomas Rodney Papers
Robert Williams Papers

Department of Archives and Manuscripts, Louisiana State University, Baton Rouge
Bisland Family Papers, 1817
David Bradford Letters, 1798–1805
Liddell Family Papers, 1847–48
Mathews Family Papers, 1797, 1834–42

Massachusetts Historical Society, Boston
Winthrop Sargent Papers

Unpublished Master's Theses and Dissertation

Fowler, William B. "The History of Jefferson College of Washington, Mississippi, Prior to the War for Southern Independence." Master's thesis, Louisiana State University, 1937.

Hatfield, Joseph T. "The Public Career of William C. C. Claiborne." PhD diss., Emory University, 1962.

Stokes, Beatrice M. "John Bisland, Mississippi Planter, 1776–1821." Master's thesis, Louisiana State University, 1941.

Public Documents

Adams County Board of Supervisors. *Transcription of County Archives of Mississippi, No. 2, Adams County (Natchez): Minutes of the County Court, 1802–1804*. Jackson, MS: N.p., 1942.

———. *Transcription of County Archives of Mississippi, No. 2, Adams County (Natchez): Minutes of the Court of General Quarter Sessions of the Peace, 1799–1801*. Jackson, MS: N.p., 1942.

Addison, W. Innes, ed. *The Matriculation Albums of the University of Glasgow from 1728 to 1858*. Glasgow: MacLehose, 1913.

———, ed. *A Roll of the University of Glasgow from 31st December 1727 to 31st December 1897, with Short Bibliographical Notes*. Glasgow: MacLehose, 1898.

Anderson, Peter John, ed. *Lists of Officers of the University and King's College of Aberdeen, 1495–1860*. Aberdeen, Scotland: University of Aberdeen, 1893.

———, ed. *Officers and Graduates of the University and King's College of Aberdeen*. Aberdeen, Scotland: Melne and Hutchison, 1893.

———, ed. *Roll of Alumni in Arts of the University and King's College of Aberdeen, 1596–1860*. Aberdeen, Scotland: University of Aberdeen, 1900.

Carter, Clarence Edwin, ed. *The Territorial Papers of the United States*. Vol. 5. Washington, DC: GPO, 1937.

Claiborne, W. C. C. *Official Letter Books of W. C. C. Claiborne, 1801–1816*. Edited by Dunbar Rowland. 6 vols. Jackson, MS: State Department of Archives and History, 1917.

Cramond, William, ed. *The Church of Alves*. Elgin, Scotland: *Courant and Courier* Office, 1900.

———, ed. *The Records of Elgin, 1234–1800*. 2 vols. Aberdeen, Scotland: Milne and Hutchison, 1903.

Craven, J. B. *History of the Episcopal Church in the Diocese of Moray*. Kirkwall, Scotland: Pierce, 1889.

Crèvecoeur, J. Hector St. John. *Letters from an American Farmer*. Garden City, NY: Doubleday.

Discoveries Made in Exploring the Missouri, Red River and Washita, by Captains Lewis and Clark, Doctor Sibley, and William Dunbar, Esq. with a Statistical Account of the Countries Adjacent. Natchez, MS: Marschalk, 1806.

Dunbar, E., ed. *Social Life in Former Days Chiefly in the Province of Moray, Illustrated by Letters and Family Papers*. 2 vols. Edinburgh: Edmonston and Douglas, 1865–66.

Dunbar, William. *Life, Letters and Papers of William Dunbar of Elgin, Morayshire, Scotland, and Natchez, Mississippi*. Edited by Eron Rowland. Jackson: Press of the Mississippi Historical Society, 1930.

Ellicott, Andrew. *The Journal of Andrew Ellicott.* Chicago: Quadrangle Books, 1962.

Forbes, Duncan, ed. *Ane Account of the Familie of Innes.* Aberdeen, Scotland: Spaulding Club, 1864.

Holmes, Jack D. L., ed. *Documentos ineditos para la historia de la Luisiana, 1792–1810.* Madrid: Ediciones Jose Pormu Turanzas, 1963.

Innes, Cosmo, ed. *Selections from the Records of the University and King's College of Aberdeen, 1796–1854.* Aberdeen, Scotland: Spaulding Club, 1854.

Jefferson, Thomas. *The Writings of Thomas Jefferson.* Memorial ed. 20 vols. Edited by Andrew A. Lipscomb and Albert Ellery Bergh. Washington, DC: Thomas Jefferson Memorial Association of the United States, 1903.

———. *The Writings of Thomas Jefferson: Being His Autobiography, Correspondence, Reports, Messages, Addresses, and Other Writings, Official and Private.* Edited by H. A. Washington. Vol. 4. Washington, DC: Taylor and Maury, 1854.

Jensen, Merrill, ed. *American Colonial Documents to 1776.* Vol. 9 of *English Historical Documents.* Edited by Douglas C. Davis. New York: Oxford University Press, 1955.

McMurtrie, Douglas C., ed. *The Mississippi Militia Law of 1799: A Note on This Natchez Imprint of February, 1799, Accompanied by a Complete Facsimile of the Apparently Unique Copy of the Law Preserved in the Archivo General de Indios at Seville, Spain.* Chicago: John Calhoun Club, 1933.

Mississippi Territory. General Assembly. An Act Empowering the Board of Trustees of Jefferson College to Elect New Trustees. *Acts Passed by the Second General Assembly of the Mississippi Territory, during Their First Session.* Jackson, MS: Marschalk, 1804.

———. An Act Supplementary to an Act Entitled "An Act Providing for the Inspection of Cotton," Passed the 10th day of March, 1803. *Acts Passed by the Second General Assembly of the Mississippi Territory, during Their First Session.* Jackson, MS: Marschalk, 1804.

———. An Act Supplementary to the Acts of the General Assembly Providing for the Raising of a Revenue, Passed the 30th of January 1802 and the 12th of March 1803. *Acts Passed by the Second General Assembly of the Mississippi Territory, during Their First Session.* Jackson, MS: Marschalk, 1804.

———. An Act to Establish a College in the Mississippi Territory. *Acts Passed at the Third Session of the First General Assembly of the Mississippi Territory.* Natchez, MS: Marschalk, 1804.

———. An Act to Incorporate the Mississippi Society for the Acquisition and Dissemination of Useful Knowledge. *Acts Passed by the Second General Assembly of the Mississippi Territory, during Their First Session.* Jackson, MS: Marschalk, 1804.

———. An Act to Prevent the Importation and Spreading of the Small-pox within This Territory. *Acts Passed by the Third Session of the First General Assembly of the Mississippi Territory.* Jackson, MS: Marschalk, 1804.

———. *Journals of the General Assembly of the Mississippi Territory: Journal of the Legislative Council, Second General Assembly, Second Session, October 3–*

November 19, 1803. Edited by William D. McCain. Hattiesburg, MS: Book Farm, 1940.

———. A Law Concerning Aliens and Contagious Diseases. *Laws of the Mississippi Territory, 1799*. Natchez, MS: Marschalk, 1799.

———. A Law to Provide for the Inspection of Cotton Gins, Cotton Presses and Cotton, Intended for Exportation from the Mississippi Territory. *Laws of the Mississippi Territory, September 21–October 5, 1799*. Jackson, MS: N.p., n.d.

———. *Report, in Part, of the Committee to Whom Were Referred on the 13th Ultimo, a Petition of Cato West, and Others, in Behalf of Themselves and the Other Inhabitants of the Mississippi Territory*. February 18, 1800. Jackson: Mississippi Territory House of Representatives, 1806.

Montgomery, Thomas Lynch, ed. *Forfeited Estates, Inventories and Sales*. Pennsylvania Archives. 6th series. Harrisburg, PA: Harrisburg Publishing, 1907.

The Natchez Court Records: Abstracts of Early Records, 1767–1805. Greenwood, MS: N.p., 1953.

Ree, Stephen. *Parish Ministers of the Presbytery of Elgin, 1560–1912*. Elgin, Scotland: Walker, 1912.

Richardson, James D., ed. *A Compilation of the Messages and Papers of the Presidents*. 10 vols. Washington, DC: GPO, 1897.

Rowland, Dunbar, ed. *The Mississippi Territorial Archives*, vol. 1, *1798–1804, Executive Journals of Governor Winthrop Sargent and Governor William Charles Cole Claiborne*. Nashville, TN: Brandon, 1905.

U.S. Congress. House of Representatives. *Report of the Committee on Public Lands, March 4, 1806*. 9th Cong., 1st sess., 1806. Washington, DC: Way, 1806.

Whitaker, Arthur Preston, ed. *Documents Relating to the Commercial Policy of Spain in the Floridas with Incidental Reference to Louisiana*. Deland: Florida State Historical Society, 1931.

Young, Robert. *Annals of the Parish and Burgh of Elgin, from the Twelfth Century to the Year 1876, with Some Historical and Other Notices Illustrative of the Subject*. Elgin, Scotland: *Moray Weekly News* Office, 1879.

Journal Articles

Abbey, Kathryn T. "Peter Chester's Defense of the Mississippi after the Willing Raid." *Mississippi Valley Historical Review* 22 (1935): 17–32.

Abernethy, Thomas P. "Aaron Burr in Mississippi." *Journal of Southern History* 11 (1949): 9–21.

Adam, Margaret I. "Eighteenth Century Highlands and the Poverty Problem." *Scottish Historical Review* 19 (1921): 1–20.

———. "The Highland Emigration of 1770." *Scottish Historical Review* 16 (1919): 280–92.

Allen, Milford F. "Thomas Jefferson and the Louisiana-Arkansas Frontier." *Arkansas Historical Quarterly* 20 (1961): 39–64.

Bacarisse, Charles A. "Baron de Bastrop." *Southwestern Historical Quarterly* 58 (1955): 319–30.

Brown, P. Hume. "Scotland in the Eighteenth Century." *Scottish Historical Review* 6 (1909): 343–56.

Browne, C. A. "Some Historical Relations of Agriculture in the West Indies to That of the United States." *Agricultural History* 1 (1927): 23–34.

Burns, Francis P. "The Spanish Land Laws of Louisiana." *Louisiana Historical Quarterly* 11 (1928): 557–81.

Carter, Clarence E. "Some Aspects of British Administration in West Florida." *Mississippi Valley Historical Review* 1 (1914): 364–75.

Caughey, John. "The Natchez Rebellion of 1781 and Its Aftermath." *Louisiana Historical Quarterly* 16 (1933): 51–63.

———. "Willing's Expedition down the Mississippi, 1778," *Louisiana Historical Quarterly* 15 (1932): 5–36.

"Concerning Philip Nolan." *Quarterly of the Texas State Historical Association* 7 (1904): 308–17.

Cotterill, R. S. "The National Land System in the South, 1803–1812." *Mississippi Valley Historical Review* 16 (1930): 495–506.

Cox, Isaac Joslin. "The Exploration of the Louisiana Frontier, 1803–1806." *Annual Report of the American Historical Association*, 1904, 151–74.

———. "The Louisiana-Texas Frontier." Pts. 1 and 2. *Quarterly of the Texas State Historical Association* 10 (1906): 1–75; 17 (1913): 1–42, 140–87.

———. "The New Invasion of the Goths and Vandals." *Proceedings of the Mississippi Valley Historical Association* 8 (1914–15): 176–200.

Craven, Avery O. "The Agricultural Reformers of the Ante-bellum South." *American Historical Review* 33 (1928): 302–14.

Dart, Henry P., ed. "West Florida: The Capture of Baton Rouge by Galvez, September 21st, 1779." *Louisiana Historical Quarterly* 12 (1929): 255–65.

DeRosier, Arthur H., Jr. "Carpenter's Estimate on the Building of 'The Forest.'" *Journal of Mississippi History* 27 (1965): 259–64.

Dickie, John M. "The Economic Position of Scotland in 1760." *Scottish Historical Review* 18 (1920): 14–31.

Dumbell, Stanley. "Early Liverpool Cotton Imports and the Organization of the Cotton Market in the Eighteenth Century." *Economic Journal* 33 (1923): 362–73.

Dunbar, William. "Meteorological Observations for One Entire Year." *Transactions of the American Philosophical Society* 6 (1804): 9–23.

———. "Monthly and Annual Results of Meteorological Observations." *Transactions of the American Philosophical Society* 6 (1804): 188–89.

Gratz, Simon, ed. "Thomas Rodney." Pts. 1 and 2. *Pennsylvania Magazine of History and Biography* 43 (1919); 44 (1920).

Gray, L. C. "Economic Efficiency and Competitive Advantages of Slavery under the Plantation System." *Agricultural History* 4 (1930): 31–47.

Hamilton, Peter J. "Running Mississippi's South Line." *Publications of the Mississippi Historical Society* 2 (1899): 157–68.

Hamilton, William B. "Early Cotton Regulation in the Lower Mississippi Valley." *Agricultural History* 15 (1941): 20–25.

———. "Jefferson College and Education in Mississippi, 1798–1817." *Journal of Mississippi History* 3 (1941): 259–76.

———. "The Southeastern Frontier, 1795–1817, an Essay in Social History." *Journal of Southern History* 10 (1944): 389–404.

Hansen, Marcus L. "The Population of the American Outlying Regions in 1790." *Annual Report of the American Historical Association* 1 (1931): 398–408.

Haynes, Robert V. "The Revolution of 1800 in Mississippi." *Journal of Mississippi History* 19 (1957): 234–52.

Hearon, Cleo. "Mississippi and the Compromise of 1850." *Publications of the Mississippi Historical Society* 14 (1914): 7–231.

Horn, D. B. "Some Scottish Writers of History in the Eighteenth Century." *Scottish Historical Review* 40 (1961): 1–18.

Howard, C. N. "Some Economic Aspects of British West Florida, 1763–1768." *Journal of Southern History* 6 (1940): 201–21.

Hudgins, Mary D. "William Dunbar, History Maker." *Arkansas Historical Quarterly* 1 (1942): 331–41.

Hunt, Gaillard. "Office-Seeking during Jefferson's Administration." *American Historical Review* 3 (1898): 270–91.

James, James A. "Spanish Influence in the West during the American Revolution." *Mississippi Valley Historical Review* 6 (1917): 193–208.

Jenks, William L. "Territorial Legislation by Governor and Judges." *Mississippi Valley Historical Review* 5 (1918): 36–50.

Johnson, Cecil. "The Distribution of Land in British West Florida." *Louisiana Historical Quarterly* 16 (1933): 535–53.

———. "Expansion in West Florida, 1770–1779." *Mississippi Valley Historical Review* 20 (1934): 481–96.

Leonard, Irving A. "A Frontier Library, 1799." *Hispanic American Historical Review* 23 (1943): 21–51.

Loehr, Rodney C. "The Influence of English Agriculture on American Agriculture, 1775–1825." *Agricultural History* 11 (1937): 3–15.

McGroarty, William B., ed. "Diary of Captain Philip Buckner." *William and Mary College Quarterly Historical Magazine* 6 (1926): 173–207.

Meikle, Henry W. "The Learning of the Scots in the Eighteenth Century." *Scottish Historical Review* 7 (1910): 289–93.

Mitchell, Jennie O'Kelly, and Robert Dabney Calhoun. "The Marquis de Maison Rouge, the Baron de Bastrop, and Colonel Abraham Morhouse, Three Ouachita Valley Soldiers of Fortune." *Louisiana Historical Quarterly* 20 (1937): 289–463.

Moore, John Hebron. "Cotton Breeding in the Old South." *Agricultural History* 30 (1956): 95–104.

Morrison, J. K. "Early History of Jefferson College." *Publications of the Mississippi Historical Society* 2 (1899): 179–88.

Phillips, Ulrich B. "The Economic Cost of Slaveholding in the Cotton Belt." *Political Science Quarterly* 20 (1905): 257–75.

Rives, George L. "Spain and the United States in 1795." *American Historical Review* 4 (1898): 62–79.

Rowland, Dunbar. "The Mississippi Valley in American History." *Proceedings of the Mississippi Valley Historical Association* 9 (1915–16): 59–74.

Scroggs, William O. "Early Trade and Travel in the Lower Mississippi Valley." *Proceedings of the Mississippi Valley Historical Association* 2 (1909): 235–56.

———. "Rural Life in the Lower Mississippi Valley about 1803." *Proceedings of the Mississippi Valley Historical Association* 8 (1914–15): 262–77.

Shue, W. D. "The Cotton Oil Industry." *Publications of the Mississippi Historical Society* 8 (1904): 253–92.

Siebert, Wilbur H. "The Loyalists in West Florida and the Natchez District." *Proceedings of the Mississippi Valley Historical Association* 8 (1914–15): 102–22.

Smith, Robert Worthington. "Was Slavery Unprofitable in the Ante-Bellum South?" *Agricultural History* 20 (1946): 62–64.

Swearingen, Mack, ed. "Luxury at Natchez in 1801: A Ship's Manifest from the McDonogh Papers." *Journal of Southern History* 3 (1937): 188–90.

Sydnor, Charles S. "Historical Activities in Mississippi in the Nineteenth Century." *Journal of Southern History* 3 (1937): 139–60.

Taylor, Paul S. "Plantation Laborer before the Civil War." *Agricultural History* 28 (1954): 1–21.

Thompson, Edgar T. "The Climatic Theory of the Plantation." *Agricultural History* 15 (1941): 49–60.

Watson, J. W. *Morayshire Described: Being a Guide to Visitors Containing Notices of Ecclesiastical and Military Antiquities, Topographical Descriptions and the Principal Courts, Residencies, Towns, and Villages, and Genealogical Notes of the Leading Families in the County, with Map and Illustrations.* Elgin, Scotland: Russell and Watson, 1868.

Whittington, G. P., ed. "The Journal of Dr. John Sibley July–October, 1802." *Louisiana Historical Quarterly* 10 (1927): 474–97.

———, ed. "Letters of Dr. John Sibley of Louisiana to his Son Samuel Hopkins Sibley, 1803–1821." *Louisiana Historical Quarterly* 10 (1927): 498–512.

Winston, James E. "Notes on the Economic History of New Orleans, 1803–1836." *Mississippi Valley Historical Review* 11 (1924): 200–226.

Wood, Minter. "Life in New Orleans in the Spanish Period." *Louisiana Historical Quarterly* 22 (1939): 642–709.

Books

Abernethy, Thomas P. *The South in the New Nation, 1789–1819.* Baton Rouge: Louisiana State University Press, 1961.

Baily, Francis. *Journal of a Tour in Unsettled Parts of North America in 1796 and 1797.* London: Baily Bros., 1856.

Bettersworth, John K. *Mississippi: A History.* Austin, TX: Steck, 1959.

Black Agnes, or the Defense of Dunbar by Agnes, Countess of March, in the Year 1338. London: Renington, 1804.

Buck, Solon J., and Elizabeth Hawthorn Buck. *The Planting of Civilization in Western Pennsylvania.* Pittsburgh: University of Pittsburgh Press, 1939.

Cuming, Fortescue. *Sketches of a Tour to the Western Country through the States of Ohio and Kentucky: A Voyage down the Ohio and Mississippi Rivers, and a Trip through the Mississippi Territory, and Part of West Florida, Commenced at Philadelphia in the Winter of 1807 and Concluded in 1809*. Cleveland, OH: Clark, 1904.

Davis, John. *Travels in Louisiana and the Floridas in the Year 1802, Giving a Correct Picture of Those Countries*. New York: Riley, 1806.

DeRosier, Arthur H., Jr. *The Removal of the Choctaw Indians*. Knoxville: University of Tennessee Press, 1970.

Douglas, Robert. *The Land Provosts of Elgin: Historical and Biographical Sketches*. Elgin, Scotland: Walker, 1926.

Ellison, Thomas. *The Cotton Trade of Great Britain*. London: Wilson, 1886.

Ewen, C. L'Estrange. *A History of Surnames of the British Isles: A Concise Account of Their Origin, Evolution, Etymology, and Legal Status*. London: Paul, Trench, Trubner, 1931.

Flores, Dan L., ed. *Jefferson and Southwestern Exploration: The Freeman and Custis Accounts of the Red River Expedition of 1806*. Norman: University of Oklahoma Press, 1984.

Gayarré, Charles. *The American Domination*. Vol. 4 of *History of Louisiana*. New York: Widdleton, 1856.

Gray, Lewis Cecil. *History of Agriculture in the Southern United States to 1860*. 2 vols. Gloucester, MA: Smith, 1958.

Greene, Evarts Boutell. *The Revolutionary Generation, 1763–1790*. New York: Macmillan, 1945.

Hamilton, William Baskerville. *Anglo-American Law on the Frontier: Thomas Rodney and His Territorial Cases*. Durham, NC: Duke University Press, 1953.

———. *Thomas Rodney, Revolutionary and Builder of the West*. Durham, NC: Duke University Press, 1953.

Hammond, M. B. *The Cotton Industry: An Essay in American Economic History*. New York: Macmillan, 1897.

Herman, Arthur. *How the Scots Invented the Modern World: The True Story of How Western Europe's Poorest Nation Created Our World and Everything in It*. New York: Crown, 2001.

Holmes, Jack D. L. *Gayoso: The Life of a Spanish Governor in the Mississippi Valley, 1789–1799*. Baton Rouge: Louisiana State University Press, 1965.

Kane, Harnett T. *Natchez on the Mississippi*. New York: Morrow, 1947.

Kinnaird, Lawrence, ed. *Spain in the Mississippi Valley, 1765–1794*. 4 vols. Washington, DC: GPO, 1949.

Marshall, Theodora Britton, and Gladys Crail Evans. *They Found It in Natchez*. New Orleans: Pelican, 1940.

Matheson, D. *The Place Names of Elginshire*. Stirling, Scotland: MacKay, 1905.

Mathews, Catharine Van Cortlandt. *Andrew Ellicott: His Life and Letters*. New York: Grafton Press, 1908.

Monette, John W. *History of the Discovery and Settlement of the Valley of the Mississippi by the Three Great European Powers, Spain, France and Great Britain, and the Subsequent Occupation, Settlement, and Extension of Civil Government by the United States until the Year 1846*. 2 vols. New York: Harper, 1846.

Moore, John Hebron. *Agriculture in Ante-bellum Mississippi*. New York: Bookman Associates, 1958.

Murray, Elizabeth Dunbar. *Early Romances of Historic Natchez*. Natchez, MS: Natchez Printing and Stationery, 1938.

Pittman, Philip. *The Present State of the European Settlements on the Mississippi with a Geographical Description of That River Illustrated by Plans and Draughts*. London: Nourse, 1770.

Rampini, Charles. *A History of Moray and Nairn*. Edinburgh: Blackwood, 1897.

Rhind, William. *Sketches of the Past and Present State of Moray*. Edinburgh: Shortrede, 1839.

Rowland, Dunbar. *Courts, Judges, and Lawyers of Mississippi, 1798–1935*. Jackson, MS: Hederman, 1935.

———. *History of Mississippi, the Heart of the South*. 2 vols. Chicago and Jackson, MS: Clarke, 1925.

Shaw, Lachlan. *The History of the Province of Moray*. 32 vols. Glasgow: Morison, 1882.

Shields, Joseph Dunbar. *Natchez: Its Early History*. Louisville, KY: Morton, 1930.

Sinclair, John, ed. *The Statistical Account of Scotland, Drawn Up from the Communications of the Ministers of the Different Parishes*. Edinburgh: Creech, 1794.

Sydnor, Charles S. *A Gentleman of the Old Natchez Region, Benjamin L. C. Wailes*. Durham, NC: Duke University Press, 1938.

Townend, Peter, ed. *Burke's Genealogical and Heraldic History of the Peerage, Baronetage, and Knightage*. 103rd ed. London: Burke's Peerage, 1963.

Index